Knowledge Discovery from Data Streams

Chapman & Hall/CRC
Data Mining and Knowledge Discovery Series

SERIES EDITOR
Vipin Kumar
University of Minnesota
Department of Computer Science and Engineering
Minneapolis, Minnesota, U.S.A

AIMS AND SCOPE

This series aims to capture new developments and applications in data mining and knowledge discovery, while summarizing the computational tools and techniques useful in data analysis. This series encourages the integration of mathematical, statistical, and computational methods and techniques through the publication of a broad range of textbooks, reference works, and handbooks. The inclusion of concrete examples and applications is highly encouraged. The scope of the series includes, but is not limited to, titles in the areas of data mining and knowledge discovery methods and applications, modeling, algorithms, theory and foundations, data and knowledge visualization, data mining systems and tools, and privacy and security issues.

PUBLISHED TITLES

UNDERSTANDING COMPLEX DATASETS:
DATA MINING WITH MATRIX DECOMPOSITIONS
David Skillicorn

COMPUTATIONAL METHODS OF FEATURE
SELECTION
Huan Liu and Hiroshi Motoda

CONSTRAINED CLUSTERING: ADVANCES IN
ALGORITHMS, THEORY, AND APPLICATIONS
Sugato Basu, Ian Davidson, and Kiri L. Wagstaff

KNOWLEDGE DISCOVERY FOR
COUNTERTERRORISM AND LAW ENFORCEMENT
David Skillicorn

MULTIMEDIA DATA MINING: A SYSTEMATIC
INTRODUCTION TO CONCEPTS AND THEORY
Zhongfei Zhang and Ruofei Zhang

NEXT GENERATION OF DATA MINING
Hillol Kargupta, Jiawei Han, Philip S. Yu,
Rajeev Motwani, and Vipin Kumar

DATA MINING FOR DESIGN AND MARKETING
Yukio Ohsawa and Katsutoshi Yada

THE TOP TEN ALGORITHMS IN DATA MINING
Xindong Wu and Vipin Kumar

GEOGRAPHIC DATA MINING AND
KNOWLEDGE DISCOVERY, SECOND EDITION
Harvey J. Miller and Jiawei Han

TEXT MINING: CLASSIFICATION, CLUSTERING,
AND APPLICATIONS
Ashok N. Srivastava and Mehran Sahami

BIOLOGICAL DATA MINING
Jake Y. Chen and Stefano Lonardi

INFORMATION DISCOVERY ON ELECTRONIC
HEALTH RECORDS
Vagelis Hristidis

TEMPORAL DATA MINING
Theophano Mitsa

RELATIONAL DATA CLUSTERING: MODELS,
ALGORITHMS, AND APPLICATIONS
Bo Long, Zhongfei Zhang, and Philip S. Yu

KNOWLEDGE DISCOVERY FROM DATA STREAMS
João Gama

Chapman & Hall/CRC
Data Mining and Knowledge Discovery Series

Knowledge Discovery from Data Streams

João Gama

CRC Press
Taylor & Francis Group
Boca Raton London New York

CRC Press is an imprint of the
Taylor & Francis Group, an **informa** business

A CHAPMAN & HALL BOOK

Chapman & Hall/CRC
Taylor & Francis Group
6000 Broken Sound Parkway NW, Suite 300
Boca Raton, FL 33487-2742

© 2010 by Taylor and Francis Group, LLC
Chapman & Hall/CRC is an imprint of Taylor & Francis Group, an Informa business

---

Library of Congress Cataloging-in-Publication Data

Gama, João.
    Knowledge discovery from data streams / João Gama.
        p. cm. -- (Chapman & Hall/CRC data mining and knowledge discovery series)
    Includes bibliographical references and index.
    ISBN 978-1-4398-2611-9 (hardcover : alk. paper)
    1. Computer algorithms. 2. Machine learning. 3. Data mining. I. Title. II. Series.

    QA76.9.A43G354 2010
    006.3 '12--dc22
                                     2010014600

Visit the Taylor & Francis Web site at
http://www.taylorandfrancis.com

and the CRC Press Web site at
http://www.crcpress.com

Contents

List of Tables

List of Figures

List of Algorithms

Foreword

In spite of being a small country in terms of geographic area and population size, Portugal has a very active and respected artificial intelligence community, with a good number of researchers well known internationally for the high quality of their work and relevant contributions in this area.

One of these researchers is João Gama from the University of Porto. Gama is one of the leading investigators in of the current hottest research topics in machine learning and data mining: data streams.

Although other books have been published covering important aspects of data streams, these books are either mainly related to database aspects of data streams or are a collection of chapter contributions for different aspects of this issue.

This book is the first book to didactically cover in a clear, comprehensive and mathematically rigorous way the main machine learning related aspects of this relevant research field. The book not only presents the main fundamentals important to fully understand data streams, but also describes important applications. The book also discusses some of the main challenges of data mining future research, when stream mining will be at the core of many applications. These challenges will have to be addressed for the design of useful and efficient data mining solutions able to deal with real-world problems. It is important to stress that, in spite of this book being mainly about data streams, most of the concepts presented are valid for different areas of machine learning and data mining. Therefore, the book is an up-to-date, broad and useful source of reference for all those interested in knowledge acquisition by learning techniques.

André Ponce de Leon Ferreira de Carvalho
University S. Paulo

Acknowledgments

Life is the art of drawing sufficient conclusions from insufficient premises.
Samuel Butler

This book is a result of the Knowledge Discovery from Ubiquitous Data Streams project funded by the Portuguese *Fundação para a Ciência e Tecnologia*. We thank FCT that funded, in the last 5 years, research projects in this topic. The work, analysis, discussions, and debates with several students and researchers strongly influenced the issues presented here. I thank Ricardo Rocha, Ricardo Fernandes, and Pedro Medas for their work on decision trees, Pedro Rodrigues on clustering, Gladys Castillo and Milton Severo on change detection, Eduardo Spinosa, Andre Carvalho on novelty detection and Carlos Pinto and Raquel Sebastião on histograms. To all of them, Thank you!

The Knowledge Discovery in Ubiquitous Environments project, funded by the European Union under IST, was another major source of inspiration. All the meetings, events, activities, and discussions contributed to improve our vision on the role of data mining in a world in motion.

A special thanks to those who contributed material to this book. André de Carvalho contributed the Preface and reviewed the book, Albert Bifet and Ricard Gavaldà contributed Section 2.2.5.1, Mark Last contributed Section 8.4, Mohamed Gaber Section 12.4, and Chedy Raissi and Pascal Poncelet Section 7.4.1. Together with Jesus Aguilar, we organized a stream of workshops in data streams. They constitute the backbone of this book.

A word of gratitude to my family and friends, who have been the major source of support.

Chapter 1

Knowledge Discovery from Data Streams

1.1 Introduction

In the last three decades, machine learning research and practice have focused on batch learning usually using small datasets. In batch learning, the whole training data is available to the algorithm, which outputs a decision model after processing the data eventually (or most of the times) multiple times. The rationale behind this practice is that examples are generated at random according to some stationary probability distribution. Most learners use a greedy, hill-climbing search in the space of models. They are prone to high-variance and overfitting problems. Brain and Webb (2002) pointed out the relation between variance and data sample size. When learning from small datasets the main problem is variance reduction, while learning from large datasets may be more effective when using algorithms that place greater emphasis on bias management.

In most challenging applications, learning algorithms act in dynamic environments, where the data are collected over time. A desirable property of these algorithms is the ability of incorporating new data. Some supervised learning algorithms are naturally incremental, for example *k-nearest neighbors*, and *naive-Bayes*. Others, like *decision trees*, require substantial changes to make incremental induction. Moreover, if the process is not strictly stationary (as are most real-world applications), the target concept could gradually change over time. Incremental learning is a necessary property but not sufficient. Incremental learning systems must have mechanisms to incorporate concept drift, forgetting outdated data and adapting to the most recent state of nature.

What distinguishes current datasets from earlier ones is automatic data feeds. We do not just have people who are entering information into a computer. Instead, we have computers entering data into each other. Nowadays, there are applications in which the data are better modeled not as persistent tables but rather as transient data streams. Examples of such applications include network monitoring, web mining, sensor networks, telecommunications data management, and financial applications. In these applications, it is not feasible to load the arriving data into a traditional database management system (DBMS), which is not traditionally designed to directly support the continuous queries required in these applications (Babcock et al., 2002).

1.2   An Illustrative Example

Sensors distributed all around electrical-power distribution networks produce streams of data at high-speed. Electricity distribution companies usually manage that information using SCADA/DMS tools (Supervisory Control and Data Acquisition/Distribution Management Systems). One of their important tasks is to forecast the electrical load (electricity demand) for a given sub-network of consumers. Load forecast systems provide a relevant support tool for operational management of an electricity distribution network, since they enable the identification of critical points in load evolution, allowing necessary corrections within available time, and planning strategies for different horizons. This is of great economic interest, given that companies make decisions to buy or to sell energy based on these predictions.

The scenario just described is easily extended for water and gas distribution grids. In these applications, data are collected from a huge set of sensors distributed all around the networks. The number of sensors can increase over time, and, because they might come from different generations, they send information at different time scales, speeds, and granularities. Sensors usually act in adversery conditions, are prone to noise, weather conditions, communications failures, battery limits, etc. Data continuously flow possibly at high-speed, in a dynamic and time-changing environment.

Data mining in this context requires a continuous processing of the incoming data monitoring trends, and detecting changes. In this context, we can identify several relevant data mining tasks:

- Cluster Analysis

  - Identification of Profiles: Urban, Rural, Industrial, etc.;

- Predictive Analysis

  - Predict the value measured by each sensor for different time horizons;

  - Predict peeks in the demand;

- Monitoring evolution

  - Change Detection
    * Detect changes in the behavior of sensors;
    * Detect failures and abnormal activities;

Figure 1.1: Example of an electrical grid. Sensors are represented by dots. Sensors continuously measure quantities of interest corresponding to the electricity demand of a covered geographical area.

- Extreme Values, Anomaly, and Outliers Detection
  * Identification of peeks in the demand;
  * Identification of **critical points** in load evolution;
- Exploitation of background information given by the topology and geographical information of the network.

The usual approach for dealing with these tasks consists of: 1) select a finite data sample and 2) generate a static model. Several types of models have been used for such: different clustering algorithms and structures, various neural networks based models, Kalman filters, wavelets, etc. This strategy can exhibit very good performance in the next few months, but, later, the performance starts degrading, requiring retraining all decision models as times goes by. What is the problem? The problem probably is related to the use of *static decision models*. Traditional systems that are one-shot, memory-based, trained from fixed training sets, and static models are not prepared to process the highly detailed evolving data. Thus, they are neither able to continuously maintain a predictive model consistent with the actual state of nature, nor to quickly react to changes. Moreover, with the evolution of hardware components, these sensors are acquiring computational power. The challenge will be to run the predictive model in the sensors themselves.

A basic question is: How can we collect labeled examples in real-time? Suppose that at time t our predictive model made a prediction $\hat{y}_{t+k}$, for the time $t + k$, where k is the desired horizon forecast. Later on, at time $t + k$ the sensor measures the quantity of interest y_{t+k}. We can then estimate the loss of our prediction $L(\hat{y}_{t+k}, y_{t+k})$.[1] We do not need to know the true value y_i for all points in the stream. The framework can be used in situations of limited feedback, by computing the loss function and L for points where y_i is known. A typical example is fraud detection in credit card usage. The system receives and classifies requests from transactions in real-time. The prediction can be useful for the decision of whether to accept the request. Later on, companies send bank statements to the credit card users. The system receives the feedback whenever the user denounces a fraudulent transaction.

Given its relevant application and strong financial implications, electricity load forecast has been targeted by several works, mainly relying on the non-linearity and generalizing capacities of neural networks, which combine a cyclic factor and an auto-regressive one to achieve good results (Hippert et al., 2001). Nevertheless, static iteration-based training, usually applied to estimate the best weights for the network connections, is not adequate for the high-speed stream of data usually encountered.

1.3   A World in Movement

The constraints just enumerated imply to switch from one-shot learning tasks to a lifelong and spatially pervasive perspective. From this perspective, induced by ubiquitous environments, *finite training sets, static models, and stationary distributions* must be completely redefined. These aspects entail new characteristics for the data:

- Data are made available through *unlimited streams* that continuously flow, eventually at high speed, over time;

- The underlying *regularities may evolve over time* rather than be stationary;

- The data can no longer be considered as *independent and identically distributed*;

- The data are now often *spatially as well as time situated.*

But do these characteristics really change the essence of machine learning? Would not simple adaptations to existing learning algorithms suffice to cope with the new needs previously described? These new concerns might indeed appear rather abstract, and with no visible direct impact on machine learning

---

[1] As alternative we could make another prediction, using the current model, for the time $t + k$.

techniques. Quite to the contrary, however, even very basic operations that are at the core of learning methods are challenged in the new setting. For instance, consider the standard approach to cluster variables (columns in a working matrix). In a batch scenario, where all data are available and stored in a working matrix, we can apply any clustering algorithm over the *transpose* of the working matrix. In a scenario where data evolve over time, this is not possible, because the transpose operator is a blocking operator (Barbará, 2002): the first output tuple is available only after processing all the input tuples. Now, think of the computation of the entropy of a collection of data when this collection comes as a data stream which is no longer finite, where the domain (set of values) of the variables can be huge, and where the number of classes of objects is not known a priori; or think of continuous maintenance of the k-most frequent items in a retail data warehouse with three terabytes of data, hundreds of gigabytes of new sales records updated daily with millions of different items.

Then, what becomes of statistical computations when the learner can only afford one pass on each data piece because of time and memory constraints; when the learner has to decide on the fly what is relevant and must be further processed and what is redundant or not representative and could be discarded? These are a few examples of the clear need for new algorithmic approaches.

1.4   Data Mining and Data Streams

Solutions to these problems require new sampling and randomizing techniques, together with new approximate and incremental algorithms (Muthukrishnan, 2005; Aggarwal, 2007; Gama and Gaber, 2007). Some data stream models allow delete and update operators. For these models or in the presence of context change, the incremental property is not enough. Learning algorithms need forgetting operators that discard outdated information: decremental unlearning (Cauwenberghs and Poggio, 2000).

Another related conceptual framework is the *block evolution* presented by Ramakrishnan and Gehrke (2003). In the block evolution model, a database consists of a sequence of data blocks $D_1, D_2, \ldots$ that arrives sequentially. For evolving data, two classes of problems are of particular interest: model maintenance and change detection. The goal of model maintenance is to maintain a data mining model under inserts and deletes of blocks of data. In this model, older data is available if necessary. Change detection is related to quantify the difference between two sets of data and determine when the change has statistical significance.

All through this book, we focus on algorithms and problems where random access to data is not allowed or has high costs. Memory is assumed to be small with respect to the dimension of data. Hulten and Domingos (2001) present desirable properties for learning from high-speed, time-changing data streams: incrementality, on-line learning, constant time to process each example, single scan over the training set, take drift into account. In the problems we are interested in, the assumption that the observations are generated at random according to a stationary probability distribution is highly improbable. In complex systems and for large time periods, we should expect changes in the distribution of the examples. A natural approach for these *incremental tasks* is the use of *adaptive learning algorithms*, incremental learning algorithms that take into account concept drift.

Formally, we can define (`Adaptive Learning Algorithms`) as follows. Let $E_t = \{\vec{x}_i, y_i : y = f(\vec{x})\}$ be a set of examples available at time $t \in \{1, 2, 3, \ldots, i\}$. A learning algorithm is adaptive if from the sequence of examples $\{\ldots, E_{j-1}, E_j, \ldots\}$, produce a sequence of Hypothesis $\{\ldots, H_{j-1}, H_j, \ldots\}$, where each hypothesis H_i only depends on previous hypothesis H_{i-1} and the example E_i.

An adaptive learning algorithm requires two operators:

- *Increment*: the example E_k is incorporated in the decision model;

- *Decrement*: the example E_k is forgotten from the decision model.

A main issue is that machine learning algorithms will have to enter the world of **limited rationality**, e.g., rational decisions are not feasible in practice due to the finite computational resources available for making them (Simon, 1997). In addition to continuous flow of data produced in a dynamic environment, the ideas we present here might be useful in several other situations. For example, if the entire dataset is not available at the time the original decision model is built, or if the original dataset is too large to process and does not fit in memory, and applications where the characteristics of the data change over time.

In summary, knowledge discovery from data streams implies new requirements to be considered. The new constraints include:

- The algorithms will have to use *limited computational resources*, in terms of computational power, memory, communication, and processing time;

- The algorithms will have only a *limited direct access to data* and may have to communicate with other agents on *limited bandwidth* resources;

- In a community of smart devices geared to ease the life of users in real time, answers will have to be ready in an *anytime protocol*;

- Data gathering and data processing might be *distributed*.

Chapter 2

Introduction to Data Streams

Nowadays, we are in the presence of sources of data produced continuously at high speed. Examples include TCP/IP traffic, GPS data, mobile calls, emails, sensor networks, customer click streams, etc. These data sources continuously generate huge amounts of data from nonstationary distributions. Storage, maintenance, and querying data streams brought new challenges in the database and data mining communities. The database community has developed Data Stream Management Systems (DSMS) for continuous querying, compact data structures (sketches and summaries), and sub-linear algorithms for massive dataset analysis. In this chapter, we discuss relevant issues and illustrative techniques developed in stream processing that might be relevant for data stream mining.

2.1 Data Stream Models

Data streams can be seen as stochastic processes in which events occur continuously and independently from each another. Querying data streams is quite different from querying in the conventional relational model. A key idea is that operating on the data stream model does not preclude the use of data in conventional stored relations: data might be *transient*. What makes processing data streams different from the conventional relational model? The main differences are summarized in Table 2.1. Some relevant differences include:

1. The data elements in the stream arrive on-line.

2. The system has no control over the order in which data elements arrive, either within a data stream or across data streams.

3. Data streams are potentially unbounded in size.

4. Once an element from a data stream has been processed, it is discarded or archived. It cannot be retrieved easily unless it is explicitly stored in memory, which is small relative to the size of the data streams.

In the streaming model (Muthukrishnan, 2005) the input elements $f_1, f_2, \ldots, f_j, \ldots$ arrive sequentially, item by item, and describe an underlying

Table 2.1:   Comparison between Database Management Systems and Data Stream Management Systems.

Data Base Management Systems	Data Stream Management Systems
Persistent relations	Transient streams (and persistent relations)
One-time queries	Continuous queries
Random access	Sequential access
Access plan determined by query processor and physical DB design	Unpredictable data characteristics and arrival patterns

function F. Streaming models differ on how f_i describes F. Regarding these models, we can distinguish between:

1. **Insert Only Model**: once an element f_i is seen, it can not be changed.

2. **Insert-Delete Model**: elements f_i can be deleted or updated.

3. **Additive Model**: each f_i is an increment to $F[j] = F[j] + f_i$.

2.1.1   Research Issues in Data Stream Management Systems

From the point of view of data stream management systems, several research issues emerge. These issues have implications on data stream management systems, such as:

- Approximate query processing techniques to evaluate queries that require unbounded amount of memory.

- Sliding window query processing both as an approximation technique and as an option in the query language.

- Sampling to handle situations where the flow rate of the input stream is faster than the query processor.

- The meaning and implementation of blocking operators (e.g., aggregation and sorting) in the presence of unending streams.

These types of queries require techniques for storing summaries or synopsis information about previously seen data. There is a trade-off between the size of summaries and the ability to provide precise answers.

2.1.2   An Illustrative Problem

A problem that clearly illustrates the issues in a streaming process is the problem of finding the maximum value (MAX) or the minimum value (MIN) in a sliding window over a sequence of numbers. When we can store in memory all the elements of the sliding window, the problem is trivial and we can find the exact solution. When the size of the sliding window is greater than the

Table 2.2: Differences between traditional and stream data query processing.

	Traditional	Stream
Number of passes	Multiple	Single
Processing Time	Unlimited	Restricted
Memory Usage	Unlimited	Restricted
Type of Result	Accurate	Approximate
Distributed?	No	Yes

available memory, there is no exact solution. For example, suppose that the sequence is monotonically decreasing and the aggregation function is MAX. Whatever the window size, the first element in the window is always the maximum. As the sliding window moves, the exact answer requires maintaining all the elements in memory.

2.2 Basic Streaming Methods

Data streams are unbounded in length. However, this is not the only problem. The domain of the possible values of an attribute can also be very large. A typical example is the domain of all pairs of IP addresses on the Internet. It is so huge, that it makes exact storage intractable, as it is impractical to store all data to execute queries that reference past data. Some results on tail inequalities provided by statistics are useful in these contexts. The basic general bounds on the tail probability of a random variable (that is, the probability that a random variable deviates largely from its expectation) include the Markov, Chebyshev and Chernoff inequalities (Motwani and Raghavan, 1997). A summary of the differences between traditional and stream data processing is presented in Table 2.2.

It is impractical to store all data to execute queries that reference past data. These types of queries require techniques for storing summaries or synopsis information about previously seen data. There is a trade-off between the size of summaries and the ability to provide precise answers. We are faced with problems whose solution requires $O(N)$ space. Suppose we have restricted memory. How can we solve these problems using less space than $O(N)$?

Algorithms that process data streams are typically *sub-linear* in time and space, but they provide an answer which is in some sense approximate. There are three main constraints to consider: the amount of memory used to store information, the time to process each data element, and the time to answer the query of interest. In general, we can identify two types of approximate answers:

- ϵ Approximation: the answer is correct within some small fraction ϵ of

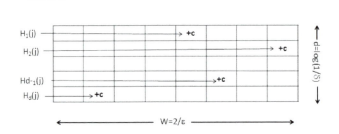

Figure 2.1: The Count-Min Sketch: The dimensions of the array depend on the desired probability level (δ), and the admissible error (ϵ).

error.

- (ϵ, δ) Approximation: the answer is within $1 \pm \epsilon$ of the correct result, with probability $1 - \delta$.

The constants ϵ and δ have a large influence on the space used. Typically, the space is $O(\frac{1}{\epsilon^2}log(1/\delta))$.

2.2.1 Illustrative Examples

2.2.1.1 Counting the Number of Occurrences of the Elements in a Stream

Cormode and Muthukrishnan (2005) present the Count-Min Sketch, a streaming algorithm for summarizing data streams. It has been used to approximately solve point queries, range queries, and inner product queries. Here we present a simple point query estimate: *Count the number of packets of each IP from the set of IPs that cross a server in a network.*

A Count-Min Sketch is an array of $w \times d$ in size (Figure 2.1). Given a desired probability level (δ), and an admissible error (ϵ), the size of the data structure is $w = 2/\epsilon$ and $d = \lceil log(1/\delta) \rceil$. Associated with each row there is a hash function $h(.)$ that uniformly maps a value x to a value in the interval $[1, \ldots, w]$.

Each entry x in the stream is mapped to one cell per row of the array of counts. It uses d hash functions to map entries to $[1, \ldots, w]$. When an update c of item j arrives, c is added to each of these cells. c can be any value: positive values for inserts, and negative values for deletes.

At any time we can answer point queries like: *How many times have we observed a particular IP?* To answer such a query, we determine the set of d cells to which each of the d hash-functions map: $CM[k, h_k(IP)]$. The estimate is given by taking the minimum value among these cells:

$\hat{x}[IP] = min(CM[k, h_k(IP)])$. This estimate is always optimistic, that is $x[j] \leq \hat{x}[j]$, where $x[j]$ is the true value. The interesting fact is that the estimate is upper bounded by $\hat{x}[j] \leq x[j] + \epsilon \times ||x||$, with probability $1 - \delta$.

2.2.1.2 Counting the Number of Distinct Values in a Stream

Another counting problem is the *distinct values* query: Find the number of distinct values in a stream of a random discrete variable.

Assume that the domain of the attribute is $\{0, 1, \ldots, M-1\}$. The problem is trivial if we have space linear in M. Is there an approximate algorithm using space $log(M)$?

The basic assumption is the existence of a hash function $h(x)$ that maps incoming values $x \in [0, \ldots, N-1]$ uniformly across $[0, \ldots, 2^L - 1]$, where $L = O(logN)$. Let $lsb(y)$ denote the position of the least-significant 1-value bit in the binary representation of y. A value x is mapped to $lsb(h(x))$. The algorithm maintains a `Hash Sketch`, that is a bitmap vector of L bits, initialized to zero. For each incoming value x, set the $lsb(h(x))$ to 1.

At each time-stamp t, let R denote the position of rightmost zero in the bitmap. R is an indicator of $log(d)$, where d denotes the number of distinct values in the stream: $d = 2^R$. In fact, Flajolet and Martin (1985) prove that, for large enough streams, $E[R] = log(\phi d)$, where $\phi = 0.7735$, so $d = 2^R/\phi$. This result is based on the uniformity of $h(x)$: $Prob[BITMAP[k] = 1] = Prob[10^k] = 1/2^{k+1}$. Assuming d distinct values, it is expected $d/2$ to map to BITMAP[0], $d/4$ to map to BITMAP[1], and $d/2^r$ map to BITMAP[r-1].

In the following, we present an illustrative example of the `Hash Sketch` algorithm application. Assume the hash function $h(x) = 3x + 1 \mod 5$. Suppose that the first element of the stream is 1.

$$x = 1 \rightarrow h(x) = 4 \rightarrow 0100 \rightarrow lsb(h(x)) = 2$$

and the BITMAP is set to:

5	4	3	2	1	0
0	0	0	1	0	0

Assume than the input stream is $1, 3, 2, 1, 2, 3, 4, 3, 1, 2, 3, 1, \ldots$. Applying the hash function to the elements of the stream, we obtain $h(Stream) = 4, 5, 2, 4, 2, 5, 3, 5, 4, 2, 5, 4, \ldots$. The position of the least-significant 1 bit is: $lsb(h(x)) = 2, 0, 1, 2, 1, 0, 0, 0, 2, 1, 0, 2, \ldots$. After processing the first 12 elements of the stream, the bitmap would look like:

5	4	3	2	1	0
0	0	0	1	1	1

In this case, R, the position of the rightmost 1, is 2 and $d = 4$.

2.2.2 Bounds of Random Variables

An estimator is a function of the observable sample data that is used to estimate an unknown population parameter. We are particularly interested in interval estimators that compute an interval for the true value of the parameter, associated with a confidence $1 - \delta$. Two types of intervals are:

- Absolute approximation: $\overline{X} - \epsilon \leq \mu \leq \overline{X} + \epsilon$, where ϵ is the absolute error;

- Relative approximation: $(1-\delta)\overline{X} \leq \mu \leq (1+\delta)\overline{X}$, where δ is the relative error.

An interesting result from statistics is the *Chebyshev Inequality*.

Theorem 2.2.1 (Chebyshev) *Let X be a random variable with standard deviation σ, the probability that the outcome of X is no less than $k\sigma$ away from its mean is no more than $1/k^2$:*

$$P(|X - \mu| \leq k\sigma) \leq \tfrac{1}{k^2}$$

No more than $1/4$ of the values are more than 2 standard deviations away from the mean, no more than $1/9$ are more than 3 standard deviations away, no more than $1/25$ are more than 5 standard deviations away, and so on.

Two results from the statistical theory useful in most of the cases are:

Theorem 2.2.2 (Chernoff Bound) *Let $X_1, X_2, \ldots, X_n$ be independent random variables from Bernoulli experiments. Assuming that $P(X_i = 1) = p_i$. Let $X_s = \sum_{i=1}^{n} X_i$ be a random variable with expected value $\mu_s = \sum_{i=1}^{n} np_i$. Then for any $\delta > 0$:*

$$P[X_s > (1 + \delta)\mu_s] \leq \left(\frac{e^\delta}{(1 + \delta)^{1+\delta}}\right)^{\mu_s} \qquad (2.1)$$

From this theorem, it is possible to derive the absolute error (Motwani and Raghavan, 1997):

$$\epsilon \leq \sqrt{\frac{3\overline{\mu}}{n} ln(2/\delta)} \qquad (2.2)$$

Theorem 2.2.3 (Hoeffding Bound) *Let $X_1, X_2, \ldots, X_n$ be independent random variables. Assume that each x_i is bounded, that is $P(X_i \in R = [a_i, b_i]) = 1$. Let $S = 1/n \sum_{i=1}^{n} X_i$, whose expected value is $E[S]$. Then, for any $\epsilon > 0$,*

$$P[S - E[S] > \epsilon] \leq e^{-\frac{2n^2\epsilon^2}{R^2}} \qquad (2.3)$$

From this theorem, we can derive the absolute error (Motwani and Raghavan, 1997):

$$\epsilon \leq \sqrt{\frac{R^2 ln(2/\delta)}{2n}} \qquad (2.4)$$

Chernoff and Hoeffding bounds are independent from the distribution generating examples. They are applicable in all situations where observations are

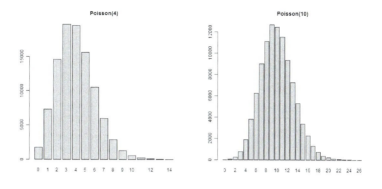

Figure 2.2: Frequency distribution of two Poisson random variables with $\lambda = 4$ and $\lambda = 10$.

independent and generated by a stationary distribution. Due to their generality they are conservative, that is, they require more observations than when using distribution dependent bounds. Chernoff bound is multiplicative and its error is expressed as a relative approximation. The Hoeffding bound is additive and the error is absolute. While the Chernoff bound uses the sum of events and requires the expected value for the sum, the Hoeffding bound uses the expected value and the number of observations.

2.2.3 Poisson Processes

A Poisson process is a stochastic process in which events occur continuously and independently from each another. Examples that are well-modeled as Poisson processes include the radioactive decay of atoms, telephone calls arriving, page view requests to a website, items bought in a supermarket, etc.

A random variable x is said to be a Poisson random variable with parameter λ if x takes values $0, 1, 2, \ldots, \infty$ with:

$$p_k = P(x = k) = e^{-\lambda} \frac{\lambda^k}{k!}$$

$P(x = k)$ increases with k from 0 till $k \leq \lambda$ and falls off beyond λ. The mean and variance are $E(X) = Var(X) = \lambda$ (see Figure 2.2).

Some interesting properties of Poisson processes are:

- The number of points t_i in an interval (t_1, t_2) of length $t = t_2 - t_1$ is a Poisson random variable with parameter λt;

- If the intervals (t_1, t_2) and (t_3, t_4) are non-overlapping, then the number of points in these intervals are independent;

- If $x_1(t)$ and $x_2(t)$ represent two independent Poisson processes with parameters $\lambda_1 t$ and $\lambda_2 t$, their sum $x_1(t) + x_2(t)$ is also a Poisson process with parameter $(\lambda_1 + \lambda_2)t$.

2.2.4   Maintaining Simple Statistics from Data Streams

The recursive version of the sample mean is well known:

$$\bar{x}_i = \frac{(i-1) \times \bar{x}_{i-1} + x_i}{i} \tag{2.5}$$

In fact, to incrementally compute the mean of a variable, we only need to maintain in memory the number of observations (i) and the sum of the values seen so far $\sum x_i$. Some simple mathematics allow us to define an incremental version of the standard deviation. In this case, we need to store 3 quantities: i, the number of data points; $\sum x_i$, the sum of the i points; and $\sum x_i^2$, the sum of the squares of the i data points. The equation to continuously compute σ is:

$$\sigma_i = \sqrt{\frac{\sum x_i^2 - \frac{(\sum x_i)^2}{i}}{i-1}} \tag{2.6}$$

Another useful measure that can be recursively computed is the correlation coefficient. Given two streams x and y, we need to maintain the sum of each stream ($\sum x_i$ and $\sum y_i$), the sum of the squared values ($\sum x_i^2$ and $\sum y_i^2$), and the sum of the crossproduct ($\sum (x_i \times y_i)$). The exact correlation is:

$$corr(a,b) = \frac{\sum (x_i \times y_i) - \frac{\sum x_i \times \sum y_i}{n}}{\sqrt{\sum x_i^2 - \frac{\sum x_i^2}{n}} \sqrt{\sum y_i^2 - \frac{\sum y_i^2}{n}}} \tag{2.7}$$

We have defined the *sufficient statistics* necessary to compute the mean, standard deviation, and correlation on a time series. The main interest in these formulas is that they allow us to maintain exact statistics (mean, standard deviation, and correlation) over an eventually infinite sequence of numbers without storing in memory all the numbers.

2.2.5   Sliding Windows

Most of the time, we are not interested in computing statistics over all the past, but only over the *recent* past. The simplest situation is the *sliding windows* of fixed size. These types of windows are similar to *first in, first out* data structures. Whenever an element j is observed and inserted into the window, another element $j - w$, where w represents the window size, is forgotten.

Several window models have been presented in the literature. Babcock, Datar, and Motwani (2002) defines two basic types of sliding windows:

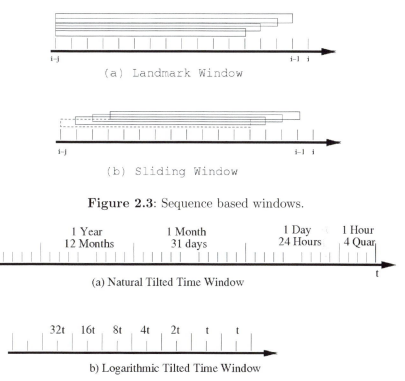

(a) Landmark Window

(b) Sliding Window

Figure 2.3: Sequence based windows.

(a) Natural Tilted Time Window

b) Logarithmic Tilted Time Window

Figure 2.4: Tilted time windows. The top figure presents a *natural tilted time window*, the figure in the bottom presents the *logarithm tilted windows*.

- **Sequence based.** The size of the window is defined in terms of the number of observations. Two different models are *sliding windows* of size j and *landmark windows*;

- **Timestamp based.** The size of the window is defined in terms of *duration*. A timestamp window of size t consists of all elements whose timestamp is within a time interval t of the current time period.

Computing statistics over sliding windows requires storing all elements inside the window in memory. Suppose we want to maintain the standard deviation of the values of a data stream using only the last 100 examples, that is, in a fixed time window of dimension 100. After seeing observation 1000, the observations inside the time window are:

$$x_{901}, x_{902}, x_{903}, \ldots, x_{999}, x_{1000}$$

Sufficient statistics after seeing the 1000th observation:

$$A = \sum_{i=901}^{1000} x_i; \ B = \sum_{i=901}^{1000} x_i^2$$

Whenever the 1001th value is observed, the time window moves 1 observation and the updated sufficient statistics are: $A = A + x_{1001} - x_{901}$ and

$B = B + x_{1001}^2 - x_{901}^2$.

Note that we need to store in memory the observations inside the window. Due to the necessity to forget old observations, we need to maintain in memory all the observations inside the window. The same problem applies for time windows whose size changes with time. In the following sections we address the problem of maintaining approximate statistics over sliding windows in a stream, without storing in memory all the elements inside the window.

2.2.5.1   Computing Statistics over Sliding Windows: The ADWIN Algorithm

The ADWIN (ADaptive sliding WINdow) (Bifet and Gavaldà, 2006, 2007) is a change detector and estimator algorithm using an adaptive size sliding window. It solves in a well-specified way the problem of tracking the average of a stream of bits or real-valued numbers. ADWIN keeps a variable-length window of recently seen items, with the property that the window has the maximal length statistically consistent with the hypothesis *there has been no change in the average value inside the window.*

More precisely, an older fragment of the window is dropped if and only if there is enough evidence that its average value differs from that of the rest of the window. This has two consequences: one, a change is reliably declared whenever the window shrinks; and two, that at any time the average over the existing window can be reliably taken as an estimation of the current average in the stream (barring a very small or very recent change that is still not statistically visible).

The inputs to ADWIN are a confidence value $\delta \in (0, 1)$ and a (possibly infinite) sequence of real values x_1, x_2, x_3, ..., x_t, ... The value of x_t is available only at time t. Each x_t is generated according to some distribution D_t, independently for every t. We denote with μ_t the expected value of x_t when it is drawn according to D_t. We assume that x_t is always in $[0, 1]$; by an easy rescaling, we can handle any case in which we know an interval $[a, b]$ such that $a \le x_t \le b$ with probability 1. Nothing else is known about the sequence of distributions D_t; in particular, μ_t is unknown for all t.

The algorithm ADWIN uses a sliding window W with the most recently read x_i. Let $\hat{\mu}_W$ denote the (known) average of the elements in W, and μ_W the (unknown) average of μ_t for $t \in W$. We use $|W|$ to denote the length of a (sub)window W.

The algorithm ADWIN is presented in Figure 1. The idea behind the ADWIN method is simple: whenever two 'large enough' subwindows of W exhibit 'distinct enough' averages, one can conclude that the corresponding expected values are different, and the older portion of the window is dropped. The meaning of 'large enough' and 'distinct enough' can be made precise again by using the Hoeffding bound. The test eventually boils down to whether the average of the two subwindows is larger than a variable value ϵ_{cut} computed as follows:

$$m \quad := \quad \frac{2}{1/|W_0| + 1/|W_1|}$$

$$\epsilon_{cut} \quad := \quad \sqrt{\frac{1}{2m} \cdot \ln \frac{4|W|}{\delta}} \ .$$

where m is the harmonic mean of $|W_0|$ and $|W_1|$.

Algorithm 1: The ADWIN Algorithm.

---

begin
     Initialize Window W;
     foreach $(t) > 0$ **do**
         $W \leftarrow W \cup \{x_t\}$ (i.e., add x_t to the head of W);
         repeat
            | Drop elements from the tail of W
         until $|\hat{\mu}_{W_0} - \hat{\mu}_{W_1}| < \epsilon_{cut}$ *holds for every split of W into*
         $W = W_0 \cdot W_1$
     Output $\hat{\mu}_W$
end

The main technical result in Bifet and Gavaldà (2006, 2007) about the performance of ADWIN is the following theorem, that provides bounds on the rate of false positives and false negatives for ADWIN:

Theorem 2.2.4 *With ϵ_{cut} defined as above, at every time step we have:*

1. *(False positive rate bound). If μ_t has remained constant within W, the probability that* ADWIN *shrinks the window at this step is at most δ;*

2. *(False negative rate bound). Suppose that for* some *partition of W in two parts W_0W_1 (where W_1 contains the most recent items) we have $|\mu_{W_0} - \mu_{W_1}| > 2\epsilon_{cut}$. Then with probability $1 - \delta$* ADWIN *shrinks W to W_1, or shorter.*

This theorem justifies us in using ADWIN in two ways:

- As a *change detector*, since ADWIN shrinks its window if and only if there has been a significant change in recent times (with high probability);

- As an *estimator* for the current average of the sequence it is reading since, with high probability, older parts of the window with a significantly different average are automatically dropped.

ADWIN is parameter and assumption free in the sense that it automatically detects and adapts to the current rate of change. Its only parameter is a

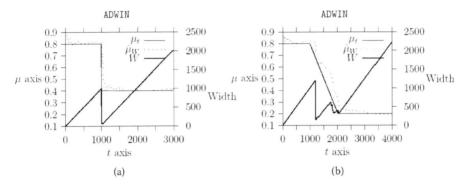

Figure 2.5: Output of algorithm `ADWIN` for different change rates: (a) Output of algorithm `ADWIN` with abrupt change; (b) Output of algorithm `ADWIN` with slow gradual changes.

confidence bound δ, indicating how confident we want to be in the algorithm's output, inherent to all algorithms dealing with random processes.

Also important, `ADWIN` does not maintain the window explicitly, but compresses it using a variant of the exponential histogram technique in Datar et al. (2002). This means that it keeps a window of length W using only $O(\log W)$ memory and $O(\log W)$ processing time per item, rather than the $O(W)$ one expects from a naïve implementation.

Let us consider how `ADWIN` behaves in two special cases: sudden (but infrequent) changes, and slow gradual changes. Suppose that for a long time μ_t has remained fixed at a value μ, and that it suddenly jumps to a value $\mu' = \mu + \epsilon$. By part (2) of Theorem 2.2.4 one can derive that the window will start shrinking after $O(\mu \ln(1/\delta)/\epsilon^2)$ steps, and in fact will be shrunk to the point where only $O(\mu \ln(1/\delta)/\epsilon^2)$ examples prior to the change are left. From then on, if no further changes occur, no more examples will be dropped so the window will expand unboundedly.

In case of a gradual change with slope α following a long stationary period at μ, observe that the average of W_1 after n_1 steps is $\mu + \alpha n_1/2$; we have:

$$\epsilon = \alpha n_1/2 \geq O(\sqrt{\mu \ln(1/\delta)/n_1})$$

iff $n_1 = O(\mu \ln(1/\delta)/\alpha^2)^{1/3}$. So n_1 steps after the change the window will start shrinking, and will remain at approximately size n_1 from then on. A dependence on α of the form $O(\alpha^{-2/3})$ may seem odd at first, but one can show that this window length is actually optimal in this setting, even if α is known: it minimizes the sum of variance error (due to short window) and error due to out-of-date data (due to long windows in the presence of change). Thus, in this setting, `ADWIN` provably adjusts automatically the window setting to its optimal value, up to multiplicative constants.

Figure 2.5 illustrates these behaviors. In Figure 2.5(a), a sudden change from $\mu_{t-1} = 0.8$ to $\mu_t = 0.4$ occurs, at $t = 1000$. One can see that the window size grows linearly up to $t = 1000$, that ADWIN cuts the window severely 10 steps later (at $t = 1010$), and that the window expands again linearly after time $t = 1010$. In Figure 2.5(b), μ_t gradually descends from 0.8 to 0.2 in the range $t \in [1000, 2000]$. In this case, ADWIN cuts the window sharply at t around 1200 (i.e., 200 steps after the slope starts), keeps the window length bounded (with some random fluctuations) while the slope lasts, and starts growing it linearly again after that. As predicted by theory, detecting the change is harder in slopes than in abrupt changes.

2.2.6 Data Synopsis

With new data constantly arriving even as old data is being processed, the amount of computation time per data element must be low. Furthermore, since we are limited to bounded amount of memory, it may not be possible to produce exact answers. High-quality approximate answers can be an acceptable solution. Two types of techniques can be used: data reduction and sliding windows. In both cases, they must use data structures that can be maintained incrementally. The most commonly used techniques for data reduction involve *sampling*, *synopsis* and *histograms*, and *wavelets*.

2.2.6.1 Sampling

Sampling is a common practice for selecting a subset of data to be analyzed. Instead of dealing with an entire data stream, we select instances at periodic intervals. Sampling is used to compute statistics (expected values) of the stream. While sampling methods reduce the amount of data to process, and, by consequence, the computational costs, they can also be a source of errors. The main problem is to obtain a *representative* sample, a subset of data that has approximately the same properties of the original data.

How to obtain an unbiased sampling of the data? In statistics, most techniques require knowing the length of the stream. For data streams, we need to modify these techniques. The key problems are the *sample size* and *sampling method*.

The simplest form of sampling is *random sampling*, where each element has equal probability of being selected. The *reservoir sampling* technique (Vitter, 1985) is the classic algorithm to maintain an online random sample. The basic idea consists of maintaining a sample of size k, called the reservoir. As the stream flows, every new element has a probability k/n of replacing an old element in the reservoir.

Analyze the simplest case: sample size $k = 1$. The probability that the ith item is the sample from a stream length n:

$$\tfrac{1}{2} \times \tfrac{2}{3} \ldots \times \tfrac{i}{i+1} \times \ldots \times \tfrac{n-2}{n-1} \times \tfrac{n-1}{n} = 1/n$$

Algorithm 2: The Reservoir Sampling Algorithm.

---

input: S: a stream of values

         k: size of the reservoir

begin

     /* Creates uniform sample of fixed size k */

     Insert the first k elements into the reservoir;

     foreach $v \in S$ **do**

         Let i be the position of v;

         Generate a random integer M in the range $1, \ldots, i$;

         if $M \leq k$ **then**

             Insert v in the reservoir;

             Delete an instance from the reservoir at random.

end

A usual improvement consists of determining the number of elements to skip before the next is added to the reservoir, instead of flipping a coin for each element. Extensions to maintain a sample of size k over a count-based sliding window of the n most recent data items from data streams appear in Babcock et al. (2002).

Min-Wise Sampling. Another sampling approach is the Min-Wise Sampling strategy (Broder et al., 2000). For each element of the stream, pick a random number in the range $[0, 1]$, and retain the elements with the smallest random number seen so far. It is straightforward, that all elements have the same probability of being selected, and therefore the sample is uniform. The advantage of this procedure is its applicability in distributed streams, by merging results and picking the retained elements with smaller numbers.

Load Shedding. Sampling is also useful to *slow down* data. Load shedding techniques has been studied to adjust the data transmission rate controlling the congestion of stream applications in computer networks (Tatbul et al., 2003). These techniques are used in the context of continuous queries. Whenever the arrival rate of the stream might overload the system, some fractions of data are discarded. Load shedding techniques focus o when to discard data, if tuples might be dropped at any point of their processing states, and how much load to shed based on measures of quality of service.

Sampling is useful to slow-down data, but might be problematic in monitoring problems, because it reduces the probability of detecting changes and anomalies.

2.2.6.2   Synopsis and Histograms

Synopsis and histograms are summarization techniques that can be used to approximate the frequency distribution of element values in a data stream. They are commonly used to capture attribute value distribution statistics for query optimizers (like range queries). A histogram is defined by a set of non-overlapping intervals. Each interval is defined by the boundaries and a frequency count. The reference technique is the V-Optimal histogram (Guha et al., 2004). It defines intervals that minimize the frequency variance within each interval. Sketches are special case of synopsis, which provide probabilistic guarantees on the quality of the approximate answer (e.g., the answer is 10 ± 2 with probability 95%). Sketches have been used to solve the k-hot items (Cormode and Muthukrishnan, 2003), dicussed in Section 7.2.

2.2.6.3 Wavelets

Wavelet transforms are mathematical techniques in which signals are represented as a weighted sum of simpler, fixed building waveforms at different scales and positions. Wavelets express a times series in terms of translation and scaling operations over a simple function called *mother wavelet*. While scaling compresses or stretches the mother wavelet, translation shifts it along the time axis.

Wavelets attempt to capture trends in numerical functions. Wavelets decompose a signal into a set of coefficients. The decomposition does not preclude information loss, because it is possible to reconstruct the signal from the full set of coefficients. Nevertheless, it is possible to eliminate small coefficients from the wavelet transform introducing small errors when reconstructing the original signal. The reduced set of coefficients are of great interest for streaming algorithms.

A wavelet transform decomposes a signal into several groups of coefficients. Different coefficients contain information about characteristics of the signal at different scales. Coefficients at coarse scale capture global trends of the signal, while coefficients at fine scales capture details and local characteristics.

The simplest and most common transformation is the Haar wavelet (Jawerth and Sweldens, 1994). It is based on the multiresolution analysis principle, where the space is divided into a sequence of nested subspaces. Any sequence $(x_0, x_1, \ldots, x_{2n}, x_{2n+1})$ of even length is transformed into a sequence of two-component-vectors $((s_0, d_0), \ldots, (s_n, d_n))$. The process continues, by separating the sequences s and d, and recursively transforming the sequence s. One stage of the Fast Haar-Wavelet Transform consists of:

$$\begin{bmatrix} s_i \\ d_i \end{bmatrix} = 1/2 \begin{bmatrix} 1 & 1 \\ 1 & -1 \end{bmatrix} \times \begin{bmatrix} x_i \\ x_{i+1} \end{bmatrix}$$

As an illustrative example, consider the sequence $f = (2, 5, 8, 9, 7, 4, -1, 1)$. Applying the Haar transform:

- **Step 1**
  $s_1 = (2 + 5, 8 + 9, 7 + 4, -1 + 1)/2$, $d_1 = (2 - 5, 8 - 9, 7 - 4, -1 - 1)/2$
  $s_1 = (7, 17, 11, 0)/2$, $\mathbf{d_1} = \{-1.5, -.5, 1.5, -1\}$

- **Step 2**
  $s_2 = ((7 + 17)/2, (11 + 0)/2)/2$, $d_2 = ((7 - 17)/2, (11 - 0)/2)/2$
  $s_2 = (24/2, 11/2)/2$, $\mathbf{d_2} = \{-2.5, -2.75\}$

- **Step 3**
  $s_3 = ((24 + 11)/4)/2$, $d_3 = \{((24 - 11)/4)/2\}$
  $s_3 = 4.375$, $\mathbf{d}_3 = \{1.625\}$

The sequence $\{4.375, 1.625, -2.5, -2.75, -1.5, -.5, 1.5, -1\}$ are the coefficients of the expansion. The process consists of adding/subtracting pairs of numbers, divided by the normalization factor.

Wavelet analysis is popular in several streaming applications, because most signals can be represented using a small set of coefficients. Matias et al. (1998) present an efficient algorithm based on multi-resolution wavelet decomposition for building histograms with application to database problems, like selectivity estimation. In the same research line, Chakrabarti et al. (2001) propose the use of *wavelet-coefficient synopses* as a general method to provide approximate answers to queries. The approach uses multi-dimensional wavelets synopsis from relational tables. Guha and Harb (2005) propose one-pass wavelet construction streaming algorithms with provable error guarantees for minimizing a variety of error-measures including all weighted and relative l_p norms. Marascu and Masseglia (2009) present an outlier detection method using the two most significant coefficients of Haar wavelets.

2.2.6.4   Discrete Fourier Transform

The Discrete Fourier transform (DFT) (Brigham, 1988) of a time sequence $x_1, x_2, \ldots, x_w$ is a sequence $DFT(x) = X = X_1, X_2, \ldots, X_{w-1}$ of complex numbers given by

$$X_F = \frac{1}{\sqrt{w}} \sum_{i=0}^{w-1} x_i e^{j2\pi F_i/w}, \text{ where } j = \sqrt{-1}.$$

The inverse Fourier transform of X is given by:

$$x_i = \frac{1}{\sqrt{w}} \sum_{F=0}^{w-1} X_F e^{j2\pi F_i/w}.$$

A DFT decomposes a sequence of values into components of different frequencies. An interesting property is that DFT preserves the Euclidean distance between any two sequences. Since for most time series the first few coefficients contain most of the energy we would expect that those coefficients retain the raw shape of the sequence.

There are several efficient and fast Fourier transform algorithms (FFT). Their complexity is $O(n \times log(n))$ while to compute the discrete Fourier transform from the definition is $O(N^2)$ (Brigham, 1988).

2.3 Illustrative Applications

2.3.1 A Data Warehouse Problem: Hot-Lists

Assume we have a retail data warehouse. The actual size of the data warehouse is 3 TB of data, and hundreds of gigabytes of new sales records are updated daily. The order of magnitude of the different items is millions.

The *hot-list* problem consists of identifying the most (say 20) popular items. Moreover, we have restricted memory: we can have a memory of hundreds of bytes only. The goal is to continuously maintain a list of the top-k most frequent elements in a stream. Here, the goal is the *rank* of the items. The absolute value of counts is not relevant, but their relative position. A first and trivial approach consists of maintaining a count for each element in the alphabet and when query returns the k first elements in the sorted list of counts. This is an exact and efficient solution for small alphabets. For large alphabets it is very space (and time) inefficient; there will be a large number of zero counts.

Misra and Gries (1982) present a simple algorithm (Algorithm 3) that maintains partial information of interest by monitoring only a small subset m of elements. We should note that $m > k$ but $m \ll N$ where N is the cardinality of the alphabet. When a new element i arrives, if it is in the set of monitored elements, increment the appropriate counter; otherwise, if there is some counter with count zero, it is allocated to the new item, and the counter set to 1, otherwise decrement all the counters.

Later, Metwally et al. (2005) present the `Space-saving` algorithm (Algorithm 4), an interesting variant of the Misra and Gries (1982) algorithm. When a new element i arrives, if it is in the set of monitored elements, increment the appropriate counter; otherwise remove the element with fewer hits, and include i with a counter initialized with the counts of the removed element plus one.

Both algorithms are efficient for very large alphabets with skewed distributions. The advantage of the `Space-saving` comes up if the popular elements evolve over time, because it tends to give more importance to recent observations. The elements that are growing more popular will gradually be pushed to the top of the list. Both algorithms continuously return a list of the top-k elements. This list might be only an approximate solution. Metwally et al. (2005) report that, even if it is not possible to guarantee top-k elements, the algorithm can guarantee top-k' elements, with $k' \approx k$. If we denote by c_i the count associated with the most recent monitored element, any element i is *guaranteed* to be among the top-m elements if its guaranteed number of hits, $count_i - c_i$, exceeds $count_{m+1}$. Nevertheless, the counts maintained by both are not liable, because only the rank of elements is of interest.

Algorithm 3: The `Frequent` Algorithm.

---

input: S: A Sequence of Examples
begin
    foreach *example* $(e) \in S$ **do**
        if e *is monitored* **then**
            Increment $Count_e$;
        else
            if *there is a* $Count_j == 0$ **then**
                Replace element j by e and initialize $Count_e = 1$;
            else
                Subtract 1 to each $Count_i$;
end

Algorithm 4: The `Space-Saving` Algorithm.

---

input: S: A Sequence of Examples
begin
    foreach *example* $(e) \in S$ **do**
        if e *is monitored* **then**
            Increment $Count_e$;
        else
            Let e_m be the element with least hits min;
            Replace e_m with e with $count_e = min + 1$;
end

2.3.2 Computing the Entropy in a Stream

Entropy measures the randomness of data. A number of recent results in the networking community have used entropy in analyzing IP network traffic at the packet level (Chakrabarti et al., 2006, 2007).

Wagner and Plattner (2005) present a very nice description of the connections between *randomness* of traffic sequences and propagation of malicious events. In that paper, the authors wrote:

> *When a fast scanning worm propagates through the Internet, the propagation activity looks like this: a smaller number of infected hosts tries to find other hosts to be infected by attempting to connect to them in a random fashion. This scanning activity is different from normal Internet traffic. The connection between entropy and worm propagation is that worm traffic is more uniform or structured than normal traffic in some respects and a more random in others. The change in IP address characteristics seen on a flow level (i.e. when packets belonging to a TCP connection or*

Algorithm 5: Basic Estimator for the Entropy Norm.

---

input: S: A Sequence of Examples
begin

> Randomly sample a position j in the stream;
> Let r be the count how many times a_j appears subsequently;
> Output $X = \frac{r}{m} \times log(\frac{m}{r}) - \frac{(r-1)}{m} \times log(\frac{m}{r-1})$;

end

> *UDP data stream with same source/destination IP address and port numbers are reported aggregated into one flow) is relatively intuitive: infected, scanning hosts try to connect to a lot of other hosts. If these flows grow to be a significant part of the set of flows seen in total, the source IP addresses of the scanning hosts will be seen in many flows and since they are relatively few hosts, the source IP address fields will contain less entropy per address seen than normal traffic. On the other hand the target IP addresses seen in flows will be much more random than in normal traffic.*

The authors developed an entropy-based approach that determines and reports entropy contents of traffic parameters such as IP addresses. Changes in the entropy content indicate a massive network event.

The problem we address here is how to compute entropy in high-speed streams with very large alphabets. Consider a large sequence of characters $S = \langle a_1, a_2, a_3, \ldots, a_m \rangle$ where each $a_j \in \{1, \ldots n\}$. Let f_i be the frequency of i in the sequence. The goal is to compute the empirical entropy:

$$H(S) = -\sum_i \frac{f_i}{m} log(\frac{f_i}{m}) = -\sum_i p_i log(p_i)$$

.

This is an easy problem, if we have $O(n)$ space: compute each f_i exactly. More challenging is if n is huge, m is huge, and we have only one pass over the input. The challenge is approximately compute $H(S)$ in space sublinear in m, the stream length, and n, the alphabet size. We do not require an exact answer. A (ϵ, δ) approximation, that is, an answer that is $(1 \pm \epsilon) \times H(S)$ with probability $1 - \delta$ is enough.

Chakrabarti et al. (2007) proposed a method to solve this problem. To understand their proposal, consider Algorithm 5. The expected value of X, when computed from large substrings, is an unbiased estimator for the entropy: $E[X] = H(S)$. This estimate is not very reliable, but it can be improved by taking the average of many repetitions using different random samples. Nevertheless, the quality of this estimate is problematic for low entropy streams.

To overcome this difficulty, Chakrabarti et al. (2007) propose another approach. The authors observe that low entropy streams occur when one of the tokens is much more frequent than all the others. They propose to decompose entropy as:

$$H(S) = -p_a \times log_2(p_a) + (1 - p_a) \times H(S') \tag{2.8}$$

where p_a is the frequency of the most frequent element in S and S' is the substream of S after removing a. In low entropy streams, a is the *boring guy*.

How can we find p_a and $H(S')$ online in one pass? Remember that $H(S')$ can be computed, if we know S', using the simple estimator described in Algorithm 5. The problem is that a, the *boring guy* (if there is one), is not known in advance.

Based on the Min-Wise sampling strategy (described in Section 2.2.6.1), Chakrabarti et al. (2007) propose the algorithm presented in Algorithm 6. The main idea is to keep two samples, and two sets of statistics: $(token_1, tag_1, freq_1)$ and $(token_2, tag_2, freq_2)$ to compute the estimator. Both sets contain a token, a random number in the esprit of Min-Wise sampling (see Section 2.2.6.1), and the frequency of the token. These statistics are such that $tag_1 < tag_2$ and $token_1$ will be sample from S, and $token_2$ will be sample from $S' = S \setminus \{token_1\}$.

Algorithm 6: The Maintain Samples Algorithm.

---

input: S: A Sequence of Examples
begin
    foreach *example* $(e) \in S$ **do**
        Let x = random();
        if $e == token_1$ **then**
            if $x < tag_1$ **then**
                $tag_1 = x; token_1 = e; freq_1 = 1;$
            else
                $freq_1 = freq_1 + 1;$
        else
            if $e == token_2$ **then**
                $freq_2 = freq_2 + 1;$
            if $x < tag_1$ **then**
                $tag_2 = tag_1; token_2 = token_1; freq_2 = freq_1; tag_1 = x;$
                $token_1 = e; freq_1 = 1;$
            else
                if $x < tag_2$ **then**
                    $tag_2 = x; token_2 = e; freq_2 = 1;$
end

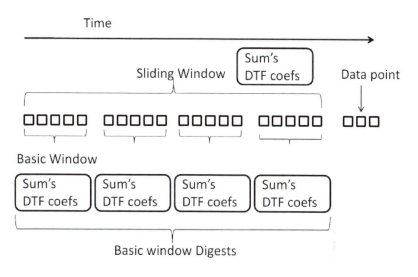

Figure 2.6: The three aggregation levels in StatStream.

2.3.3 Monitoring Correlations Between Data Streams

Zhu and Shasha (2002) present the StatStream system for monitoring tens of thousands of high-speed time-series data streams in an online fashion and making decisions based on them. In addition to single stream statistics such as average and standard deviation, over sliding windows, StatStream also finds high correlations among all pairs of streams for a given period of time.

StatStream implements efficient methods for solving these problems based on Discrete Fourier Transforms and a three-level time interval hierarchy. The time intervals considered are:

- **Data points** - the smallest unit of time over which the system collects data;

- **Basic windows** - a consecutive subsequence of time points over which the system maintains a digest incrementally;

- **Sliding window** - a user-defined subsequence of basic windows over which the user wants statistics.

Figure 2.6 shows the relation between the three levels. Let w be the size of the sliding window. Suppose $w = kb$, where b is the length of a basic window and k is the number of basic windows inside the sliding window. Let $S[0], S[1], \ldots, S[k-1]$ denote the sequence of basic windows inside the sliding window. The elements of a basic window $S[i] = s[(t-w) + ib + 1 : (t-w) + (i+1)b]$. The sliding window moves over basic windows, when a new basic window $S[k]$ is full filled in, $S[0]$ expires.

Simple Statistics. Moving averages always involve w points. For each basic window `StatStream` maintain the digest $\sum(S[i])$. When the new basic window $S[k]$ is available and the sliding window moves, the sum is updated as: $\sum_{new}(s) = \sum_{old}(s) + \sum S[k] - \sum S[0]$. Maximum, minimum, and standard deviation are computed in a similar way.

Monitoring Correlation. A useful normalization of a series $x_1, \ldots, x_w$ over a sliding window of size w is: $\hat{x}_i = \frac{x_i - \bar{x}}{\sigma_x}$ where $\sigma_x = \sqrt{\sum_{i=1}^{w}(x_i - \bar{x})^2}$. The correlation coefficient of two time series can be reduced to the Euclidean distance between their normalized series:

$$corr(x, y) = 1 - \frac{1}{2}d^2(\hat{x}, \hat{y})$$

where $d(\hat{x}, \hat{y})$ is the Euclidean distance between $\hat{x}$ and $\hat{y}$. The proof is based on $\sum_{i=1}^{w}\hat{x}_i^2 = 1$ and $corr(x, y) = \sum_{i=1}^{w}\hat{x}_i \cdot \hat{y}_i$.

By reducing the correlation coefficient to the Euclidean distance, we need to identify the sequences with correlation coefficients higher than a user specified threshold. Let the DFT (see Section 2.2.6.4) of the normalized form of two time series x and y be $\hat{X}$ and $\hat{Y}$ respectively. Let $d_n(\hat{X}, \hat{Y})$ be the Euclidean distance between series $\hat{X}_1, \hat{X}_2, \ldots, \hat{X}_n$ and $\hat{Y}_1, \hat{Y}_2, \ldots, \hat{Y}_n$. Then

$$corr(x, y) \geq 1 - \epsilon^2 \Rightarrow d_n(\hat{X}, \hat{Y}) \leq \epsilon$$

where $n, (n << w)$ refers to the number of DFT coefficients retained. From this result, we can examine the correlations of only those stream pairs for which $d_n(\hat{X}, \hat{Y}) \leq \epsilon$ holds. We will get a superset of highly correlated pairs and there will be no false negatives.

The technique can be extended to report stream pairs of high negative correlation:

$$corr(x, y) \leq -1 + \epsilon^2 \Rightarrow d_n(-\hat{X}, \hat{Y}) \leq \epsilon$$

Incremental Maintenance of DFT Coefficients. The DFT coefficients $\hat{X}$ of the normalized sequence can be computed from the DFT coefficients X of the original sequence: $\hat{X}_0 = 0$ and $\hat{X}_i = \frac{X_i}{\sigma_x}$.

Let X_m^{old} be the m-th DFT coefficient of the series in sliding window $x_0, x_1, \ldots, x_{w-1}$ and X_m^{new} be that coefficient of the series $x_1, x_2, \ldots, x_w$, $X_m^{new} = e^{\frac{j2\pi m}{w}}(X_m^{old} + \frac{x_w - x_0}{\sqrt{w}})$.

This can be extended to an update on the basic windows when the sliding window moves. Let X_m^{old} be the m-th DFT coefficient of the series in sliding window $x_0, x_1, \ldots, x_{w-1}$ and X_m^{new} be that coefficient of the series $x_b, x_{b+1}, \ldots, x_w, x_{w+1}, \ldots, x_{w+b-1}$.

$$X_m^{new} = e^{\frac{j2\pi mb}{w}}X_m^{old} + \frac{1}{\sqrt{w}}\left(\sum_{i=0}^{b-1}e^{\frac{j2\pi m(b-i)}{w}}x_{w+i} - \sum_{i=0}^{b-1}e^{\frac{j2\pi m(b-i)}{w}}x_i\right).$$

To update the DFT coefficients incrementally, `StatStream` should keep the following n summaries for the basic windows:

$$\sum_{i=0}^{b-1} e^{\frac{j2\pi m(b-i)}{w}} x_i, m = 1, \ldots, n$$

Reducing the space of correlated streams. The feature space of the DFT coefficients on normalized sequences is bounded: $|\hat{X}_i| \leq \frac{\sqrt{2}}{2}, i = 1, \ldots, n$. By using DFT on normalized sequences, we map the original sequences into a bounded feature space. `StatStream` superimposes an $\hat{n}$ grid in the DFT feature space by partition that spaces into cells with the same size and shape. Each stream is mapped to a cell based on its first $\hat{n}$ normalized co-efficients. Suppose a stream x is hashed to cell $(c_1, c_2, \ldots, c_{\hat{n}})$. To report the streams whose correlation coefficients with x less to the threshold $1 - \epsilon^2$, only streams hashed to cells adjacent to cell $(c_1, c_2, \ldots, c_{\hat{n}})$ need to be examined. High negative correlations with x must be hashed to cells adjacent to cell $(-c_1, -c_2, \ldots, -c_{\hat{n}})$. After hashing the streams to cells, the number of stream pairs to be examined is greatly reduced. We can compute their Euclidean distance and correlation based on the first $\hat{n}$ DFT coefficients.

2.3.4 Monitoring Threshold Functions over Distributed Data Streams

The problem consists of monitoring data produced in a sensor network. The sensors monitor the concentration of air pollutants. Each sensor maintains a data vector with measurements of the concentration of various pollutants $(CO_2, SO_2, O_3,$ etc.). A function on the average of the data vectors determines the Air Quality Index (AQI). The goal consists of triggering an alert whenever the AQI exceeds a given threshold.

The problem involves computing a function over the data collected in all sensors. A trivial solution consists of sending data to a central node. This might be problematic due to the huge volume of data collected in each sensor and the large number of sensors.

Sharfman, Schuster, and Keren (2007) present a distributed algorithm to solve this type of problem. They present a geometric interpretation of the problem. Figures 2.7 illustrates the vector space. The gray dots corresponds to the sensor's measurements, and the black dot to the aggregation vector. The gray region corresponds to the alarm region. The goal is to detect whenever the cross is inside the gray region.

The method is based on local computations with reduced communications between sensors. The base idea is that the aggregated function is always in-side the convex-hull of the vector space (see Figure 2.8 A and B). Suppose that all points share a reference point. Each sensor can compute a sphere with diameter the actual measurement of the sensor and the reference point. If all spheres are in the normal region, the aggregated value is also in the

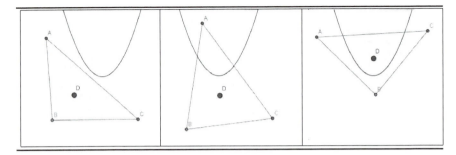

Figure 2.7: The vector space. The gray dots (A,B,C) correspond to the sensor's measurements and the black dot (D) to the aggregation vector. The gray region corresponds to the alarm region. The center figure illustrates a normal air condition. The right figure presents an alarm condition, even though none of the sensors are inside the alarm region.

normal region. This holds, because the convex-hull of all vertex is bounded by the union of the spheres (see Figure 2.8 C and D). In the case that a sphere is not monochromatic, the node triggers the re-calculation of the aggregated function. The algorithm only uses local constraints! Mostly only local computations are required and this minimizes the communications between sensors.

Algorithm 7: The Monitoring Threshold Functions Algorithm (sensor node).

---

begin
    Broadcast Initial position
    Compute an initial reference point
    foreach *new measurement* **do**
        Compute the sphere and check its color
        if *sphere non-monochromatic* **then**
            Broadcast the actual measurement
            Recompute a new reference point
end

2.4 Notes

The research on Data Stream Management Systems started in the database community, to solve problems like continuous queries in transient data. The

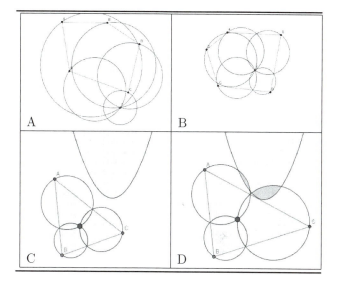

Figure 2.8: The bounding theorem. The convex-hull of sensors is bounded by the union of spheres. Sensors only need to communicate their measurements when the spheres are non-monochromatic.

most relevant projects include: The *Stanford StREam DatA Manager* (Stanford University) with focus on data management and query processing in the presence of multiple, continuous, rapid, time-varying data streams. At MIT, the `Aurora` project was developed to build a single infrastructure that can efficiently and seamlessly meet the demanding requirements of stream-based applications. It focuses on real-time data processing issues, such as quality of service (QoS)- and memory-aware operator scheduling, semantic load shedding for dealing with transient spikes at incoming data rates. Two other well known systems include `Telegraph` developed at University of Berkeley, and `NiagaraCQ` developed at University of Wisconsin. We must also refer to the `Hancock` project, developed at AT&T Research labs, where a C-based domain-specific language was designed to make it easy to read, write, and maintain programs that manipulate huge amounts of data.

Chapter 3

Change Detection

Most of the machine learning algorithms assume that examples are generated at random, according to some stationary probability distribution. In this chapter, we study the problem of learning when the distribution that generates the examples changes over time. Embedding change detection in the learning process is one of the most challenging problems when learning from data streams. We review the Machine Learning literature for learning in the presence of drift, discuss the major issues to detect and adapt decision problems when learning from streams with unknown dynamics, and present illustrative algorithms to detect changes in the distribution of the training examples.

3.1   Introduction

In many applications, learning algorithms act in dynamic environments where the data flows continuously. If the process is not strictly stationary (as most of real-world applications), the target concept could change over time. Nevertheless, most of the work in Machine Learning assumes that training examples are generated at random according to some stationary probability distribution. Basseville and Nikiforov (1993) present several examples of real problems where change detection is relevant. These include user modeling, monitoring in bio-medicine and industrial processes, fault detection and diagnosis, safety of complex systems, etc.

The *Probably Approximately Correct - PAC* learning (Valiant, 1984) framework assumes that examples are independent and randomly generated according to some probability distribution D. In this context, some model-class learning algorithms (like Decision Trees, Neural Networks, some variants of k-Nearest Neighbors, etc.) could generate hypotheses that converge to the Bayes-error in the limit, that is, when the number of training examples increases to infinite. All that is required is that D must be stationary; the distribution must not change over time.

Our environment is naturally dynamic, constantly changing in time. Huge amounts of data are being continuously generated by various dynamic systems or applications. Real-time surveillance systems, telecommunication systems, sensor networks and other dynamic environments are such examples. Learning algorithms that model the underlying processes must be able to track this behavior and adapt the decision models accordingly.

3.2   Tracking Drifting Concepts

Concept drift means that the concept about which data is being collected may shift from time to time, each time after some minimum permanence. Changes occur over time. The evidence of drift in a concept is reflected in some way in the training examples. Old observations, which reflect the behavior of nature in the past, become irrelevant to the current state of the phenomena under observation and the learning agent must forget that information.

Suppose a supervised learning problem, where the learning algorithm observes sequences of pairs $(\vec{x}_i, y_i)$ where $y_i \in \{C_1, C_2, ..., C_k\}$. At each time stamp t the learning algorithm outputs a class prediction $\hat{y}_t$ for the given feature vector $\vec{x}_t$. Assuming that examples are independent and generated at random by a stationary distribution $\mathcal{D}$, some model class algorithms (e.g., decision trees, neural networks, etc.) can approximate $\mathcal{D}$ with arbitrary accuracy (bounded by the *Bayes error*) whenever the number of examples increases to infinite.

Suppose now the case where $\mathcal{D}$ is not stationary. The data stream consists of sequences of examples $e_i = (\vec{x}_i, y_i)$. Suppose further that from time to time, the distribution that is generating the examples changes. The data stream can be seen as sequences $< S_1, S_2, ..., S_k, ... >$ where each element S_i is a set of examples generated by some stationary distribution $\mathcal{D}_i$. We designate as *context* each one of these sequences. In that case, and in the whole dataset, no learning algorithm can guarantee arbitrary precision. Nevertheless, if the number of observations within each sequence S_i is large enough, we could approximate a learning model to $\mathcal{D}_i$. The main problem is to detect change points whenever they occur. In real problems between two consecutive sequences S_i and S_{i+1} there could be a transition phase where some examples of both distributions appear mixed. An example generated by a distribution $\mathcal{D}_{i+1}$ is noise for distribution $\mathcal{D}_i$. This is another difficulty faced by change detection algorithms. They must differentiate *noise* from *change*. The difference between noise and examples of another distribution is *persistence*: there should be a consistent set of examples of the new distribution. Algorithms for change detection must combine *robustness* to noise with *sensitivity* to concept change.

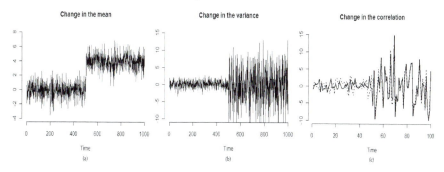

Figure 3.1: Three illustrative examples of change: (a) Change in the mean; (b) Change in variance; (c) Change in correlation.

3.2.1 The Nature of Change

The nature of change is diverse and abundant. In this section, we identify two dimensions for analysis. The *causes* of change, and the *rate* of change. In a first dimension, the causes of change, we can distinguish between changes due to modifications in the context of learning, because of changes in hidden variables, from changes in the characteristic properties in the observed variables. Existing Machine Learning algorithms learn from observations described by a finite set of attributes. In real-world problems, there can be important properties of the domain that are not observed. There could be *hidden* variables that influence the behavior of nature (Harries et al., 1998). Hidden variables may change over time. As a result, concepts learned at one time can become inaccurate. On the other hand, there could be changes in the characteristic properties of the nature.

The second dimension is related to the *rate of change*. The term *Concept Drift* is more associated to gradual changes in the target concept (for example the rate of changes in prices), while the term *Concept Shift* refers to abrupt changes. Usually, detection of abrupt changes is easier and requires few examples for detection. Gradual changes are more difficult to detect. At least in the first phases of gradual change, the perturbations in data can be seen as noise by the detection algorithm. To be resilient to noise, they often require more examples to distinguish change from noise. In an extreme case, if the rate of change is larger than our ability to learn, we cannot learn anything. In the other side, slow changes can be confused with stationarity.

We can formalize concept drift as a change in the joint probability $P(\vec{x}, y)$, which can be decomposed in:

$$P(\vec{x}, y) = P(y|\vec{x}) \times P(\vec{x})$$

We are interested in changes in the y values given the attribute values $\vec{x}$, that is $P(y|\vec{x})$.

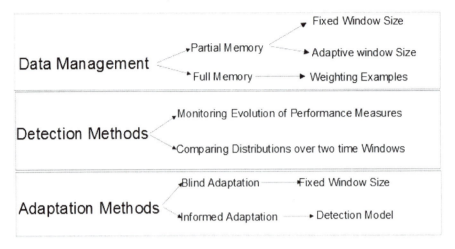

Figure 3.2: Main dimensions in change detection methods in data mining.

Lazarescu et al. (2004) defines concept drift in terms of consistency and persistence. Consistency refers to the change $\epsilon_t = \theta_t - \theta_{t-1}$ that occurs between consecutive examples of the target concept from time $t - 1$ to t, with θ_t being the state of the target function in time t. A concept is *consistent* if ϵ_t is smaller or equal than a consistency threshold ϵ_c. A concept is *persistent* if it is consistent during p times, where $p \geq \frac{w}{2}$ and w is the size of the window. The drift is therefore considered *permanent* (real) if it is both consistent and persistent. Virtual drift is consistent but it is not persistent. Noise has neither consistency nor persistence. Whenever a change in the underlying concept generating data occurs, the class-distribution changes, at least in some regions of the instance space. Nevertheless, it is possible to observe changes in the class-distribution without concept drift. This is usually referred as *virtual drift* (Widmer and Kubat, 1996). In practice, the decision model needs to be updated, regardless of whether the concept change is real or virtual.

3.2.2   Characterization of Drift Detection Methods

There are several methods in Machine Learning to deal with changing concepts: Klinkenberg and Renz (1998); Klinkenberg and Joachims (2000); Klinkenberg (2004); Widmer and Kubat (1996); Zeira et al. (2004). All of these methods assume that the most recent examples are the relevant ones. In general, approaches to cope with concept drift can be analyzed into four dimensions: data management, detection methods, adaptation methods, and decision model management (see Figure 3.2).

3.2.2.1 Data Management

The data management methods characterize the information about data stored in memory to maintain a decision model consistent with the actual state of the nature. We can distinguish:

- **Full Memory.** Methods that store in memory sufficient statistics over all the examples. Examples include weighting the examples accordingly to their age. Weighted examples are based on the simple idea that the importance of an example should decrease with time. A simple strategy consists in multipling the sufficient statistics by a fading factor α $(0 < \alpha < 1)$. Suppose that at time i, the stored sufficient statistic is S_{i-1} and we observe example x_i. Assuming an aggregation function $G(x, S)$, the fading factor acts like: $S_i = G(x_{i-1}, \alpha \times S_{x_i})$. Thus, the oldest information has less importance. Koychev (2000, 2002) presents methods for linear decay, while Klinkenberg (2004) present exponential decay method. This last method weights the examples solely based on their age using an exponential aging function: $w_\lambda(x) = exp(-\lambda i)$, where example x was found i time steps ago. The parameter λ controls how fast the weights decrease. For larger values of λ less weight is assigned to the examples and less importance they have. If $\lambda = 0$, all the examples have the same weight.

- **Partial Memory.** Methods that store in memory only the most recent examples. Examples are stored in a *first-in first-out (fifo)* data structure. Examples in the *fifo* define a time-window over the stream of examples. At each time step, the learner induces a decision model using only the examples that are included in the window. The key difficulty is how to select the appropriate window size. A small size window, which reflects accurately the current distribution, can assure a fast adaptability in phases with concept changes but in more stable phases it can affect the learner performance; while a large window would produce good and stable learning results in periods of stability but can not react quickly to concept changes.

  1. **Fixed Size Windows.** These methods store in memory a fixed number of the most recent examples. Whenever a new example is available, it is stored in memory and the oldest one is discarded. This is the simplest method to deal with concept drift and can be used as a baseline for comparisons.

  2. **Adaptive Size Windows.** In this method, the set of examples in the window is variable. It is used in conjunction with a detection model. The most common strategy consists of decreasing the size of the window whenever the detection model signals drift and increasing otherwise.

Dynamic environments with non-stationary distributions require the forgetfulness of the observations not consistent with the actual behavior of the nature. Drift detection algorithms must not only adapt the decision model to newer information but also forget old information. The memory model also indicates the *forgetting mechanism*. Weighting examples corresponds to a *gradual* forgetting. The relevance of old information is less and less important. Time windows correspond to *abrupt* forgetting (weight equal 0). The examples are deleted from memory. We can combine, of course, both forgetting mechanisms by weighting the examples in a time window (see Klinkenberg (2004)).

3.2.2.2   Detection Methods

The Detection Model characterizes the techniques and mechanisms for drift detection. One advantage detection model, is that they can provide meaningful description (indicating change-points or small time-windows where the change occurs) and quantification of the changes. They may follow two different approaches:

1. Monitoring the evolution of performance indicators. Some indicators (e.g., performance measures, properties of the data, etc.) are monitored over time (see Klinkenberg and Renz (1998); Zeira et al. (2004) for a good overview of these indicators).

2. Monitoring distributions on two different time-windows. A reference window, which usually summarizes past information, and a window over the most recent examples (Kifer et al., 2004).

Most of the work in drift detection follows the first approach. Relevant work in this approach is the FLORA family of algorithms developed by (Widmer and Kubat, 1996). FLORA2 includes a window adjustment heuristic for a rule-based classifier. To detect concept changes, the accuracy and the coverage of the current learner are monitored over time and the window size is adapted accordingly. In the context of information filtering, Klinkenberg and Renz (1998) propose monitoring the values of three performance indicators: *accuracy*, *recall*, and *precision* over time, and their posterior comparison to a confidence interval of standard sample errors for a moving average value (using the last M batches) of each particular indicator. Klinkenberg and Joachims (2000) present a theoretically well-founded method to recognize and handle concept changes using properties of Support Vector Machines. The key idea is to select the window size so that the estimated generalization error on new examples is minimized. This approach uses unlabeled data to reduce the need for labeled data; it does not require complicated parameterization and it works effectively and efficiently in practice.

An example of the latter approach, in the context of learning from Data Streams, has been presented by Kifer et al. (2004). The author proposes algorithms (statistical tests based on Chernoff bound) that examine samples drawn from two probability distributions and decide whether these distributions are different. In the same line, system VFDTc (Gama et al., 2006) has the ability to deal with concept drift, by continuously monitoring differences between two class-distributions of the examples: the class-distribution when a node was a leaf and the weighted sum of the class-distributions in the leaves descendant of that node.

The Cumulative Sum Algorithm. The cumulative sum (CUSUM algorithm) is a sequential analysis technique due to Page (1954). It is typically used for monitoring change detection. CUSUM was announced in Biometrika a few years after the publication of the SPRT algorithm (Wald, 1947). It is the classical change detection algorithm that gives an alarm when the mean of the input data is significantly different from zero. The CUSUM input can be any filter residual, for instance the prediction error from a Kalman filter. The CUSUM test is as follows:

$$g_0 = 0$$

$$g_t = max(0, g_{t-1} + (r_t - v))$$

The decision rule is: **if** $g_t > \lambda$ **then alarm and** $g_t = 0$. This formula only detects changes in the positive direction. When negative changes need to be found as well, the *min* operation should be used instead of the *max* operation. In this case, a change is detected when the value of S is below the (negative) value of the threshold value.

The CUSUM test is memoryless, and its accuracy depends on the choice of parameters v and λ. Both parameters are relevant to control the trade-off between earlier detecting true alarms by allowing some false alarms. Low values of v allows faster detection, at the cost of increasing the number of false alarms.

A variant of the previous algorithm is the Page-Hinkley (PH) test. This is a sequential analysis technique typically used for monitoring change detection in signal processing. It allows efficient detection of changes in the normal behavior of a process which is established by a model. The PH test is a sequential adaptation of the detection of an abrupt change in the average of a Gaussian signal (Mouss et al., 2004). This test considers a cumulative variable m_T, defined as the cumulated difference between the observed values and their mean till the current moment:

$$m_T = \sum_{t=1}^{T}(x_t - \bar{x}_T - \delta) \; where \; \bar{x}_T = \frac{1}{T}\sum_{t=1}^{T} x_t$$

Here δ corresponds to the magnitude of changes that are allowed. The minimum value of this variable is also computed with the following formula: $M_T = min(m_t, t = 1 \ldots T)$. As a final step, the test monitors the difference between M_T and m_T: $PH_T = m_T - M_T$. When this difference is greater than a given threshold (λ) we alarm a change in the distribution. The threshold

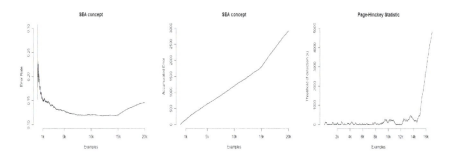

Figure 3.3: Illustrative example of the Page-Hinkley test. The left figure plots the on-line error rate of a learning algorithm. The center plot is the accumulated on-line error. The slope increases after the occurrence of a change. The right plot presents the evolution of the PH statistic.

λ depends on the admissible false alarm rate. Increasing λ will entail fewer false alarms, but might miss some changes. Figure 3.3 presents an illustrative example using the Page-Hinkley test.

The slope of the line that approximates the PH statistic provides information about the *velocity* of change. Abrupt and rapid changes correspond to high slope values. Slow and gradual changes correspond to lower values of the slope.

3.2.2.3 Adaptation Methods

The Adaptation model characterizes the adaptation of the decision model. Here, we consider two different approaches:

1. *Blind Methods*: Methods that adapt the learner at regular intervals without considering whether changes have really occurred. Examples include methods that weight the examples according to their age and methods that use time-windows of fixed size.

2. *Informed Methods*: Methods that only modify the decision model after a change was detected. They are used in conjunction with a detection model.

Blind methods adapt the learner at regular intervals without considering whether changes have really occurred. Examples of this approach are *weighted examples* and *time windows* of fixed size. Weighted examples are based on the simple idea that the importance of an example should decrease with time (references related to this approach can be found in: Klinkenberg and Renz (1998); Klinkenberg and Joachims (2000); Lanquillon (2001); Maloof and Michalski (2000); Widmer and Kubat (1996)).

3.2.2.4   Decision Model Management

Model management characterizes the number of decision models needed to maintain in memory. The key issue here is the assumption that data generated comes from multiple distributions, at least in the transition between contexts. Instead of maintaining a single decision model several authors propose the use of multiple decision models. A seminal work is the system presented by Kolter and Maloof (2003). The Dynamic Weighted Majority algorithm (DWM) is an ensemble method for tracking concept drift. DWM maintains an ensemble of base learners, predicts target values using a weighted-majority vote of these *experts*, and dynamically creates and deletes experts in response to changes in performance. DWM maintains an ensemble of predictive models, each with an associated weight. Experts can use the same algorithm for training and prediction, but are created at different time steps so they use different training set of examples. The final prediction is obtained as a weighted vote of all the experts. The weights of all the experts that misclassified the example are decreased by a multiplicative constant β. If the overall prediction is incorrect, a new expert is added to the ensemble with weight equal to the total weight of the ensemble. Finally, all the experts are trained on the example. Later, the same authors present the AddExp algorithm (Kolter and Maloof, 2005), a variant of DWM extended for classification and regression, able to prune some of the previous generated experts. All these algorithms are further detailed in Chapter 10.

Another important aspect is the *granularity* of decision models. When drift occurs, it does not have impact in the whole instance space, but in particular regions. Adaptation in global models (like naive Bayes, discriminant functions, SVM) require reconstruction of the decision model. Granular decision models (like decision rules and decision trees[1] can adapt parts of the decision model. They only need to adapt those parts that cover the region of the instance space affected by drift. An instance of this approach is the CVFDT algorithm (Hulten et al., 2001) that generates alternate decision trees at nodes where there is evidence that the splitting test is no longer appropriate. The system replaces the old tree with the new one when the last becomes more accurate.

3.2.3   A Note on Evaluating Change Detection Methods

Error rate is one of the most relevant criteria for classifier evaluation. To evaluate the performance of change detection methods when data evolves over time, other performance metrics are needed. Relevant criteria for change detection methods include:

- Probability of True detection: capacity to detect and react to drift;

---

[1]Nodes in a decision tree correspond to hyper-rectangles in particular regions of the instance space.

- Probability of False alarms: resilience to false alarms when there is no drift, that is, not detecting drift when there is no change in the target concept;

- Delay in detection: the number of examples required to detect a change after the occurrence of a change.

3.3 Monitoring the Learning Process

In most real-world applications of Machine Learning, data is collected over time. For large time periods, it is hard to assume that examples are independent and identically distributed. At least in complex environments it is highly probable that class-distributions change over time. In this work we assume that examples arrive one at a time. The framework could be easily extended to situations where data comes in batches of examples. We consider the on-line learning framework: when an example becomes available, the decision model must take a decision (e.g., a prediction). Only after the decision has been taken, the environment reacts providing feedback to the decision model (e.g., the class label of the example). In the PAC learning model (Mitchell, 1997), it is assumed that if the distribution of the examples is stationary, the error rate of the learning algorithm (p_i) will decrease when the number of examples (i) increases.[2] This sentence holds for any learning algorithm with infinite-capacity (e.g., decision trees, neural networks, etc.). A significant increase in the error of the algorithm when trained using more examples, suggests a change in the intrinsic properties in the process generating examples and that the actual decision model is no longer appropriate.

3.3.1 Drift Detection Using Statistical Process Control

Suppose a sequence of examples, in the form of pairs $(\vec{x}_i, y_i)$. For each example, the actual decision model predicts $\hat{y}_i$, that can be either True ($\hat{y}_i = y_i$) or False ($\hat{y}_i \neq y_i$). For a set of examples, the error is a random variable from Bernoulli trials. The binomial distribution gives the general form of the probability for the random variable that represents the number of errors in a sample of n examples. For each point i in the sequence, the error-rate is the probability of observing False, p_i, with standard deviation given by $s_i = \sqrt{p_i(1 - p_i)/i}$. The drift detection method manages two registers during the training of the learning algorithm, p_{min} and s_{min}. For each new processed example i, if $p_i + s_i$ is lower than $p_{min} + s_{min}$ these values are updated.

---

[2] For an infinite number of examples, the error rate will tend to the Bayes error.

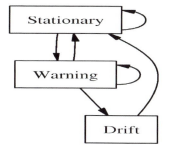

Figure 3.4: The space state transition graph.

For a sufficient large number of examples, the binomial distribution is closely approximated by a normal distribution with the same mean and variance. Considering that the probability distribution is unchanged when the context is static, then the $1 - \alpha/2$ confidence interval for p with $n > 30$ examples is approximately $p_i \pm z * s_i$. The parameter z depends on the desired confidence level.

Suppose that in the sequence of examples, there is an example j with correspondent p_j and s_j. We define three possible states for the system:

- *In-Control*: while $p_j + s_j < p_{min} + \beta * s_{min}$. The error of the system is stable. The example j is generated from the same distribution of the previous examples.

- *Out-of-Control*: whenever $p_j + s_j \geq p_{min} + \alpha * s_{min}$. The error is increasing, and reaches a level that is significantly higher from the past recent examples. With probability $1 - \alpha/2$ the current examples are generated from a different distribution.

- *Warning*: whenever the system is in between the two margins. The error is increasing but without reaching an action level. This is a non-decidable state. The causes of error increase can be due to noise, drift, small inability of the decision model, etc. More examples are needed to make a decision.

The graph describing the state transition is presented in Figure 3.4. It is not possible to move from a stationary state to a drift state without passing the warning state. However, it is possible to move from a warning state to a stationary state. For example, we can observe an increase of the error reaching the warning level, followed by a decrease. We assume that such situations correspond to a *false alarm*, most probably due to noisy data, without changing of context.

We use a warning level to define the optimal size of the context window. The context window will contain the old examples that are on the new con-

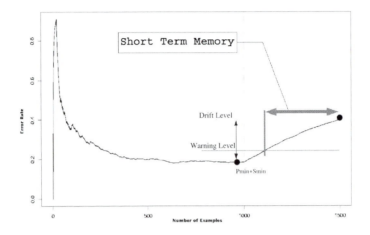

Figure 3.5: Dynamically constructed time window. The vertical line marks the change of concept.

text and a minimal number of examples on the old context. Suppose that, in the sequence of examples that traverse a node, there is an example i with correspondent p_i and s_i. In the experiments described next, the confidence level for warning has been set to 95%, that is, the warning level is reached if $p_i + s_i \geq p_{min} + 2 * s_{min}$. The confidence level for drift has been set to 99%, that is, the drift level is reached if $p_i + s_i \geq p_{min} + 3 * s_{min}$. Suppose a sequence of examples where the error of the actual model increases reaching the warning level at example k_w, and the drift level at example k_d. This is an indication of a change in the distribution of the examples. A new context is declared starting in example k_w, and a new decision model is induced using only the examples starting in k_w till k_d.

The SPC algorithm (Algorithm 8) provides information not only when drift occurs but also the *rate of change*. The distance between warning and drift provides such information. Small distances imply fast change rate while larger distances indicate slower changes. Considering only the warning zone, the ratio between the number of errors and the number of processed examples is an indication of the *rate of change*. A major characteristic is the use of the variance of the error estimate to define the action boundaries. The boundaries are not fixed but decrease as confidence in the error estimates increase. SPC can be directly implemented inside on-line and incremental algorithms, or as a wrapper to batch learners. Figure 3.5 details the dynamic window structure.

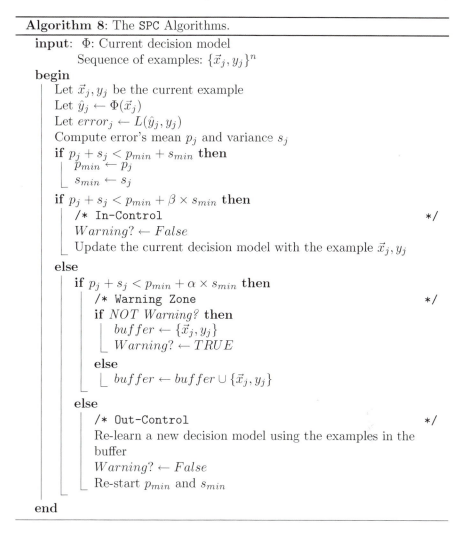

Algorithm 8: The SPC Algorithms.

---

input: Φ: Current decision model
            Sequence of examples: $\{\vec{x}_j, y_j\}^n$

begin

  Let $\vec{x}_j, y_j$ be the current example

  Let $\hat{y}_j \leftarrow \Phi(\vec{x}_j)$

  Let $error_j \leftarrow L(\hat{y}_j, y_j)$

  Compute error's mean p_j and variance s_j

  if $p_j + s_j < p_{min} + s_{min}$ **then**
    $p_{min} \leftarrow p_j$
    $s_{min} \leftarrow s_j$

  if $p_j + s_j < p_{min} + \beta \times s_{min}$ **then**
    /* In-Control   */
    $Warning? \leftarrow False$
    Update the current decision model with the example $\vec{x}_j, y_j$

  else

    if $p_j + s_j < p_{min} + \alpha \times s_{min}$ **then**
      /* Warning Zone   */
      if $NOT\ Warning?$ **then**
        $buffer \leftarrow \{\vec{x}_j, y_j\}$
        $Warning? \leftarrow TRUE$

      else
        $buffer \leftarrow buffer \cup \{\vec{x}_j, y_j\}$

    else
      /* Out-Control   */
      Re-learn a new decision model using the examples in the buffer
      $Warning? \leftarrow False$
      Re-start p_{min} and s_{min}

end

3.3.2 An Illustrative Example

The use of an artificial dataset allows us to control and evaluate experiences more precisely. The artificial dataset used, the *SEA concepts*, was first described in Street and Kim (2001). It consists of three attributes, where only two are relevant attributes: $x_i \in [0, 10]$, where $i = 1, 2, 3$. The target concept is $x_1 + x_2 \leq \beta$, where $\beta \in \{7, 8, 9, 9.5\}$. The training set has four blocks. For the first block the target concept is with $\beta = 8$. For the second, $\beta = 9$; the third, $\beta = 7$; and the fourth, $\beta = 9.5$. That is, the target concept changes over time.

Figure 3.6 illustrates the use of the SPC algorithm as a wrapper over a naive-Bayes classifier that incrementally learns the SEA concept dataset.

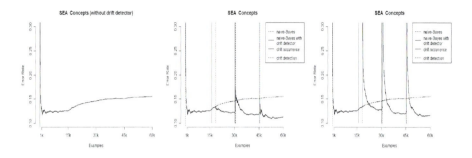

Figure 3.6: Illustrative example of using the SPC algorithm in the SEA concept dataset. All the figures plot the prequential error of a naive-Bayes in the *SEA-concepts* dataset. In the first plot there is no drift detection. In the second plot, the SPC algorithm was used to detect drift. The third plot is similar to the second one, without using buffered examples when a warning is signaled.

The vertical bars denote drift occurrence, while dotted vertical bars indicate when drift was detected. Both figures plot the classifier prequential error (see Chapter 5). In the left figure, the classifier trains with the examples stored in the buffer after the warning level was reached.

From the practical point of view, when a drift is signaled, the method defines a dynamic time window of the most recent examples used to train a new classifier. Here the key point is how fast the change occurs. If the change occurs at slow rate, the prequential error will exhibit a small positive slope. More examples are needed to evolve from the warning level to the action level and the window size increases. For abrupt changes, the increase of the prequential error will be also abrupt and a small window (using few examples) will be chosen. In any case the ability of training a new accurate classifier depends on the rate of changes and the capacity of the learning algorithm to converge to a stable model. The last aspect depends on the number of examples in the context.

3.4   Final Remarks

Change detection is one of the most relevant aspects when learning from time evolving data. The fact that data are produced on a real-time basis, or, at least, in a sequential fashion, and that the environment and the task at hand may change over time, profoundly modifies the underlying assumptions on which rest most of the existing learning techniques and demands the development of new principles and new algorithms. The challenge for data mining is to continuously maintain an accurate decision model. In this context, the assumption that examples are generated at random according to a stationary probability distribution does not hold, at least not in complex systems and for large periods of time. Old observations, which reflect the past behavior of the nature, become irrelevant to the current state of the phenomena under observation and the learning agent must forget that information.

The main research issue is how to incorporate change detection mechanisms in the learning algorithm. Embedding change detection methods in the learning algorithm is a requirement in the context of continuous flow of data. The level of *granularity* of decision models is a relevant property (Fan, 2004), because if can allow partial, fast and efficient updates in the decision model instead of rebuilding a complete new model whenever a change is detected. The ability to recognize seasonal and re-occurring patterns is an open issue.

3.5 Notes

Change detection and concept drift have attracted much attention in the last 50 years. Most of the works deal with fixed-sample problems and atmost one change model. A review of techniques, methods and applications of change detection appears in Basseville and Nikiforov (1993) and Ghosh and Sen (1991). Procedures of sequential detection of changes have been studied in statistical process control (Grant and Leavenworth, 1996). The pioneer work in this area is Shewhart (1931), who presented the *3-sigma control chart*. More efficient techniques, the cumulative sum procedures, were developed by Page (1954). Cumulative sums have been used in data mining in Pang and Ting (2004). Kalman filters associated with CUSUM appear in Schön et al. (2005), Bifet and Gavaldà (2006), and Severo and Gama (2006).

In the 1990s, concept drift was studied by several researchers in the context of finite samples. The relevant works include Schlimmer and Granger (1986), with the system STAGGER and the famous STAGGER dataset, Widmer and Kubat (1996), presenting the FLORA family of algorithms, and Harries et al. (1998), who present the Splice system for identifying context changes. Kuh et al. (1990) present bounds on the frequency of concept changes, e.g. rate of drift, that is acceptable by any learner. Pratt and Tschapek (2003) describe a visualization technique that uses brushed, parallel histograms to aid in understanding concept drift in multidimensional problem spaces.

A survey on incremental data mining model maintenance and change detection under block evolution appears in Ganti et al. (2002). Remember that in block evolution (Ramakrishnan and Gehrke, 2003), a dataset is updated periodically through insertions and deletions of blocks of records at each time.

One important application of change detection algorithms is in burst detection. Burst regions are time intervals in which some data features are un-expected. For example, gamma-ray burst in astronomical data might be associated with the death of massive starts; bursts in document streams might be valid indicators of emerging topics, strong buy-sell signals in the financial market, etc. Burst detection in text streams was discussed in Kleinberg (2004). Vlachos et al. (2005) discuss a similar problem in financial streams.

Chapter 4

Maintaining Histograms from Data Streams

Histograms are one of the most used tools in exploratory data analysis. They present a graphical representation of data, providing useful information about the distribution of a random variable. Histograms are widely used for density estimation. They have been used in approximate query answering, in processing massive datasets, to provide a quick but faster answer with error guarantees. In this chapter we present representative algorithms to learn histograms from data streams and its application in data mining.

4.1 Introduction

A histogram is visualized as a bar graph that shows frequency data. The basic algorithm to construct a histogram consists of sorting the values of the random variables and placing them into *bins*. Then we count the number of data points in each bin. The height of the bar drawn on the top of each bin is proportional to the number of observed values in that bin.

A histogram is defined by a set of non-overlapping intervals. Each interval is defined by the boundaries and a frequency count. In the context of open-ended data streams, we never observe all values of the random variable. For that reason, and allowing for consideration of extreme values and outliers, we define a histogram as a set of break points $b_1, ..., b_{k-1}$ and a set of frequency counts $f_1, ..., f_{k-1}, f_k$ that define k intervals in the range of the random variable: $[-\infty, b_1],]b_1, b_2], ...,]b_{k-2}, b_{k-1}],]b_{k-1}, \infty]$.

The most used histograms are either *equal width*, where the range of observed values is divided into k intervals of equal length ($\forall i, j : (b_i - b_{i-1}) = (b_j - b_{j-1})$), or *equal frequency*, where the range of observed values is divided into k bins such that the counts in all bins are equal ($\forall i, j : (f_i = f_j)$).

4.2 Histograms from Data Streams

When all the data are available, there are exact algorithms to construct histograms. All these algorithms require a user-defined parameter k, the number of bins. Suppose we know the range of the random variable (domain information), and the desired number of intervals k. The algorithm to construct *equal width* histograms traverse the data once; whereas in the case of *equal frequency* histograms a sort operation is required. One of the main problems of using histograms is the definition of the number of intervals. A rule that has been used is the Sturges's rule: $k = 1 + log_2(n)$, where k is the number of intervals and n is the number of observed data points. This rule has been criticized because it is implicitly using a binomial distribution to approximate an underlying normal distribution.[1] Sturge's rule has probably survived as long as it has because for moderate values of n (less than 200) it produces reasonable histograms. However, it does not work for large n. In exploratory data analysis histograms are used iteratively. The user tries several histograms using different values of the number of intervals, and chooses the one that better fits his purposes.

4.2.1 K-buckets Histograms

Gibbons et al. (1997) discuss histograms in the context of DBMS, for accelerating queries, namely range-queries. Most of the work in this area applies to static databases, using pre-computed histograms or histograms computed from time to time (e.g., every night). In these settings, histograms become quickly out-dated, providing answers with increasing errors. Gibbons et al. (1997) present approaches for incremental maintenance of approximate histograms that might be applied in databases with continuous inserts and deletes.

An illustration of the algorithm presented by Gibbons et al. (1997) for incremental maintenance of histograms with a fixed number of buckets is presented in Figure 4.1. The number of bins is defined a priori. The counts of each bin are continuously incremented or decremented as inserts and deletes occurs in the database. Histogram maintenance is based on two operators:

- *Split & Merge Operator*: triggers whenever the count in a bucket is greater than a given threshold. It occurs with inserts in the database. The bucket is divided into two, and two consecutive buckets are merged.

- *Merge & Split Operator*: triggers whenever the count in a bucket is below a given threshold. It occurs with deletes in the database. The bucket is

---

[1]Alternative rules for constructing histograms include Scott's (1979) rule for the class width: $h = 3.5sn^{-1/3}$ and Diaconis's (1981) rule for the class width: $h = 2(IQ)n^{-1/3}$ where s is the sample standard deviation and IQ is the sample interquartile range.

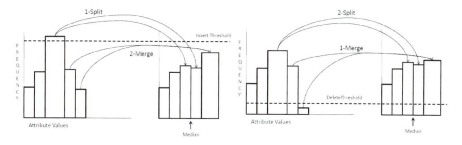

Figure 4.1: Split & Merge and Merge & Split Operators.

merged with a neighbor bucket, and the bucket with higher counts is divided into two.

4.2.2 Exponential Histograms

The *exponential histogram* (Datar et al., 2002) is another histogram frequently used to solve counting problems. Consider a simplified data stream environment where each element comes from the same data source and is either 0 or 1. The goal consists of counting the number of 1's in a sliding window. The problem is trivial if the window can fit in memory. Assume that N is the window size, can we solve the problem using $O(log(N))$ space? Datar et al. (2002) presented an exponential histogram strategy to solve this problem. The basic idea consists of using buckets of different sizes to hold the data. Each bucket has a time stamp associated with it. This time stamp is used to decide when the bucket is out of the window. Exponential histograms, other than buckets, use two additional variables, $LAST$ and $TOTAL$. The variable LAST stores the size of the last bucket. The variable $TOTAL$ keeps the total size of the buckets.

When a new data element arrives, we first check the value of the element. If the new data element is zero, ignore it. Otherwise create a new bucket of size 1 with the current time-stamp and increment the counter $TOTAL$. Given a parameter ϵ, if there are $|1/\epsilon|/2 + 2$ buckets of the same size, merge the two oldest buckets of the same size into a single bucket of double size. The largest time-stamp of the two buckets is used as the time-stamp of the newly created bucket. If the last bucket gets merged, we update the size of the merged bucket to the counter $LAST$.

Whenever we want to estimate the moving sum, we check if the oldest bucket is within the sliding window. If not, we drop that bucket, subtract its size from the variable $TOTAL$, and update the size of the current oldest bucket to the variable $LAST$. This procedure is repeated until all the buckets with the time-stamps outside of the sliding window are dropped. The estimate number of 1's in the sliding window is $TOTAL - LAST/2$.

4.2.2.1 An Illustrative Example

Assume we are interested in counting the number of 1's in a time window of length 10, allowing a relative error of 0.5. With these parameters, we should merge buckets, when there are 3 buckets of the same size: $|1/0.5|/2+2$. Assuming the illustrative stream:

Time	1	2	3	4	5	6	7	8	9	10	11	12	13	14	15
Element	1	1	1	1	0	1	0	1	1	1	1	1	1	1	0

The trace of the evolution of the exponential histogram is:

Time	Buckets	Total	Last
T1	1_1	1	1
T2	$1_1, 1_2$	2	1
T3	$1_1, 1_2, 1_3$	3	1
(merge)	$2_2, 1_3$	3	2
T4	$2_2, 1_3, 1_4$	4	2
T5	$2_2, 1_3, 1_4$	4	2
T6	$2_2, 1_3, 1_4, 1_6$	5	2
	$2_2, 2_4, 1_6$	5	2
T7	$2_2, 2_4, 1_6$	5	2
T8	$2_2, 2_4, 1_6, 1_8$	6	2
T9	$2_2, 2_4, 1_6, 1_8, 1_9$	7	2
	$2_2, 2_4, 2_8, 1_9$	7	2
	$4_4, 2_8, 1_9$	7	4
T10	$4_4, 2_8, 1_9, 1_{10}$	8	4
T11	$4_4, 2_8, 1_9, 1_{10}, 1_{11}$	9	4
	$4_4, 2_8, 2_{10}, 1_{11}$	9	4
T12	$4_4, 2_8, 2_{10}, 1_{11}, 1_{12}$	10	4
T13	$4_4, 4_{10}, 2_{12}, 1_{13}$	11	4
T14	$4_4, 4_{10}, 2_{12}, 1_{13}, 1_{14}$	12	4
(Removing out-of-date)			
T15	$4_{10}, 2_{12}, 1_{13}, 1_{14}$	8	4

4.2.2.2 Discussion

The main property of the exponential histograms is that the size grows exponentially, i.e. $2^0, 2^1, 2^2, ..., 2^h$. Datar et al. (2002) show that using the algorithm for the basic counting problem, one can adapt many other techniques to work for the sliding window model, with a multiplicative overhead of $O(log(N)/\epsilon)$ in memory and a $1 + \epsilon$ factor loss in accuracy. These include maintaining approximate histograms, hash tables, and statistics or aggregates such as sum and averages.

In this example the time scale is compressed. The most recent data is stored inside the window at the finest detail (granularity). Oldest information is stored at a coarser detail, in an aggregated way. The level of granularity depends on the application. This window model is designated as *tilted time window*. Tilted time windows can be designed in several ways. Han and Kamber (2006) present two possible variants: *natural tilted time windows*, and *logarithm tilted windows*. Illustrative examples are presented in Figure 2.4. In the first case, data is stored with granularity according to a natural time taxonomy: last hour at a granularity of fifteen minutes (4 buckets), last day in hours (24 buckets), last month in days (31 buckets) and last year in months (12 buckets). Similar time scale compression appears in the case of logarithmic tilted windows. Here, all buckets have the same size. Time is compressed using an exponential factor: $2^0, 2^1, 2^2, \ldots$. Buckets aggregate and store data from time-intervals of increasing size.

4.3   The Partition Incremental Discretization Algorithm - PiD

Gama and Pinto (2006); Pinto and Gama (2007) present the *Partition Incremental Discretization* algorithm (PiD for short) one of the first approaches for incremental discretization. PiD is composed by two layers. The first layer simplifies and summarizes the data; the second layer constructs the final histogram.

The first layer is initialized without seeing any data. The input for the initialization phase is the number of intervals (that should be much greater than the desired final number of intervals) and the range of the variable. The range of the variable is only indicative. It is used to initialize the set of breaks using an equal-width strategy. Each time we observe a value of the random variable, we update $layer_1$. The update process determines the interval corresponding to the observed value, and increments the count of this interval. Whenever the count of an interval is above a user-defined threshold (a percentage of the total number of points seen so far), a split operator triggers. The split operator generates new intervals in $layer_1$. If the interval that triggers the split operator is the first or the last a new interval with the same step is inserted. In all the other cases, the interval is split into two, generating a new interval.

The process of updating $layer_1$ works on-line, performing a single scan over the data stream. It can process infinite sequences of data, processing each example in constant time and space.

The second layer merges the set of intervals defined by the first layer. It triggers whenever it is necessary (e.g., by user action). The input for the second layer is the breaks and counts of $layer_1$, the type of histogram (equal-width or equal-frequency) and the number of intervals. The algorithm for the $layer_2$ is very simple. For equal-width histograms, it first computes the breaks of the final histogram, from the actual range of the variable (estimated in $layer_1$).

Algorithm 9: The PiD Algorithm for Updating $Layer_1$.

---

input: x: Current value of the random variable
$\quad\quad\quad$ *breaks*: vector of actual set of break points
$\quad\quad\quad$ *counts*: vector of actual set of frequency counts
$\quad\quad\quad$ NrB: Actual number of breaks
$\quad\quad\quad$ α: Threshold for Split an interval
$\quad\quad\quad$ Nr: Number of observed values seen so far

begin
$\quad$ $k \leftarrow 2 + integer((x - breaks[1])/step)$
$\quad$ **if** *(x < breaks[1])* **then**
$\quad\quad$ $k \leftarrow 1$
$\quad\quad$ $Min.x \leftarrow x$
$\quad$ **if** *(x > breaks[NrB])* **then**
$\quad\quad$ $k \leftarrow NrB$
$\quad\quad$ $Max.x \leftarrow x$
$\quad$ **while** *(x < breaks[k − 1])* **do** $k \leftarrow k - 1$
$\quad$ **while** *(x > breaks[k])* **do** $k \leftarrow k + 1$
$\quad$ counts[k] = 1 + counts[k]
$\quad$ $Nr \leftarrow 1 + Nr$
$\quad$ **if** $(1 + counts[k])/(Nr + 2) > \alpha$ **then**
$\quad\quad$ $val \leftarrow counts[k]/2$
$\quad\quad$ $counts[k] \leftarrow val$
$\quad\quad$ **if** *(k == 1)* **then**
$\quad\quad\quad$ $breaks \leftarrow append(breaks[1] - step, breaks)$
$\quad\quad\quad$ $counts \leftarrow append(val, counts)$
$\quad\quad$ **else**
$\quad\quad\quad$ **if** *(k == NrB)* **then**
$\quad\quad\quad\quad$ $breaks \leftarrow append(breaks, breaks[NrB] + step)$
$\quad\quad\quad\quad$ $counts \leftarrow append(counts, val)$
$\quad\quad\quad$ **else**
$\quad\quad\quad\quad$ $breaks \leftarrow Insert((breaks[k] + breaks[k + 1])/2, breaks, k)$
$\quad\quad\quad\quad$ $counts \leftarrow Insert(val, counts, k)$
$\quad\quad$ $NrB \leftarrow NrB + 1$
end

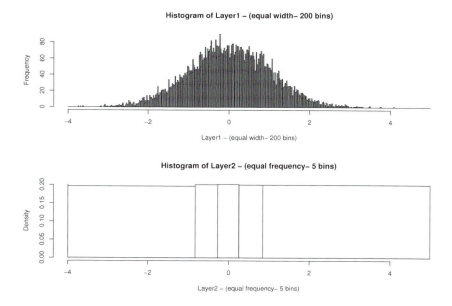

Figure 4.2: An illustrative example of the two layers in `PiD`. The input for *layer*$_1$ is the raw data stream; the input for *layer*$_2$ is the counts stored in *layer*$_1$.

The algorithm traverses the vector of breaks once, adding the counts corresponding to two consecutive breaks. For equal-frequency histograms, we first compute the exact number F of points that should be in each final interval (from the total number of points and the number of desired intervals). The algorithm traverses the vector of counts of *layer*$_1$ adding the counts of consecutive intervals till F.

The two-layer architecture (see Figure 4.2) divides the histogram problem into two phases. In the first phase, the algorithm traverses the data stream and incrementally maintains an equal-width discretization. The second phase constructs the final histogram using only the discretization of the first phase. The computational costs of this phase can be ignored: it traverses once the dicretization is obtained in the first phase. We can construct several histograms using different number of intervals, and different strategies: equal-width or equal-frequency. This is the main advantage of `PiD` in exploratory data analysis. `PiD` was used as a building block for a distributed clustering algorithm discussed in Section 12.3.2.

4.3.1 Analysis of the Algorithm

The histograms generated by `PiD` are not exact. There are two sources of error:

1. The set of boundaries. The breaks of the histogram generated in the second layer are restricted to the set of breaks defined in the first layer.

2. The frequency counters. The counters of the second layer are aggregations of the frequency counters in the first layer. If the splitting operator does not trigger, counters in the first layer are exact, and also counters in the second layer. The splitting operator can produce inexact counters. If the merge operation of the second layer aggregate those intervals, final counters are correct.

A comparative analysis of the histograms produced by `PiD` and histograms produced by exact algorithms using all the data, reveals some properties of the `PiD` algorithm. Illustrative examples are presented in Figure 4.3. Assuming an equal-width discretization (that is the split operator did not trigger) for the first layer and any method for the second layer, the error of `PiD` boundaries (that is the sum of absolute differences between boundaries between `PiD` and batch discretization) is bound, in the worst case, by: $R * N_2/(2 * N_1)$, where N_1 denotes the number of intervals of $layer_1$, N_2 the number of intervals of $layer_2$, and R is the range of the random variable. This indicates that when N_1 increases the error decreases. The algorithm guarantees that frequencies at the second layer are exact (for the second layer's boundaries). We should note that the splitting operator will always decrease the error.

The time complexity of `PiD` depends on the discretization methods used in each layer. The time complexity of the second layer is constant because its input is the first layer that has a (almost) fixed number of intervals. The time complexity for the first layer is linear in the number of examples.

4.3.2 Change Detection in Histograms

The ability to detect and react to changes in the environment producing data is a key issue in data stream processing. As we have seen in Chapter 3, one of the most used methods to react to changes consists of weighting examples: most recent examples are more important. The weight associate with one example decreases with the age of the example. The simplest strategy use, an exponential weight decay. The weight of an example at time t is given by the expression: $w_t = w_{t-1} \times \alpha$. This is accomplished by triggering a process at each k example. Every counter in the histogram is multiplied by α, a positive constant less than 1. This means that the oldest examples get less and less weight. This method does not detect changes. The adaptation process is blind.

Another approach consists of monitoring distributions from two different time windows (Kifer et al., 2004): a reference time window, that reflects the distribution observed in the past; and the current time window reflecting

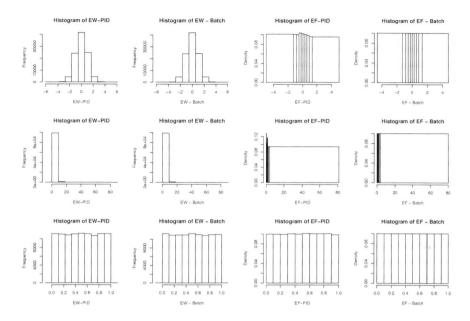

Figure 4.3: Comparison between batch histograms and `PiD` histograms. We show the histograms (using equal-width and equal-frequency) for Normal, Log-Normal, and Uniform random variables.

the distribution observed in the most recent data. Both distributions can be compared using the Kullback-Leibler (KL) divergence (Sebastião and Gama, 2007). The Kullback-Leibler divergence measures the distance between two probability distributions and so it can be used to test for change. Given a reference window with empirical probabilities p_i, and a sliding window with probabilities q_i, the KL divergence is:

$$KL(p||q) = \sum_i p(i) log_2 \frac{p(i)}{q(i)}.$$

The KL divergence is non-negative and asymmetric and as its value gets higher, the more distinct the distribution of the two variables. A higher value of the distance represents distributions that are further apart. A change is signaled whenever the Kullback-Leibler divergence is greater than a threshold value.

4.3.3 An Illustrative Example

In this section we compare the output of `PiD` against the set of intervals obtained using all the training data and the same discretization strategy of

So far, we have seen two unsupervised discretization methods: equal width and equal frequency. The distribution matrix in $layer_1$ allows us to use supervised discretization methods, like *recursive entropy discretization* (Fayyad and Irani, 1993) or *chi-merge* (Kerber, 1992; Boulle, 2004). These methods have some advantages: they are supervised, so more appropriate for classification problems, and the number of intervals of the final discretization ($layer_2$ in our case) is automatically determined.

In some learning scenarios, for example on-line learning, we need to maintain a permanent discretization in $layer_2$. Till now, $layer_1$ is updated on-line, but $layer_2$ is computed from time to time when requested. Suppose we have a $layer_1$ and a $layer_2$. Whenever a new example is available, we update $layer_1$ (and the distribution matrix) using the algorithm in Algorithm 9. It is improbable that a single observation changes the distribution in $layer_2$, so we find the corresponding interval in $layer_2$ and update the frequency counters and distribution matrix. Now we are faced with the problem: When should we reconstruct $layer_2$? We consider three cases:

- Equal-width histograms are defined by breaks b_i such that $b_{i+1} - b_i = b_{j+1} - b_j$ for each i and j. The $layer_2$ needs to be reconstructed only when the set of breaks in $layer_1$ changes. This only occurs whenever the split operator triggers. After applying the split operator, the algorithm reconstructs $layer_2$.

- Equal-frequency histograms are defined by frequencies f_i. PiD does not guarantee that all f_i are equal. Suppose that after seeing n examples, the algorithm reconstructs $layer_2$. We define two thresholds $T_{min} = min(f_i/n)$ and $T_{max} = max(f_i/n)$. Whenever we observe an interval with frequency below $(1 - \alpha) \times T_{min}$ or above $(1 + \alpha) \times T_{max}$ we reconstruct $layer_2$.[3]

- Other types of histograms, for example, entropy based or chi-merge, we have not found to be well-founded strategies. We use a very simple strategy that reconstructs $layer_2$ after seeing a pre-defined number of examples.

Most of naive Bayes implementations assume a pre-defined number of attribute-values for each attribute. The recursive entropy discretization can generate, for each attribute, different numbers of intervals at different times. The information provided by PiD allows us to use naive-Bayes in these cases. Another issue is: knowing the range of the random variable and fixing the number of intervals, equal-width discretization is naturally incremental. Why should we use PiD with equal-width in $layer_2$? What is the advantage? The advantage is that we can use a different number of intervals in $layer_2$. Most of the rules for determining the number of intervals point out that for an increasing number of examples we should use an increasing number of intervals. It is straightforward to incorporate this ability in PiD.

---

[3] A reasonable value for α seems to be 1%.

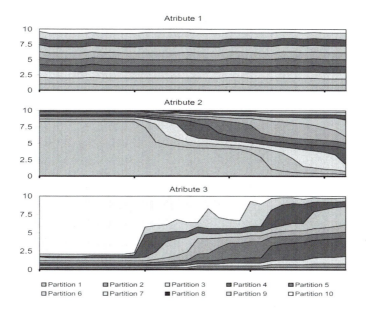

Figure 4.4: The evolution of the partitions at the second layer.

4.4.2 Time-Changing Environments

To test the incremental discretization in time-changing scenarios, we use the SEA concepts dataset (Street and Kim, 2001). This is a two-class problem, defined by three attributes. All three attributes take values between 0 and 10 but only the last two attributes are relevant. A data point belongs to class + iif $Att_2 + Att_3 \leq \theta$, where Att_2 and Att_3 represent the two last features and θ is a threshold. Drift is simulated by changing the threshold value.

In our experiences, we generate four blocks of 100k points each. For each block the threshold values were 7, 8, 10 and 11 respectively. The discretization used PiD, adopting an *equal-width* with 200 intervals for the first layer and an *equal-frequency* with 10 intervals for the second layer. The exponential decay was applied every 1000 examples with α set to 0.9. Figure 4.4 presents the evolution over time of the second layer distribution for each attribute. In Att_1 no significant changes occur; its distribution was the same in each block of data. Changes in the distribution appear in both Att_2 and Att_3. The distribution of Att_3 is almost the mirror of Att_2.

4.5   Notes

Histograms are the most basic form for density estimation. Other approaches to density estimation are kernel density estimation methods, for example, Parzen windows. A probability distribution function (pdf) or density of a random variable is a function that describes the density of probability at each point. The probability of a random variable is given by the integral of its density. Clustering, discussed in Chapter 6, is a more sophisticated technique that can be used for density estimation.

Chapter 5

Evaluating Streaming Algorithms

Nowadays, several stream learning algorithms have been developed. Most of them learn decision models that continuously evolve over time, run in resource-aware environments, and detect and react to changes in the environment generating data. One important issue, not yet conveniently addressed, is the design of experimental work to evaluate and compare decision models that evolve over time. In this chapter we present a general framework for assessing the quality of streaming learning algorithms. We defend the use of *Predictive Sequential* error estimates over a sliding window to assess performance of learning algorithms that learn from open-ended data streams in non-stationary environments. This chapter studies convergence properties and methods to comparatively assess algorithm performance.

5.1 Introduction

Most recent learning algorithms (Cormode et al., 2007; Babcock et al., 2003; Domingos and Hulten, 2000; Hulten et al., 2001; Gama et al., 2003; Ferrer-Troyano et al., 2004) maintain a decision model that continuously evolves over time, taking into account that the environment is non-stationary and computational resources are limited. Examples of public available software for learning from data streams include: the VFML (Hulten and Domingos, 2003) toolkit for mining high-speed time-changing data streams, the MOA (Kirkby, 2008) system for learning from massive datasets, Rapid-Miner (Mierswa et al., 2006) a data mining system with plug-in for stream processing, etc.

Although number of streaming learning algorithms is increasing, the metrics and the design of experiments for assessing the quality of learning models is still an open issue. The main difficulties are:

- We have a continuous flow of data instead of a fixed sample of *iid* examples;

- Decision models evolve over time instead of static models;

- Data is generated by dynamic environment non-stationary distributions instead of a stationary sample;

In a referenced paper, Dietterich (1996) proposes a straightforward technique to evaluate learning algorithms when data is abundant: *"learn a classifier from a large enough training set and apply the classifier to a large enough test set."*

Data streams are open-ended. This could facilitate the evaluation methodologies, because we have train and test sets as large as desired. The problem we address in this chapter is: *Is this sampling strategy viable in the streaming scenario?*

In this chapter we argue that the answer is *no*. Two aspects in the emerging applications and learning algorithms that have strong impact in the evaluation methodologies are the continuous evolution of decision models and the non-stationary nature of data streams. The approach we propose is based on *sequential analysis*. Sequential analysis refers to the body of statistical theory and methods where the sample size may depend in a random manner on the accumulating data (Ghosh and Sen, 1991).

5.2   Learning from Data Streams

Hulten and Domingos (2001) identify desirable properties of learning systems for efficient mining continuous, high-volume, open-ended data streams:

- Require small constant time per data example;

- Use fixed amount of main memory, irrespective to the total number of examples;

- Built a decision model using a single scan over the training data;

- Generating an anytime model independent from the order of the examples;

- Ability to deal with concept drift;

- For stationary data, ability to produce decision models that are nearly identical to the ones we would obtain using a batch learner.

From this desiderata, we can identify three dimensions that influence the learning process: *space* – the available memory is fixed; *learning time* – process incoming examples at the rate they arrive; and *generalization power* – how effective the model is at capturing the true underlying concept. In this chapter we focus in the generalization power of the learning algorithm, although we recognize that the first two dimensions have direct impact in the generalization power of the learned model.

We are in the presence of a potentially infinite number of examples. Is this fact relevant for learning? Do we need so many data points? Sampling a large training set is not enough? Figure 5.1 intend to provide useful information to

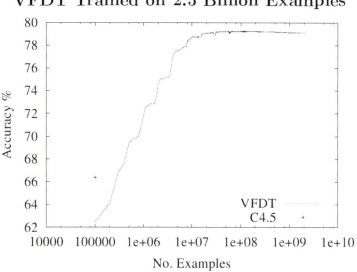

Figure 5.1: Performance evolution of VFDT in a web-mining problem. Accuracy increases with increasing number of training examples.

answer these questions, showing the accuracy's evolution of VFDT in a web-mining problem. One observes, in this particular problem, a rapid increase of the accuracy with the number of examples; using more than 1e+07 examples will not affect the accuracy, it will remain stable near 80%.

The fact that decision models evolve over time has strong implications in the evaluation techniques assessing the effectiveness of the learning process. Another relevant aspect is the resilience to overfitting: each example is processed once.

A brief look at the stream mining literature shows the diversity of evaluation methods. Table 5.1 presents a brief resume of evaluation methods. The algorithms under analysis are described in Domingos and Hulten (2000); Hulten et al. (2001); Gama et al. (2003, 2004); Ferrer-Troyano et al. (2005); Kirkby (2008); Castillo and Gama (2005), and are presented in that order.

5.3 Evaluation Issues

A key point in any intelligent system is the evaluation methodology. Learning systems generate compact representations of what is being observed. They should be able to improve with experience and continuously self-modify their

Table 5.1:   Resume of evaluation methods in stream mining literature.

Work	Evaluation Method	Memory Management	Data	Examples Train	Test	Drift
VFDT	holdout	Yes	Artif	1M	50k	No
	holdout	Yes	Real	4M	267k	No
CVFDT	holdout	Yes	Artif	1M	Yes	Yes
VFDTc	holdout	No	Artif	1M	250k	No
UFFT	holdout	No	Artif	1.5M	250k	Yes
FACIL	holdout	Yes	Artif	1M	100k	Yes
MOA	holdout	Yes	Artif	1G		No
ANB	Prequential	No	Artif			Yes

internal state. Their representation of the world is approximate. How approximate is the representation of the world? Evaluation is used in two contexts: inside the learning system to assess hypothesis, and as a wrapper over the learning system to estimate the applicability of a particular algorithm in a given problem. Three fundamental aspects are:

- What are the goals of the learning task?

- Which are the evaluation metrics?

- How to design the experiments to estimate the evaluation metrics?

For predictive learning tasks (classification and regression) the learning goal is to induce a function $\hat{y} = f(\vec{x})$. The most relevant dimension is the *generalization error*. It is an estimator of the difference between $\hat{f}$ and the unknown f, and an estimate of the loss that can be expected when applying the model to future examples.

5.3.1   Design of Evaluation Experiments

One aspect in the design of experiments that has not been conveniently addressed is that learning algorithms run in computational devices that have limited computational power. For example, existing learning algorithms assume that data fits in memory; a prohibit assumption in the presence of open-ended streams. This issue becomes much more relevant when data analysis must be done *in situ*. An illustrative example is the case of sensor networks, where data flows at high-speed and computational resources are quite limited.

Very few algorithms address the bounded memory constrain. A notable exception is VFDT (Domingos and Hulten, 2000) that can save memory by freezing less promising leaves whenever memory reaches a limit. VFDT monitors the available memory and prunes leaves (where sufficient statistics are stored) depending on recent accuracy. Kirkby (2008) presents an interesting framework to evaluate learning algorithms under memory constrains. The author proposes three environments using increasing memory, for evaluating stream mining algorithms:

- Sensor environment: hundreds of Kbytes;

- Handheld computers: tens of Mbytes;

- Server computers: several Gbytes.

The memory management is more relevant for non-parametric decision models like decision trees or support vector machines because the number of free parameters evolve with the number of training examples. For other types of models, like linear models that typically depend on the number of attributes, memory management is not so problematic in the streaming context because the size of the model does not depend on the number of examples. Kirkby (2008) defends that general purpose streaming algorithms should be evaluated in the three mentioned scenarios.

In batch learning using finite training sets, cross-validation and variants (leave-one-out, bootstrap) are the standard methods to evaluate learning systems. Cross-validation is appropriate for restricted size datasets, generated by stationary distributions, and assuming that examples are independent. In data streams contexts, where data is potentially infinite, the distribution generating examples and the decision models evolve over time, cross-validation and other sampling strategies are not applicable. Research communities and users need other evaluation strategies.

5.3.2   Evaluation Metrics

To evaluate a learning model in a stream context, two viable alternatives, presented in the literature, are:

- Holdout an independent test set. Apply the current decision model to the test set, at regular time intervals (or set of examples). The loss estimated in the holdout is an unbiased estimator.

- Predictive Sequential: *Prequential* (Dawid, 1984), where the error of a model is computed from the sequence of examples. For each example in the stream, the actual model makes a prediction based only on the example attribute-values. The prequential-error is computed based on an accumulated sum of a loss function between the prediction and observed values:

$$S_i = \sum_1^n L(y_i, \hat{y}_i)$$

We should point out that, in the prequential framework, we do not need to know the true value y_i, for all points in the stream. The framework can be used in situations of limited feedback, by computing the loss function and S_i for points where y_i is known.

The mean loss is given by: $M_i = \frac{1}{n} \times S_i$. For any loss function, we can estimate a confidence interval for the probability of error, $M_i \pm \varepsilon$, using Chernoff bound (Chernoff, 1952):

$$\varepsilon_c = \sqrt{\frac{3 \times \bar{\mu}}{n} ln(2/\delta)},$$

where δ is a user-defined confidence level. In the case of bounded loss functions, like the 0-1 loss, the Hoeffding bound (Hoeffding, 1963) can be used:

$$\varepsilon_h = \sqrt{\frac{R}{2n} \ln\left(\frac{2}{\delta}\right)},$$

where R is the range of the random variable. Both bounds use the sum of independent random variables and give a relative or absolute approximation of the deviation of X from its expectation. They are independent of the distribution of the random variable.

5.3.2.1 Error Estimators Using a Single Algorithm and a Single Dataset

Prequential evaluation provides a learning curve that monitors the evolution of learning as a process. Using holdout evaluation, we can obtain a similar curve by applying, at regular time intervals, the current model to the holdout set. Both estimates can be affected by the order of the examples. Moreover, it is known that the prequential estimator is pessimistic: under the same conditions it will report somewhat higher errors (see Figure 5.2). The prequential error estimated over all the stream might be strongly influenced by the first part of the error sequence, when few examples have been used for training the classifier. This observation leads to the following hypothesis: compute the prequential error using a forgetting mechanism. This might be achieved either using a time window of the most recent observed errors, or using fading factors.

Intuitively, the prequential error using fading factors is computed as: $E_i = \frac{S_i}{N}$ where $S_1 = L_1$ and $S_i = L_i + \alpha \times S_{i-1}$. Nevertheless, E_i converges to 0 when N tends to $+\infty$. We use a correction factor in the denominator of the equation:

$$E_i = \frac{S_i}{B_i} = \frac{L_i + \alpha \times S_{i-1}}{n_i + \alpha \times B_{i-1}}$$

where n_i is the number of examples used to compute L_i. When the loss L_i is computed for every single example, $n_i = 1$.

5.3.2.2 An Illustrative Example

The objective of this experiment is to study convergence properties of the prequential statistics using sliding window error estimates. The learning algorithm is VFDT as implemented in VFML (Hulten and Domingos, 2003). The experimental work has been done using the *Waveform* (Asuncion and

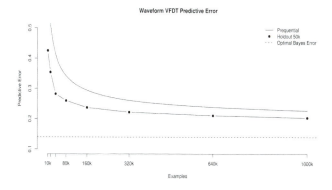

Figure 5.2: Comparison of error evolution as estimated by holdout and prequential strategies, in a stationary stream (Waveform dataset). The learning algorithm is VFDT.

Newman, 2007) dataset, because the Bayes-error is known: 14%. This is a three class problem defined by 21 numerical attributes.

Figure 5.3 plots the holdout error, the prequential error, and the prequential error estimated using sliding windows of different size. All the plots are means from 30 runs of VFDT on datasets generated with different seeds. The most relevant fact is that the window size does not matter too much: the prequential error estimated over a sliding window always converges fast to the holdout estimate. Figure 5.3 (left) plots the holdout error, the prequential error, the prequential error estimated using sliding window (50k), and the prequential error estimated using fading factor (0.975). Again, the prequential error estimated using fading factor converges fast to holdout estimate.

5.3.3 Comparative Assessment

In this section we discuss methods to compare the performance of two algorithms (A and B) in a stream. Our goal is to distinguish between random and non-random differences in experimental results.

Let S_i^A and S_i^B be the sequences of the prequential accumulated loss for each algorithm. A useful statistic that can be used with almost any loss function is: $Q_i(A, B) = log(\frac{S_i^A}{S_i^B})$. The signal of Q_i is informative about the relative performance of both models, while its value shows the strength of the differences. In an experimental study using real data from an electrical load-demand forecast problem, plotted in Figure 5.4, Q_i reflects the overall tendency but exhibits long-term influences and is not able to fast capture when a model is in a recovering phase. Two viable alternatives are sliding windows, with the known problems of deciding the window size, and fading factors. Both

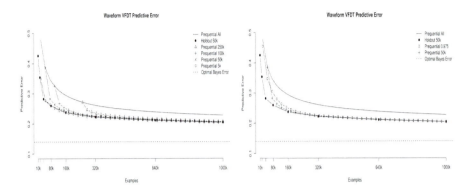

Figure 5.3: Comparison of prequential error evolution between holdout, pre-quential and prequential over sliding windows. Left plot presents the evolution of prequential error estimated using fading factors and sliding windows.

methods have been used for blind adaptation, e.g. without explicit change detection, of decision models in drift scenarios (Klinkenberg, 2004; Koychev, 2000). The formula for using fading factors with the Q_i statistic is:

$$Q_i^\alpha(A, B) = log(\frac{L_i(A) + \alpha \times S_{i-1}^A}{L_i(B) + \alpha \times S_{i-1}^B}).$$

It is interesting to observe that these two alternatives exhibit similar plots (see Figure 5.5).

The fading factors are multiplicative, corresponding to an exponential for-getting. At time-stamp t the weight of example $t - k$ is α^k. For example, using $\alpha = 0.995$ the weight associated with the first term after 3000 examples is $2.9E - 7$. In general, assuming that we can ignore the examples with weights less than ϵ, an upper bound for k (e.g. the set of "important" examples) is $log(\epsilon)/log(\alpha)$. The fading factors are memoryless, an important property in streaming scenarios. This is a strong advantage over sliding windows that require maintaining in memory all the observations inside the window.

5.3.3.1   The $0 - 1$ Loss Function

For classification problems, one of the most used tests is the McNemar test.[1] To be able to apply this test we only need to compute two quantities $n_{i,j}$: $n_{0,1}$ denotes the number of examples misclassified by A and not by B, whereas $n_{1,0}$ denotes the number of examples misclassified by B and not by A. The contingency table can be updated on the fly, which is a desirable property

---

[1]We do not argue that this is the most appropriate test for comparing classifiers. Demsar (2006) presents an in-depth analysis on statistical tests to compare classifiers in batch scenario.

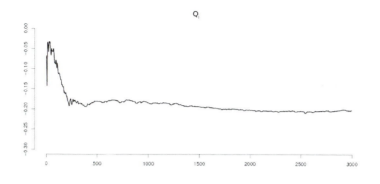

Figure 5.4: Comparison between two different neural-networks topologies in an electrical load-demand problem. The loss function is the *mean-squared error*. The figure plots the evolution of the Q_i statistic. The signal of Q_i is always negative, illustrating the overall advantage of one method over the other.

in mining high-speed data streams. The statistic

$$M = sign(n_{0,1} - n_{1,0}) \times \frac{(n_{0,1} - n_{1,0})^2}{n_{0,1} + n_{1,0}}$$

has a χ^2 distribution with 1 degree of freedom. For a confidence level of 0.99, the null hypothesis is rejected if the statistic is greater than 6.635 (Dietterich, 1996).

5.3.3.2 Illustrative Example

We have used the dataset SEA concepts (Street and Kim, 2001), a benchmark problem for concept drift. Figure 5.6 (left panel) shows the evolution of the error rate of two naive-Bayes variants: a standard one and a variant that detects and relearns a new decision model whenever drift is detected. The McNemar test was performed to compare both algorithms. The right panel shows the evolution of the statistic test computed over the entire stream. As it can be observed, once this statistic overcomes the threshold value 6.635, it never decreases below it, which is not informative about the dynamics of the process under study. Again, the problem is the long-term influences verified with the Q_i statistic. It is well known that the power of statistical tests, the probability of signaling differences where they do not exist, are highly affected by data length. Data streams are potentially unbounded, which might increase the type II errors.

To overcome this drawback, and since the fading factors are memoryless and prove to exhibit similar behaviors to sliding windows, we compute this

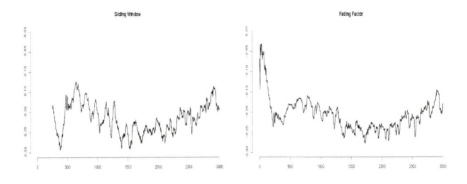

Figure 5.5: Plot of the Q_i statistic over a sliding window of 250 examples (left). The right figure plots the Q_i statistic using a fading factor of $\alpha = 0.995$.

statistic test using different window sizes and fading factors. Figure 5.7 illustrates a comparison on the evolution of a signed McNemar statistic between the two algorithms, computed over a sliding window of 1000 and 100 examples (on the top panel) and computed using a fading factor with $\alpha = 0.999$ and $\alpha = 0.99$ (on the bottom panel). It can be observed that in both cases, the statistics reject the null hypothesis almost at the same point. The use of this statistical test to compare stream-learning algorithms shows itself feasible by applying sliding-window or fading-factors techniques. Nevertheless, for different forgetting factors we got different results about the significance of the differences.

5.3.4   Evaluation Methodology in Non-Stationary Environments

An additional problem of the holdout method comes from the non-stationary properties of data streams. Non-stationarity or **concept drift** means that the concept about which data is obtained may shift from time to time, each time after some minimum permanence. The permanence of a concept is designated as **context** and is defined as a set of consecutive examples from the stream where the underlying distribution is stationary. Without loss of generality, we restrict this work to methods for explicit change detection because they are informative about the dynamics of the process generating data. In that case, some useful evaluation metrics include: *i)* probability of false alarms; *ii)* probability of true alarms; *ii)* delay in detection.

5.3.4.1   The Page-Hinkley Algorithm

Several tests for change detection have been presented in the literature (Basseville and Nikiforov, 1993; Widmer and Kubat, 1996; Klinkenberg,

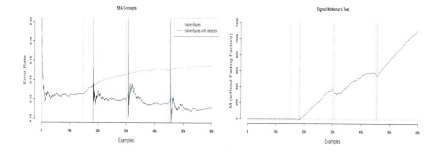

Figure 5.6: The evolution of signed McNemar statistic between two algorithms. Vertical dashed lines indicate drift in data, and vertical lines indicate when drift was detected. The left panel shows the evolution of the error rate of two naive-Bayes variants: a standard one and a variant that detects and relearns a new model whenever drift is detected. The right panel shows the evolution of the signed McNemar statistic computed for these two algorithms.

2004; Koychev, 2000; Gama et al., 2004). One of the most referred is the Page-Hinkley test (PH) (described in Section 3.2.2.2), a sequential analysis technique typically used for monitoring change detection (Page, 1954) in signal processing.

5.3.4.2 Illustrative Example

Figure 5.8 illustrates how PHT works. The top figure plots the trace of the prequential error of a naive-Bayes classifier (using data from the first concept of the SEA dataset (Street and Kim, 2001)). A concept drift occurs at point 15000 which leads to an error increment. The PHT allows us to detect the significant increase of the error. The bottom figure represents the evolution of the statistic test PH_t and the detection threshold (λ). As it can be observed, the PH statistic test follows the increase of the error rate. The λ parameter should guarantee that the algorithm, while it is resilient to false alarms, can detect and react to changes as soon as they occur, decreasing the detection delay time. Controlling this detection threshold parameter we establish a tradeoff between the false positive alarms and the missed detections.

As described before in this book the use of fading factors, as a smooth forgetting mechanism, may be an advantage in change detection algorithms. In a drift scenario, as new data is available, older observations are less useful. Using fading factors, e.g. attributing less weight to past observations, the change detection algorithm will focus on the most recent data, which in a drift scenario may lead to fast detections. For detection purposes, we monitor the evolution of the error rate of a naive-Bayes classifier (using again the SEA concepts dataset). The formula used to embed fading factors in the Page-

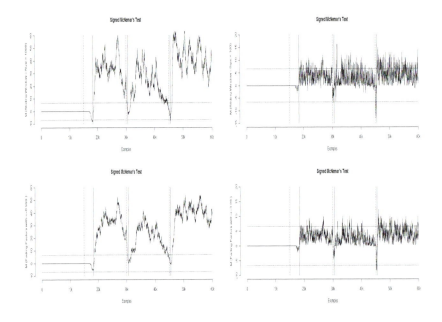

Figure 5.7: The evolution of signed McNemar statistic between the two algorithms. The top panel shows the evolution of the signed McNemar statistic computed over a sliding window of 1000 and 100 examples and the bottom panel shows the evolution of the signed McNemar statistic computed using a fading factor with $\alpha = 0.999$ and $\alpha = 0.99$, respectively. The dotted line is the threshold for a significance level of 99%. For different forgetting factors we got different results about the significance of the differences.

Hinkley test is: $m_T = \alpha \times m_{T-1} + (x_t - \hat{x}_T - \delta)$. To detect increases in the error rate (due to drifts in data) we compute the PHT, setting δ and λ parameters to 10^{-3} and 2.5, respectively. Figure 5.9 shows the delay time for this test: (a) without fading factors, (b) and (c) using different fading factors. The advantage of the use of fading factors in the PHT can be easily observed in this figure. The exponential forgetting results in small delay times without compromise miss detections.

     We can control the rate of forgetting using different fading factors; as close to one is the α value of the fading factor the less it will forget data. We evaluate the PHT using different fading factors to assess the delay time in detection. Figure 5.9 (b) and c)) shows the delay time in detection of concept drifts. We had used the PHT and different fading factors ($\alpha = 1 - 10^{-5}$ and $\alpha = 1 - 10^{-4}$, respectively) to detect these changes. Table 5.2 presents the delay time in detection of concept drifts in the same dataset used in Fgure 5.9. As the fading factor increases, one can observe that the delay time also increases,

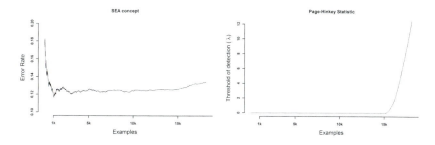

Figure 5.8: Experiments in SEA dataset illustrating the first drift at point 15000. The left figure shows the evolution of the naive-Bayes error rate. The right figure represents the evolution of the Page-Hinkley test statistic and the detection threshold λ.

Table 5.2: Delay times in drift scenarios using different *fading factors*. We observe false alarms only for $1 - \alpha = 10^{-4}$. The number of false alarms is indicated in parenthesis.

Drifts	Fading Factors $(1 - \alpha)$					
	10^{-4}	10^{-5}	10^{-6}	10^{-7}	10^{-8}	0
1st drift	1045 (1)	1609	2039	2089	2094	2095
2nd drift	654 (0)	2129	2464	2507	2511	2511
3rd drift	856 (1)	1357	1609	1637	2511	1641

which is consistent with the design of experiments. The closer one is to the α value of the fading factor, the greater is the weight of the old data, which will lead to higher delay times. The feasible values for α are between $1 - 10^{-4}$ and $1 - 10^{-8}$ (with $\alpha = 1 - 10^{-8}$ the delay times are not decreased and with $\alpha = 1 - 10^{-4}$ the delay time decreases dramatically but with false alarms). We may focus on the resilience of this test to false alarms and on its ability to reveal changes without miss detections. The results obtained with this dataset were very consistent and precise, supporting that the use of fading factors improves the accuracy of the Page-Hinkley test.

5.4   Lessons Learned and Open Issues

Assessing machine learning algorithms is one of the most relevant and difficult problems, even in the case of static models. The prequential statistic is a general methodology to evaluate learning algorithms in streaming scenarios, where learning requires dynamic models that evolves over time. The lessons learned in this chapter are:

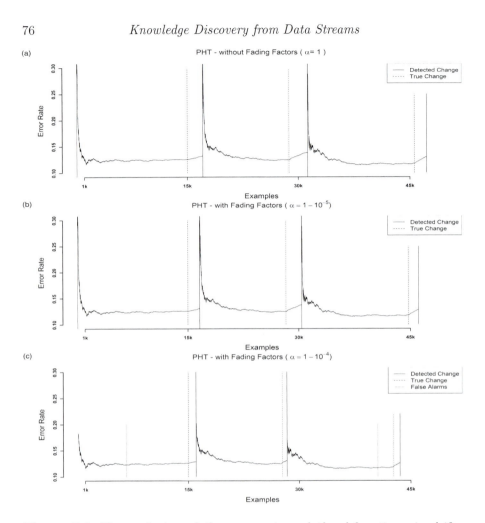

Figure 5.9: The evolution of the error rate and the delay times in drift detection using the Page-Hinkley test and different fading factors. The top panel shows the delay times using the PH test without fading factors. The middle and bottom panels show the delay times using fading factors with $\alpha = 1 - 10^{-5}$ and $\alpha = 1 - 10^{-4}$, respectively.

- The prequential error allows us to monitor the evolution of learning process;

- The prequential error requires some sort of forgetting mechanism, like sliding windows or fading factors;

- Both forgetting techniques converge toward the holdout estimate;

- Fading factors are faster and use less memory than sliding windows;

- Forgetting techniques are useful in statistical hypothesis testing, reducing type II errors;

- Forgetting techniques are useful in change detection. They might improve detection rates, maintaining the capacity of being resilient to false alarms when there are no drifts.

The main problem in the evaluation methods when learning from dynamic and time-changing data streams consists of monitoring the evolution of the learning process. In this work we defend the use of predictive sequential error estimates using fading factors to assess performance of stream learning algorithms in presence of non-stationary data. The prequential method is a general methodology to evaluate learning algorithms in streaming scenarios. In those applications where the observed target value is available later in time, the prequential estimator can be implemented inside the learning algorithm. This opens interesting opportunities: the system would be capable of monitoring the evolution of the learning process itself and self-diagnosing the evolution of it. In this chapter we focus on loss as performance criteria. Nevertheless, other criteria, imposed by data stream characteristics, must be taken into account. Memory is one of the most important constraints. Learning algorithms run in fixed memory. They need to manage the available memory, eventually discarding parts of the required statistics or parts of the decision model. We need to evaluate the memory usage over time, and its impact on accuracy.

5.5   Notes

Performance assessment, design of experimental work, and model selection, are fundamental topics in science in general and in statistics (Bhattacharyya and Johnson, 1977), artificial intelligence (Cohen, 1995), machine learning (Mitchell, 1997), data mining (Hastie et al., 2000), in particular. The topic of model selection (Schaffer, 1993) is obviously of great interest. Some general methods include *Occam's razor* (Domingos, 1998), *minimum description length* (Grünwald, 2007), *Bayesian information score* (Akaike, 1974), *risk minimization* (Vapnik, 1995), etc. A theoretical comparison between some of these methods appears in (Kearns et al., 1997). Some referential works in the area of Machine Learning, with high criticism to some usual practices, appear in (Dietterich, 1996; Salzberg, 1997), and more recently in (Demsar, 2006). More advanced topics in evaluation and model selection include the *receiver operating characteristic*, ROC curves and the AUC metric (Hand and Till, 2001; Fürnkranz and Flach, 2005).

The computational learning theory community has studied, analyzed and developed several on-line learning algorithms. Most of these works have the purpose of characterizing their theoretical limitations and possibilities. A recent book, Cesa-Bianch and Lugosi (2006), presents a relevant discussion on these topics.

Chapter 6

Clustering from Data Streams

Roughly speaking, *clustering* is the process of grouping objects into different groups, such that the common properties of data in each subset are high, and between different subsets are low. Clustering methods are widely used in data mining. They are either used to get insight into data distribution or as a preprocessing step for other algorithms. The most common approaches use distance between examples as similarity criteria. These approaches require space that is quadratic in the number of observations, which is prohibitive in the data stream paradigm.

The data stream clustering problem is defined as *to maintain a continuously consistent good clustering of the sequence observed so far, using a small amount of memory and time.* The issues are imposed by the continuous arriving data points, and the need to analyze them in real time. These characteristics require incremental clustering, maintaining cluster structures that evolve over time. Moreover, the data stream may continuously evolve, and new clusters might appear, others disappear, reflecting the dynamics of the stream.[1]

6.1 Introduction

Major clustering approaches in traditional cluster analysis include:

- *Partitioning* algorithms: construct a partition of a set of objects into k clusters, that minimize an objective function (e.g., the sum of squares' distances to the centroid representative). Examples include k-means (Farnstrom et al., 2000), and k-medoids;

- *Micro-clustering* algorithms: divide the clustering process into two phases, where the first phase is online and summarizes the data stream in local models (micro-clusters) and the second phase generates a global cluster model from the micro-clusters. Examples of these algorithms include BIRCH (Zhang et al., 1996) and CluStream (Aggarwal et al., 2003);

---

[1]Based on joint work with Pedro Pereira Rodrigues.

79

- *Density-based* algorithms are based on connectivity between regions and density functions. This type of algorithm finds clusters of arbitrary shapes, e.g., DBSCAN (Birant and Kut, 2007), and OPTICS (Peter Kriegel et al., 2003);

- *Grid-based* algorithms: based on a multiple-level granularity structure. View instance space as grid structures, e.g., Fractal Clustering (Barbará and Chen, 2000), and STING (Hinneburg and Keim, 1999);

- *Model-based* algorithms: find the best fit of the model to all the clusters. Good for conceptual clustering, e.g., COBWEB (Fisher, 1987), and SOM (Kaski and Kohonen, 1994).

Barbará (2002) identifies four basic requirements in data stream clustering algorithms: *i)* Compactness of representation; *ii)* Fast, incremental processing of new data points; *iii)* Tracking cluster changes; *iv)* Clear and fast identification of *outliers*.

In a seminal paper, Aggarwal et al. (2003) separate the clustering process into two steps. The first step works on-line and generates micro-clusters. This step requires efficient process for storing summary statistics. The second step works off-line, and generates the macro-clusters. It uses the summary statistics to provide clusters as per user-requirements. It is very efficient since it uses only the micro-clusters, allowing users to explore different aggregations and track clusters evolution.

As a final recommendation, that might be used in all the other tasks, Barbará (2002) wrote: *"Successfully applying the techniques to real data sets: This point requires the collaboration of data mining researchers with domain experts, in order to carefully evaluate the results and determine if they produce usable knowledge for the application at hand."*

6.2 Clustering Examples

Clustering examples is the most common task in unsupervised learning. The standard techniques are *partitioning clustering*, which requires knowing the number of desired clusters in advance; and *hierarchical clustering*, that generates a hierarchy of embedded clusters.

6.2.1 Basic Concepts

A powerful idea in clustering from data streams is the concept of *cluster feature - CF*. A cluster feature, or *micro-cluster*, is a compact representation of a set of points. A CF structure is a triple (N, LS, SS), used to store the sufficient statistics of a set of points:

- N is the number of data points;

- LS is a vector of the same dimension of data points that store the linear sum of the N points;

- SS is a vector of the same dimension of data points that store the square sum of the N points.

The properties of cluster features are:

- **Incrementality**
  If a point x is added to the cluster, the sufficient statistics are updated as follows:

$$LS_A \leftarrow LS_A + x$$
$$SS_A \leftarrow SS_A + x^2$$
$$N_A \leftarrow N_A + 1$$

- **Additivity**
  if A_1 and A_2 are disjoint sets, merging them is equal to the sum of their parts. The additive property allows us to merge sub-clusters incrementally.

$$LS_C \leftarrow LS_A + LS_B$$
$$SS_C \leftarrow SS_A + SS_B$$
$$N_C \leftarrow N_A + N_B.$$

A CF entry has sufficient information to calculate the norms

$$L_1 = \sum_{i=1}^{n} |x_{a_i} - x_{b_i}|$$

$$L_2 = \sqrt{\sum_{i=1}^{n} (x_{a_i} - x_{b_i})^2}$$

and basic measures to characterize a cluster:

- **Centroid**, defined as the gravity center of the cluster:

$$\vec{X}0 = \frac{LS}{N}$$

- **Radius**, defined as the average distance from member points to the centroid:

$$R = \sqrt{\frac{\sum_1^N (\vec{x}_i - \vec{X}0)^2}{N}}.$$

Algorithm 10: The `Leader` Clustering Algorithm.

---

    input : X: A Sequence of Examples x_i
               δ: Control Distance parameter.
    output: Centroids of the k Clusters
    begin
        Initialize the set of centroids $C = x_1$
        foreach $x_i \in X$ **do**
            Find the cluster c_r whose center is close to x_i
            if $d(x_i, C_r) < \delta$ **then**
                 $C = C \bigcup x_i$

    end

6.2.2 Partitioning Clustering

6.2.2.1 The Leader Algorithm

The simplest single-pass partitioning algorithm is known as the `Leader` (Spath, 1980) clustering algorithm. It uses a user-specified distance threshold that specifies the maximum allowed distance between an example and a centroid. At any step, the algorithm assigns the current example to the most similar cluster (the *leader*) if their distance is below the threshold. Otherwise the example itself is added as a leader. The `Leader` algorithm is a one-pass and fast algorithm, and does not require prior information about the number of clusters. However, it is an unstable algorithm; its performance depends too much on the order of the examples and a correct guess of the distance threshold which requires prior knowledge.

6.2.2.2 Single Pass k-Means

k-means is the most widely used clustering algorithm. It constructs a partition of a set of objects into k clusters, that minimize some objective function, usually a squared error function, which imply round-shape clusters. The input parameter k is fixed and must be given in advance, which limits its real applicability to streaming and evolving data.

Farnstrom et al. (2000) propose a *single pass k-means* algorithm. The main idea is to use a buffer where points of the dataset are kept in a compressed way. The data stream is processed in blocks. All available space on the buffer is filled with points from the stream. Using these points, find k centers such that the sum of distances from data points to their closest center is minimized. Only the k centroids (representing the clustering results) are retained, with the corresponding k cluster features. In the following iterations, the buffer is initialized with the k-centroids, found in previous iteration, weighted by the k cluster features, and incoming data points from the stream. The *single pass k-means* is incremental, improving its solution given additional data. It uses a

Algorithm 11: Algorithm for Single Pass k-Means Clustering.

input : S: A Sequence of Examples
         k: Number of desired Clusters.
output: Centroids of the k Clusters
begin
     Randomly initialize cluster means.
     Each cluster has a discard set that keeps track of the sufficient statistics.
     while *TRUE* **do**
         Fill the buffer with examples
         Execute iterations of k-means on points and discard set in the buffer, until convergence.
         /* For this clustering, each discard set is treated like a regular point weighted with the number of points in the discard set. */
         foreach *group* **do**
             update sufficient statistics of the discard set with the examples assigned to that group
         Remove points from the buffer
end

fixed size buffer and can be described in Algorithm 11. Farnstrom et al. (2000) conclude: *"The main positive result is that the single pass k-means algorithm, with a buffer of size 1% of the input dataset, can produce clusters of almost the same quality as the standard multiple pass k-means, while being several times faster."*

The *very fast k-means* algorithm (VFKM) (Domingos and Hulten, 2001) uses the Hoeffding bound (Hoeffding, 1963) to determine the number of examples needed in each step of a k-means algorithm. VFKM runs as a sequence of k-means runs, with increasing number of examples until the Hoeffding bound is satisfied.

Guha et al. (2003) present an analytical study on k-median clustering data streams. The proposed algorithm makes a single pass over the data stream and uses small space. It requires $O(nk)$ time and $O(n\epsilon)$ space where k is the number of centers, n is the number of points and $\epsilon < 1$. They have proved that any k-median algorithm that achieves a constant factor approximation cannot achieve a better run time than $O(nk)$.

6.2.3 Hierarchical Clustering

One major achievement in this area of research was the BIRCH (*Balanced Iterative Reducing and Clustering using Hierarchies*) system (Zhang et al., 1996). The BIRCH system compresses data, building a hierarchical structure

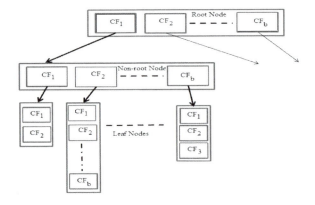

Figure 6.1: The Clustering Feature Tree in BIRCH. **B** is the maximum number of CFs in a level of the tree.

the CF-tree, where each node is a tuple (Clustering Feature) that contains the sufficient statistics describing a set of data points, and compresses all information of the CFs below in the tree. BIRCH only works with continuous attributes. It was designed for very large datasets, explicitly taking into account time and memory constraints. For example, not all data points are used for clustering, dense regions of data points are treated as sub-clusters. BIRCH might scan data twice to refine the CF-tree, although it can be used with a single scan of data. It proceeds in two phases. The first phase scans the database to build an initial in-memory CF tree, a multi-level compression of the data that tries to preserve the inherent clustering structure of the data (see Figure 6.1). The second phase uses an arbitrary clustering algorithm to cluster the leaf nodes of the CF-tree.

BIRCH requires two user-defined parameters: B the branch factor or the maximum number of entries in each non-leaf node; and T the maximum diameter (or radius) of any CF in a leaf node. The maximum diameter T defines the examples that can be *absorbed* by a CF. Increasing T, more examples can be absorbed by a micro-cluster and smaller CF-Trees are generated. When an example is available, it traverses down the current tree from the root, till finding the appropriate leaf. At each non-leaf node, the example follow the *closest*-CF path, with respect to norms L_1 or L_2. If the closest-CF in the leaf cannot absorb the example, make a new CF entry. If there is no room for a new leaf, split the parent node. A leaf node might be expanded due to the constraints imposed by B and T. The process consists of taking the two farthest CFs and creating two new leaf nodes. When traversing backup the CFs are updated.

BIRCH tries to find the best groups with respect to the available memory, while it minimizes the amount of input and output. The CF-tree grows by aggregation, getting with only one pass over the data a result of complexity O(N). However, Sheikholeslami et al. (1998) show that it does not perform well in the presence of non-spherical clusters.

6.2.4 Micro Clustering

An interesting extension of BIRCH to data streams is the CluStream system (Aggarwal et al., 2003). As in BIRCH, the system is divided in two components: one on-line and another off-line. Micro-clusters are locally kept, having statistical information of data and time stamps. The CF are extended with temporal information (CFT): the sum of time stamps, and the sum of the squares of time stamps. For each incoming data point, the distance to the centroids of existing CFs is computed. The data point is absorbed by an existing CF if the distance to the centroid falls within the *maximum boundary* of the CF. The *maximum boundary* is defined as a factor t of the *radius* deviation of the CF; otherwise, the data point starts a new micro-cluster. CluStream only maintains the most recent q micro-clusters. Whenever a new micro-cluster is generated, the oldest one is deleted or merged with the closest cluster.

CluStream can generate approximate clusters for any user-defined time granularity. This is achieved by storing the CFT at regular time intervals, referred to as snapshots. Suppose the user wants to find clusters in the stream based on a history of length h. The off-line component can analyze the snapshots stored at the snapshots t, the current time, and $(t - h)$ by using the additive property of CFT. The important problem is when to store the snapshots of the current set of micro-clusters. Two examples of time frames are presented in Figure 2.4 (see Chapter 2). For example, the natural time frame stores snapshots each quarter, 4 quarters are aggregated in hours; 24 hours are aggregated in days, etc. The aggregation level is domain dependent and explores the additive property of CFT.

Aggarwal, Han, Wang, and Yu (2003) propose to store snapshots in a pyramidal form. Snapshots are classified into *orders* varying from 1 to $log(t)$, where t is the current time stamp. The order of a particular class of snapshots defines the level of granularity at which the snapshots are maintained. The order of a snapshot is obtained as follows. Given a positive integer α a snapshot is of order i if its time stamp is divisible by α^i. We note that a snapshot might have several *orders*. For example, assume $\alpha = 2$, the snapshot taken at time-stamp 8, has orders 0, 1, 2, and 3. The system only stores the $\alpha + 1$ most recent snapshots of order i. The pyramidal framework guarantees that:

- The maximum order of a snapshot stored at time t is $log_\alpha(t)$;

- The maximum number of snapshots maintained at time t is $(\alpha + 1) \times log_\alpha(t)$;

- For any time window of length h, at least one stored snapshot can be found within $2 \times h$ units of the current time.

6.2.4.1   Discussion

The idea of dividing the clustering process into two layers, where the first layer generates local models (micro-clusters) and the second layer generates global models from the local ones, is a powerful idea that has been used elsewhere. Three illustrative examples are:

The *Clustering on Demand* framework (Dai et al., 2006) is a system for clustering time series. The first phase consists of one data scan for online statistics collection and compact multi-resolution approximations, which are designed to address the time and the space constraints in a data stream environment. The second phase applies a clustering algorithm over the summaries. Furthermore, with the multi-resolution approximations of data streams, flexible clustering demands can be supported. The *Clustering Using REpresentatives* system (Guha et al., 1998) is a hierarchical algorithm that generates partial clusters from samples of data in a first phase, and in the second phase clusters the partial clusters. It uses multiple representative points to evaluate the distance between clusters, being able to adjust to arbitrarily shaped clusters. The *On Demand Classification of Data Streams* algorithm (Aggarwal et al., 2006) uses the two-layer model for classification problems. The first layer generates the micro-clusters as in CluStream, with the additional information of class labels. A labeled data point can only be added to a micro-cluster belonging to the same class.

6.2.4.2   Monitoring Cluster Evolution

Promising research lines are tracking changes in clusters. Spiliopoulou et al. (2006) presents system MONIC, for detecting and tracking change in clusters. MONIC assumes that a cluster is an object in a geometric space. It encompasses changes that involve more than one cluster, allowing for insights on cluster change in the whole clustering. The transition tracking mechanism is based on the degree of overlapping between the two clusters. The concept of *overlap* between two clusters, X and Y, is defined as the normed number of common records weighted with the age of the records. Assume that cluster X was obtained at time t_1 and cluster Y at time t_2. The degree of overlapping between the two clusters is given by:

$$overlap(X, Y) = \frac{\sum_{a \in X \cap Y} age(a, t_2)}{\sum_{x \in X} age(x, t_2)}$$

The degree of overlapping allows inferring properties of the underlying data stream. Cluster transition at a given time point is a change in a cluster discovered at an earlier timepoint. MONIC considers transitions internal and external transitions, that reflect the dynamics of the stream. Examples of cluster transitions include: the cluster survives, the cluster is absorbed, a cluster disappears, a new cluster emerges.

Algorithm 12: Algorithm for Fractal Clustering: Initialization Phase.

---

input : S: A Set S of Examples

$\quad\quad\quad$ k: A Distance Threshold k.

begin

$\quad$ Make $k = 0$

$\quad$ Make $d_0 = d$

$\quad$ Randomly choose a point P in S.

$\quad$ **while** S *is not Empty* **do**

$\quad\quad$ Mark P as belonging to Cluster C_k

$\quad\quad$ Starting at P and in a recursive depth-first

$\quad\quad$ Find the nearest neighbor of P such that $dist(P\prime, P) < d$

$\quad\quad$ **if** $P\prime$ *exist* **then**

$\quad\quad\quad$ Put $P\prime$ in Cluster C_k

$\quad\quad\quad$ Update the average distance between $(\hat{d})$ pairs of points in C_k

$\quad\quad\quad$ Make $d = d_0 \times \hat{d}$

$\quad\quad$ **else**

$\quad\quad\quad$ backtrack to the previous point in the search

$\quad\quad$ $k = k + 1$

end

6.2.5 Grid Clustering

In grid clustering the instance space is divided into a finite and potentially large number of cells that form a grid structure. All clustering operations are performed in the grid structure which is independent of the number of data points. Grid clustering is oriented toward spatio-temporal problems. Illustrative examples that appear in the literature are (Wang et al., 1997; Hinneburg and Keim, 1999; Park and Lee, 2004).

The Fractal Clustering (FC) system (Barbará and Chen, 2000) is a grid-based algorithm that defines clusters as sets of points that exhibit high self-similarity. Note that, if the attributes of a dataset obey uniformity and independence properties, its intrinsic dimension equals the embedding dimension E. On the other hand, whenever there is a correlation between two or more attributes, the intrinsic dimension of the dataset is accordingly lower. Thus, $\mathcal{D}$ is always smaller than or equal to E. A dataset exhibiting fractal behavior is self-similar over a large range of scales (Schroeder, 1991; Sousa et al., 2007). The fractal behavior of self-similar real datasets leads to a distribution of distances that follows a power law (Faloutsos et al., 2000). Given a dataset S of N elements and a distance function $d(s_i, s_j)$, the average number k of neighbors within a distance r is proportional to r raised to $\mathcal{D}$. Thus, the number of pairs of elements within distance r (the pair-count $PC(r)$), follows a power

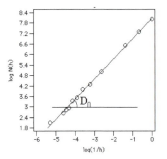

Figure 6.2: The box-counting plot: log-log plot $n(r)$ versus r. D_0 is the Hausdorff fractal dimension.

law, where K_p is a proportionality constant:

$$PC(r) = K_p \cdot r^{\mathcal{D}} \qquad (6.1)$$

Observe that by evaluating the distances between every two elements of a dataset S we can plot a graph of $PC(r)$ versus r to depict the distribution of distances in S. For a self-similar (fractal) dataset, the distribution of distances plotted in log-log scale is straight for a significant range of r, such that the slope of the best-fitting line corresponds to the exponent in Equation 6.1 and closely approaches the intrinsic dimension $\mathcal{D}$ of the dataset (Sousa et al., 2007). However, computing $PC(r)$ for different values of r requires measuring the distance between every pair of elements in S, that is, a $O(N^2)$ problem where N is the number of elements in the dataset.

6.2.5.1   Computing the Fractal Dimension

The standard process to compute the fractal dimension is the *box-counting plot* method. A set of N points, each with d dimensions, is embedded in a d-dimensional grid which cells have sizes of size r. Denote the frequency of points that fall in the i-th cell by p_i. The Hausdorff fractal dimension is given by:

$$D_0 = \lim_{r \to 0} \frac{log(n(r))}{log(1/r)}$$

If $n(r)$ is the number of cells occupied by points in the data set, the plot of $n(r)$ versus r in log-log scales is called the *box-counting plot*. The negative value of the slope of that plot corresponds to the Hausdorff fractal dimension.

6.2.5.2   Fractal Clustering

The Fractal Clustering system (Barbará and Chen, 2000) clusters data incrementally, assigning the data points to the group in which that assignment produces less fractal impact, the group in which the fractal dimension

---

Algorithm 13: Algorithm for Fractal Clustering: Incremental Step.

input : S: A Set of Examples that fit in memory
begin

> **foreach** $P \in S$ **do**
>
>> **foreach** $i \in \{1, \ldots, k\}$ **do**
>>
>>> $C'_i \leftarrow C_i \bigcup \{p\}$
>>> Compute $F_d(C'_i)$
>>> Find $\hat{i} = min_i(|F_d(C'_i) - F_d(C_i)|)$
>>> **if** $|F_d(C'_{\hat{i}}) - F_d(C_{\hat{i}})| > \tau$ **then**
>>>> └ Discard p as noise
>>>
>>> **else**
>>>> └ Place p in cluster $C_{\hat{i}}$

end

Algorithm 14: Algorithm for Fractal Clustering: Tracking Cluster Changes.

input : S: A Set of Examples that fit in memory
begin

> Initialize the count of successfully clustered points: $r = 0$
> **foreach** $P \in S$ **do**
>
>> Use FC to cluster the point
>> **if** P *is not an outlier* **then**
>>> └ $r \leftarrow r + 1$
>
> $s \leftarrow \frac{3(1+\epsilon)}{\epsilon^2} \times ln(2/\delta)$
> **if** $r \leq s$ **then**
>> └ Initialize clusters using this set S of examples
>
> $p \leftarrow \frac{r}{n}$

end

---

is less affected. The FC algorithm has two distinct phases. The initialization phase, where the initial clusters are defined, each with sufficient points so that the fractal dimension can be computed. The second phase incrementally adds new points to the set of initial clusters. The initialization phase uses a traditional distance-based algorithm. The initialization algorithm is presented in Algorithm 12. After the initial clustering phase, the incremental step (Algorithm 13) process points in a stream. For each point, the *fractal impact* in cluster C_i is computed as $|F_d(C'_i) - F_d(C_i)|$. The quantity $min_i(|F_d(C'_i) - F_d(C_i)|$ is the *Minimum Fractal Impact (MFI)* of the point. If the MFI of the point is larger than a threshold τ the point is rejected as outlier, otherwise it is included in that cluster.

FC algorithm processes data points in batches. A key issue, whenever a new batch is available, is *Is the current set of clusters appropriate for the incoming batch?* Barbará and Chen (2001) extended the FC algorithm to track the evolution of clusters. The key idea is to count the number of successful clustered points to guarantee high-probability clusters. Successful clustered points are those with MFI greater than τ. Using Chernoff bound, the number of successful clustered points must be greater than $\frac{3(1+\epsilon)}{\epsilon^2} \times ln(2/\delta)$. The algorithm to track the evolution of the clusters is presented in Algorithm 14.

6.3   Clustering Variables

Most of the work in incremental clustering of data streams has been concentrated on example clustering rather than variable clustering. Clustering variables (e.g., time series) is a very useful tool for some applications, such as sensor networks, social networks, electrical power demand, stock market, etc. The distinction between clustering examples and clustering variables is not an issue in batch clustering, since *examples* and *variables* can be easily transposed. In the context of high-speed data streams, the standard matrix transposition is not applicable. Transpose is a block operator. Clustering variables in data streams requires different algorithms.

The basic idea behind clustering streaming time series is to find groups of variables that behave similarly through time. This similarity is usually measured in terms of distances between time series, such as the Euclidean distance or the correlation. However, when applying variable clustering to data streams, a system can never be supported on total knowledge of available data, since it is always evolving and multiple passes over the data are impossible. Thus, these distances must be incrementally computed. Let $X = \langle x_1, x_2, ..., x_n \rangle$ be the complete set of n data streams and $X^t = \langle x_1^t, x_2^t, ..., x_n^t \rangle$ be the example containing the observations of all streams x_i at the specific time t. The goal of an incremental clustering system for multiple time series is to find (and make available at any time t) a partition P of those streams, where streams in the same cluster tend to be more alike than streams in different clusters. In a hierarchical approach to the problem, with the benefit of not having to previously define the target number of clusters, the goal is to continuously maintain a structured hierarchy of clusters. An example partition could be defined as $P^t = \{\{\{x_1\}, \{x_3, x_5\}\}, \{x_2, x_4\}\}$, stating that data streams x_1, x_3, x_5 have some similarity between them (more pronounced between x_3 and x_5), being at the same time somehow dissimilar from x_2 and x_4. In fact, most of the works published in clustering of data streams refer to example clustering and very few works refer to variable clustering. One of the first works for this task was presented by Rodrigues, Gama, and Pedroso (2008), with the system ODAC.

6.3.1 A Hierarchical Approach

In this section, we discuss the ODAC *(Online Divisive-Agglomerative Clustering)* system. This is an algorithm for incremental clustering of streaming time series that constructs a hierarchical tree-shaped structure of clusters using a top-down strategy. The leaves are the resulting clusters, and each leaf groups a set of variables. The union of the leaves is the complete set of variables. The intersection of leaves is the empty set.

The system uses two major operators for expansion and aggregation of the tree-based structure, based on the dynamics of the process generating data. A cluster expansion occurs in stationary phases of the stream. When a cluster receives more information we can define more detailed clusters. The variables in a cluster are divided into two new clusters. In non-stationary phases, whenever the stream correlation structure changes, the system can detect that the correlation structure in the most recent data differs from the one observed in the past. In that case the merge operator triggers and two sibling clusters are merged into one.

ODAC continuously monitors the diameter of existing clusters. The *diameter* of a cluster is the maximum distance between variables of that cluster. For each existing cluster, the system finds the two variables defining the diameter of that cluster. If a given heuristic condition is met on this diameter, the system splits the cluster and assigns each of the chosen variables to one of the new clusters, becoming the *pivot* variable for that cluster. Afterwards, all remaining variables on the old cluster are assigned to the new cluster which has the closest pivot. New leaves start new statistics, assuming that only forthcoming information will be useful to decide whether or not this cluster should be split. Each node c_k will then represent relations between streams using examples $X^{i_k..s_k}$, where i_k is the time at which the node was created and s_k is the time at which the node was split (or current time t for leaf nodes). This feature increases the system's ability to cope with changing concepts as, later on, a test is performed to check if the previously decided split still represents the structure of variables. If the diameters of the children leaves are greater than the parent's diameter, then the previously taken decision may no longer reflect the structure of data. The system merges the two leaves on the parent node, restarting statistics. Algorithm 15 presents an overview of ODAC. The forthcoming sections describe the inner core of the system.

6.3.1.1 Growing the Hierarchy

The system must analyze distances between incomplete vectors, possibly without having any of the previous values available. Thus, these distances must be incrementally computed. Since decisions must have statistical support, it uses the Hoeffding bound, forcing the criterion - the distance measure - to be scaled (Hoeffding, 1963). It uses the Pearson correlation coefficient (Pearson, 1896) between time series as *similarity* measure, as done by Leydesdorff (2005). Deriving from the correlation between two time series a and b calculated

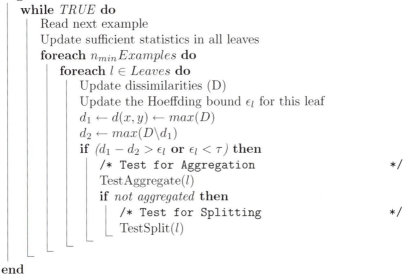

Algorithm 15: The ODAC Global Algorithm.

---

begin
    while *TRUE* **do**
        Read next example
        Update sufficient statistics in all leaves
        foreach $n_{min} Examples$ **do**
            foreach $l \in Leaves$ **do**
                Update dissimilarities (D)
                Update the Hoeffding bound ϵ_l for this leaf
                $d_1 \leftarrow d(x,y) \leftarrow max(D)$
                $d_2 \leftarrow max(D \backslash d_1)$
                if $(d_1 - d_2 > \epsilon_l$ **or** $\epsilon_l < \tau)$ **then**
                    `/* Test for Aggregation`   `*/`
                    TestAggregate(l)
                    if *not aggregated* **then**
                        `/* Test for Splitting`   `*/`
                        TestSplit(l)

end

---

in Wang and Wang (2003), the factors used to compute the correlation can be updated incrementally, achieving an exact incremental expression for the correlation:

$$corr(a,b) = \frac{P - \frac{AB}{n}}{\sqrt{A_2 - \frac{A^2}{n}}\sqrt{B_2 - \frac{B^2}{n}}} \qquad (6.2)$$

The *sufficient statistics* needed to compute the correlation are easily updated at each time step: $A = \sum a_i$, $B = \sum b_i$, $A_2 = \sum a_i^2$, $B_2 = \sum b_i^2$, $P = \sum a_i b_i$. In ODAC, the dissimilarity between variables a and b is measured by an appropriate metric, the *Rooted Normalized One-Minus-Correlation* given by

$$rnomc(a,b) = \sqrt{\frac{1 - corr(a,b)}{2}} \qquad (6.3)$$

with range $[0, 1]$. We consider the cluster's *diameter* to be the highest dissimilarity between two time series belonging to the same cluster.

The main procedure of the ODAC system grows a tree-shaped structure that represents the hierarchy of the clusters present in the data. It processes each example only once. The system incrementally updates, at each new example arrival, the sufficient statistics needed to compute the dissimilarity matrix. The dissimilarity matrix for each leaf is only computed when it is being tested for splitting or aggregation, after receiving a minimum number of examples. When processing a new example, only the leaves are updated, avoiding computation of unneeded dissimilarities; this speeds up the process every time the structure grows.

Splitting Criteria. One problem that usually arises with this sort of model is the definition of a minimum number of observations necessary to assure convergence. A common way of doing this includes a user-defined parameter; after a leaf has received at least n_{min} examples, it is considered ready to be tested for splitting. Another approach is to apply techniques based on the Hoeffding bound (Hoeffding, 1963) to solve this problem. Remember from section 2.2.2 that after n independent observations of a real-valued random variable r with range R, and with confidence $1 - \delta$, the true mean of r is at least $\bar{r} - \epsilon$, where $\bar{r}$ is the observed mean of the samples and $\epsilon = \sqrt{\frac{R^2 ln(1/\delta)}{2n}}$.

As each leaf is fed with a different number of examples, each cluster c_k will possess a different value for ϵ, designated ϵ_k. Let $d(a, b)$ be the distance measure between pairs of time series, and $D_k = \{(x_i, x_j) \mid x_i, x_j \in c_k, i < j\}$ be the set of pairs of variables included in a specific leaf c_k. After seeing n samples at the leaf, let $(x_1, y_1) \in \{(x, y) \in D_k \mid d(x, y) \geq d(a, b), \forall (a, b) \in D_k\}$ be the pair of variables with maximum dissimilarity within the cluster c_k, and in the same way considering $D'_k = D_k \backslash \{(x_1, y_1)\}$.

Let $(x_2, y_2) \in \{(x, y) \in D'_k \mid d(x, y) \geq d(a, b), \forall (a, b) \in D'_k\}$, $d_1 = d(x_1, y_1)$, $d_2 = d(x_2, y_2)$ and $\Delta d = d_1 - d_2$ be a new random variable, consisting of the difference between the observed values through time. Applying the Hoeffding bound to Δd, if $\Delta d > \epsilon_k$, we can confidently say that, with probability $1 - \delta$, the difference between d_1 and d_2 is larger than zero, and select (x_1, y_1) as the pair of variables representing the diameter of the cluster. That is:

$$d_1 - d_2 > \epsilon_k \Rightarrow diam(c_k) = d_1 \qquad (6.4)$$

With this rule, the ODAC system will only split the cluster when the true diameter of the cluster is known with statistical confidence given by the Hoeffding bound. This rule triggers the moment the leaf has been fed with enough examples to support the decision. Although a time series is not a purely random variable, ODAC models the time series first-order differences in order to reduce the negative effect of autocorrelation on the Hoeffding bound. Moreover, with this approach, the missing values can be easily treated with a zero value, considering that, when unknown, the time series is constant.

Resolving Ties. The rule presented in Equation 6.4 redirects the research to a different problem. There might be cases where the two top-most distances are nearly or completely equal. To distinguish between the cases where the cluster has many variables nearly equidistant and the cases where there are two or more highly dissimilar variables, a tweak must be done. Having in mind the application of the system to a data stream with high dimension, possibly with hundreds or thousands of variables, we turn to a heuristic approach. Based on techniques presented in Domingos and Hulten (2000), we introduce a parameter to the system, τ, which determines how long we will let the system check for the real diameter until we force the splitting and aggregation tests. At any time, if $\tau > \epsilon_k$, the system overrules the criterion of Equation 6.4, assuming the leaf has been fed with enough examples, hence it should consider the highest distance to be the real diameter.

Expanding the Tree. When a split point is reported, the pivots are variables x_1 and y_1 where $d_1 = d(x_1, y_1)$, and the system assigns each of the remaining variables of the old cluster to the cluster which has the closest pivot. The sufficient statistics of each new cluster are initialized. The total space required by the two new clusters is always less than the one required by the previous cluster. Algorithm 16 sketches the splitting procedure.

Algorithm 16: ODAC: The TestSplit Algorithm.

---

input: l: A leaf in the Cluster Structure
$X = \{x_1, \ldots, x_j\}$: Set of variables in l
begin

$\quad d_1 \leftarrow d(x_1, y_1) = \text{argmax}_{d(x,y)}(D_k)$

$\quad d_2 \leftarrow \text{argmax}_{d(x,y)}(D_k \backslash \{d(x_1, y_1)\})$

$\quad \bar{d} \leftarrow$ the average of all distances in the cluster

$\quad d_0 \leftarrow$ the minimum distance between variables $\in l$

$\quad$ **if** $(d_1 - d_0)|(d_1 - \bar{d}) - (\bar{d} - d_0)| > \epsilon_k$ **then**

$\quad\quad$ create two new leaves: C_x and C_y

$\quad\quad$ with x_1 and y_1 as pivots: $x_1 \in C_x \wedge y_1 \in C_y$

$\quad\quad$ **foreach** $x_i \in X$ **do**

$\quad\quad\quad$ /* assign variables to the cluster with the
$\quad\quad\quad\quad$ closest pivot.   */

$\quad\quad\quad$ **if** $d(x_i, x_1) \leq d(x_i, y_1)$ **then**

$\quad\quad\quad\quad$ ⌊ Assign x_i to C_x

$\quad\quad\quad$ **else**

$\quad\quad\quad\quad$ ⌊ Assign x_i to C_y

end

6.3.1.2 Aggregating at Concept Drift Detection

Whenever new data points are available, only the statistics of the leafs of the current structure are updated. This fact implies that the decision to expand the structure is based on the data corresponding to a time window over the stream. Each node has its own time window. The time windows associated with deeper nodes correspond to more recent data.

In the case of stationary data, where the correlation structure between time-series remains constant, the splitting criterion guarantees that the diameter of a cluster should decrease whenever an expansion of a cluster occurs. In fact, the diameter of each of the two new clusters should be less or equal than the parent's diameter. Nevertheless, usual real-world problems deal with non-stationary data streams, where time series that were correlated in the past are

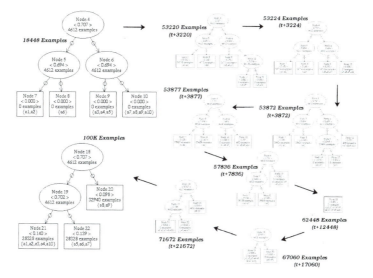

Figure 6.3: ODAC structure evolution in a time-changing dataset. Start: First concept is defined for the dataset; 50000 exs (t): Concept drift occurs in the dataset; 53220 exs (t + 3220): ODAC detects changes in the structure; 62448 exs (t + 12448, s): ODAC collapses all structure; 71672 exs (t + 21672, s + 9224): ODAC gathers second concept and stabilizes; End: Second concept remains in the dataset and the correct final structure of the second concept was discovered.

no longer correlated to each other in the current time period. The strategy adopted in ODAC is based on the analysis of the diameters. No computation is needed between the variables of the two siblings. For each given leaf c_k, we should search to see if the split decision that created it still represents the structure of data. Thus, we shall test the diameters of c_k, c_k's sibling (c_s) and c_k's parent (c_j), assuming that the sum of the children's diameters should not be as large as two times the diameter of the parent. We define a new random variable $\Delta a = 2 \cdot diam(c_j) - (diam(c_k) + diam(c_s))$. Applying the Hoeffding bound to this random variable, if $\Delta a > \epsilon$ then the condition is met, so the splitting decision is still a good approach. Given this, we choose to aggregate on c_j if:

$$2 \cdot diam(c_j) - (diam(c_k) + diam(c_s)) < \epsilon \qquad (6.5)$$

supported by the confidence given by the parent's consumed data. The system decreases the number of clusters as previous division is no longer supported and might not reflect the best divisive structure of data. The resulting leaf starts new computations and a concept drift is detected. Figure 6.3 illustrates the evolution of a cluster structure in time-changing data.

6.3.1.3   Analysis of the Algorithm

An interesting fact in ODAC is that the time to process incoming examples and the space needed to store the sufficient statistics at leaves decrease whenever an expansion of the structure triggers. To understand this observation, consider a leaf with n variables. The leaf is expanded, originating two new leaves. Assume that n_1 and n_2 are the variables in each new leaf, $n = n_1 + n_2$. By the triangular inequality: $n^2 < n_1^2 + n_2^2$. This observation implies that the space for sufficient statistics always decreases after an expansion. In the worst case scenario, the reduction is $n - 1$, while in the best case scenario, the reduction is $(n/2)^2$.

6.4   Notes

One of the first incremental clustering algorithms is the COBWEB system (Fisher, 1987). It is included in the group of hierarchical conceptual clustering algorithms. COBWEB is an incremental system that uses a hill-climbing search. It incorporates objects, one by one, in a classification tree, where each node is a probabilistic concept representing a class of objects. Whenever a new observation is available, the object traverses the tree, updating counts of sufficient statistics while descending the nodes. At each intermediate cluster, one of several operators is chosen: classify an object according to an existent cluster, create a new cluster, combine two clusters or divide one cluster into several ones. The search is guided by the *cluster utility* evaluation function. Using COBWEB in streams is problematic because every instance translates into a terminal node in the hierarchy, which is infeasible for large datasets.

Another relevant work is described in Kaski and Kohonen (1994), who developed the concept of self-organizing maps (SOM), a projection-based algorithm that maps examples from a k-dimensional space to a low-dimensional (typically two dimensional) space. The map seeks to preserve the topological properties of the input space. The model was first described as an artificial neural network by Teuvo Kohonen, and is sometimes called a Kohonen map.

Elnekave et al. (2007) present an incremental system for clustering mobile objects. It incrementally clusters trajectories of moving objects in order to recognize groups of objects with similar periodic (e.g., daily) mobile patterns.

Chapter 7

Frequent Pattern Mining

Frequent itemset mining is one of the most active research topics in knowledge discovery from databases. The pioneer work was market basket analysis, especially the task to mine transactional data describing the shopping behavior of customers. Since then, a large number of efficient algorithms were developed. In this chapter we review some of the relevant algorithms and their extensions from itemsets to item sequences.

7.1 Introduction to Frequent Itemset Mining

Let $A = \{a_1, \ldots, a_m\}$ be a set of **items**. Items may be products, special equipment items, service options etc. Any subset $I \subseteq A$ is called an **item set**. An item set may be any set of products that can be bought together. Let $T = (t_1, \ldots, t_n)$ be a set of **transactions** denoted by **transaction database**. Each transaction is a pair $\langle tid_i, k - items_i \rangle$ where $k - item_i \subseteq A$ is a set of k items. A transaction database can list, for example, the sets of products bought by the customers of a supermarket in a given period of time, the set of pages visited by a user of a site in one session, etc. Every transaction is an itemset, but some itemsets may not appear in T.

Let $I \subseteq A$ be an itemset and T a transaction database over A. A transaction $t \in T$ **covers** the itemset I or the itemset I is **contained in** transaction t if and only if $I \subseteq t$.

The set $K_T(I) = \{k \in \{1, \ldots, n\} \mid I \subseteq t_k\}$ is called the **cover** of I w.r.t. T. The cover of an itemset is the index set of the transactions that cover it.

The value $s_T(I) = |K_T(I)|$ is called the **(absolute) support** of I with respect to T. The value $\sigma_T(I) = \frac{1}{n}|K_T(I)|$ is called the **relative support** of I w.r.t. T. The support of I is the number or fraction of transactions that contain it. Sometimes $\sigma_T(I)$ is also called the *(relative) frequency* of I in T.

The Frequent Item Set Mining problem can be formally defined as:

- **Given:**

    - a set $A = \{a_1, \ldots, a_m\}$ of items;
    - a vector $T = (t_1, \ldots, t_n)$ of transactions over A;

Table 7.1: A transaction database, with 10 transactions, and the enumeration of all possible frequent itemsets using the minimum support of $s_{min} = 3$ or $\sigma_{min} = 0.3 = 30\%$.

TID	Item set
1	$\{a, d, e\}$
2	$\{b, c, d\}$
3	$\{a, c, e\}$
4	$\{a, c, d, e\}$
5	$\{a, e\}$
6	$\{a, c, d\}$
7	$\{b, c\}$
8	$\{a, c, d, e\}$
9	$\{b, c, e\}$
10	$\{a, d, e\}$

0 items	1 item	2 items	3 items
$\emptyset$: 10	$\{a\}$: 7	$\{a, c\}$: 4	$\{a, c, d\}$: 3
	$\{b\}$: 3	$\{a, d\}$: 5	$\{a, c, e\}$: 3
	$\{c\}$: 7	$\{a, e\}$: 6	$\{a, d, e\}$: 4
	$\{d\}$: 6	$\{b, c\}$: 3	
	$\{e\}$: 7	$\{c, d\}$: 4	
		$\{c, e\}$: 4	
		$\{d, e\}$: 4	

– a number σ_{min} such that $0 < \sigma_{min} \leq 1$, the **minimum support**.

- **Goal:**

    – the set of **frequent item sets**, that is, the set $\{I \subseteq A \mid \sigma_T(I) \geq \sigma_{min}\}$.

Since their introduction in Agrawal, Imielinski, and Swami (1993), the frequent itemset (and association rule) mining problems have received a great deal of attention. Within the past decade, hundreds of research papers have been published presenting new algorithms or improvements on existing algorithms to solve these mining problems more efficiently.

7.1.1 The Search Space

The search space of all itemsets contains exactly $2^{|A|}$ different itemsets. It can be represented by a subset-lattice, with the empty itemset at the top and the set containing all items at the bottom. If $|A|$ is large enough, then the naive approach to generate and count the supports of all itemsets over the database can't be achieved within a reasonable period of time. The main property exploited by most algorithms is that support is monotone decreasing with respect to the extension of an itemset. Given a transaction database T over I, let $X, Y \subseteq I$ be two itemsets. Then, $X \subseteq Y \Rightarrow support(Y) \leq support(X)$. This is an immediate consequence of $cover(X) \subseteq cover(Y)$. Hence, if an itemset is infrequent, all of its supersets must be infrequent. Also, the property *all subsets of a frequent item set are frequent* holds. This is the *monotonicity property* of support.

Apriori was the first algorithm for mining itemsets and association rules. It was introduced in Agrawal et al. (1993), and Agrawal and Srikant (1994). It uses a level wise, generate and test approach. It starts by generating the set F_1 of itemsets of size 1. The itemsets of size $k + 1$ are obtained by the

Table 7.2: A transaction database, with 10 transactions, and the search space to find all possible frequent itemsets using the minimum support of $s_{\min} = 3$ or $\sigma_{\min} = 0.3 = 30\%$.

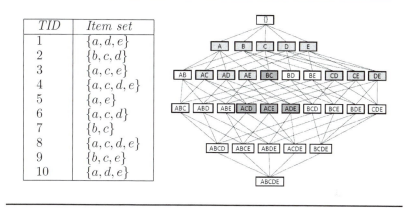

TID	Item set
1	$\{a, d, e\}$
2	$\{b, c, d\}$
3	$\{a, c, e\}$
4	$\{a, c, d, e\}$
5	$\{a, e\}$
6	$\{a, c, d\}$
7	$\{b, c\}$
8	$\{a, c, d, e\}$
9	$\{b, c, e\}$
10	$\{a, d, e\}$

itemsets of size k in two passes. First, a self-join over the set F_k. The union $X \cup Y$ of itemsets $X, Y \in F_k$ is generated if they have the same $k - 1$-prefix. This step can be done efficiently if the itemsets are in lexicographic order. In the prune step, $X \cup Y$ is only inserted into F_{k+1} if all of its k-subsets occur in F_k. After that, we need to count the supports of all candidate $k + 1$-itemsets. The database is scanned, one transaction at a time, and the supports of all candidate itemsets that are included in that transaction are incremented. All itemsets that turn out to be frequent are inserted into F_{k+1}. The algorithm performs a breadth-first search through the search space.

Table 7.2 presents a transaction database and the enumeration of all possible frequent itemsets using the minimum support of $s_{\min} = 3$ or $\sigma_{\min} = 0.3 = 30\%$. There are $2^5 = 32$ possible item sets over $A = \{a, b, c, d, e\}$. In this transaction database there are 16 frequent item sets.

The `Apriori` level wise approach implies several scans over the database to compute the support of candidate frequent itemsets. As an alternative, several algorithms significantly reduce this by generating collections of candidate itemsets in a depth-first strategy. The first algorithm proposed is the `Eclat` (Equivalent CLASS Transformation) algorithm by Zaki (2000) and the `FP-growth` algorithm by Han, Pei, Yin, and Mao (2004). The latter approach, described in Section 7.3.3, uses a prefix-tree (a trie) to store itemsets (Figure 7.1). It avoids the self-joins required in `Apriori` for candidate generation. To generate all possible extensions of an itemset by a single item, simply append the item to the suffix-tree. This search scheme generates each candidate item set at most once. It has been used as a building block in frequent itemsets and sequence mining from data streams.

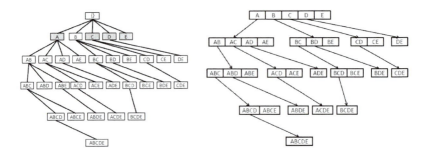

Figure 7.1: The search space using the depth-first and corresponding prefix tree for five items.

7.1.2 The `FP-growth` Algorithm

The depth-first strategy and suffix-trees used in `FP-growth` are used in most frequent patterns algorithms used in data streams. We give here a compact description of the algorithm. The pseudo-code[1] of `FP-tree` algorithm is presented in Algorithm 17. It performs two scans over the database. The first scan computes the set of frequent items (1-itemsets) and their support counts. The set of frequent items is sorted in the inverse order of their support and stored in an array L. The frequent pattern tree, FP-tree, is constructed as follows. First, create the root node of the tree, labeled with *null*. For each transaction in the database, the items are processed in descending support order, and a branch is created for each transaction. Every node in the FP-tree additionally stores a counter which keeps track of the number of transactions that share that node. When considering the branch to be added for a transaction, the count of each node along the common prefix is incremented by 1, and nodes for the items in the transaction following the prefix are created and linked accordingly.

The reason of the first database scan and process transactions in support descending order is that the more frequently occurring items are arranged closer to the root of the FP-tree and thus are more likely to be shared. This way, the FP-tree representation of the database is kept as small as possible.

7.1.3 Summarizing Itemsets

The *monotonicity property* of support suggests a compressed representation of the set of frequent itemsets:

- **Maximal frequent itemsets**: An item set is maximal if it is frequent, but none of its proper supersets is frequent.

---

[1] Following Han, Pei, Yin, and Mao (2004).

Algorithm 17: The `FP-Tree` Algorithm.

---

input: DB: A Transaction Database;
  σ: minimum support threshold;

begin

  Scan database DB once

  Collect F, the set of frequent items and the support of each item

  Sort F in support-descending order as $Flist$

  Create the root of FP-tree, T, and label it as *null*

  foreach *transaction* $(t) \in DB$ **do**

    Select the frequent items in t

    Sort them according to $Flist$

    Let $[i|It]$ be the sorted frequent items in t

    Call *insert_tree*$([i|Its], T)$

end

Function *insert_tree*$([i|Its], T)$

if T *has a child* N *labeled* i **then**

  Increment N's count by 1

else

  Create a new node, N, with its count initialized to 1,

  its parent link linked to T,

  and its node link linked to the nodes with the same label i

  if *Its is nonempty* **then**

    Call *insert_tree*(Its, N)

- **Closed frequent itemsets**: A frequent set is called *closed* iff it has no frequent supersets with the *same frequency*.

In the example of table 7.2, the maximal item sets are: $\{b, c\}\{a, c, d\}\{a, c, e\}$ $\{a, d, e\}$. All frequent itemsets are a subset of at least one of these sets.

The following relationship holds between these sets: $Maximal \subseteq Closed \subseteq Frequent$. The maximal itemsets are a subset of the closed itemsets. From the maximal itemsets it is possible to derive all frequent itemsets (not their support) by computing all non-empty intersections. The set of all closed item sets preserves the knowledge about the support values of all frequent itemsets.

7.2 Heavy Hitters

In Section 2.3.1 we have described two algorithms: the `Space Saving` algorithm (Metwally et al., 2005) and the `Frequent` algorithm (Misra and Gries, 1982) algorithm to solve top-k queries – find the k most popular items in a stream.

Here, we discuss a somewhat different problem. Given a stream S of n items $t_1, \ldots, t_n$, find those items whose frequency is greater than $\phi \times N$. The frequency of an item i is $f_i = |\{j|t_j = i\}|$. The exact ϕ-frequent items comprise the set $\{i|f_i > \phi \times N\}$. Heavy hitters are in fact singleton items.

Suppose, $\phi = 0.5$, i.e., we want to find a *majority element*. An algorithm to solve this problem can be stated as follows: store the first item and a counter, initialized to 1. For each subsequent item, if it is the same as the currently stored item, increment the counter. If it differs, and the counter is zero, then store the new item and set the counter to 1; else, decrement the counter. After processing all items, the algorithm guarantees that if there is a majority vote, then it must be the item stored by the algorithm. The correctness of this algorithm is based on a pairing argument: if every non-majority item is paired with a majority item, then there should still remain an excess of majority items.

The algorithm proposed in Karp et al. (2003) generalizes this idea to an arbitrary value of ϕ. We first note, that in any dataset there are no more than $1/\phi$ heavy hitters. The algorithm proceeds as follows (see Algorithm 18). At any given time, the algorithm maintains a set K of frequently occurring items and their counts. Initially, this set is empty. As we read an element from the sequence, we either increment its count in the set K, or insert it in the set with a count of 1. Thus, the size of the set K can keep growing. To bound the memory requirements, we do a special processing when $|K| > 1/\phi$. The algorithm decrements the count of each element in the set K and deletes elements whose count has become zero. The key property is that any element which occurs at least $N \times \phi$ times in the sequence is in the set $|K|$. Note, however, that not all elements occurring in K need to have frequency greater than $N \times \phi$. The set K is a superset of the frequent items we are interested in. To find the precise set of frequent items, another pass can be taken on the sequence, and the frequency of all elements in the set K can be counted. The algorithm identifies a set K of $\lfloor 1/\phi \rfloor$ symbols guaranteed to contain $I(x, \phi)$, using $O(1/\phi)$ memory cells.

Most of these algorithms identify all true heavy hitters, but not all reported items are necessarily heavy hitters. They are prone to *false positives*. The only way to guarantee the non-zero counters correspond to true heavy hitters is a second scan over the stream.

Cormode and Muthukrishnan (2003) present a method which works for *Insert-only* and *Insert-delete* streams, that is, can cope with addition and removal of items. Cormode and Hadjieleftheriou (2009) perform a thorough experimental study of the properties of the most relevant heavy hitters algorithms. The author concludes: *The best methods can be implemented to find frequent items with high accuracy using only tens of kilobytes of memory, at rates of millions of items per second on cheap modern hardware.*

Cormode, Korn, Muthukrishnan, and Srivastava (2008) discuss hierarchical heavy hitters (ϕ-HHH) in streaming data. Given a hierarchy and a support

---

Algorithm 18: The `Karp` Algorithm.

---

input: S: A Sequence of elements; ϕ: Support;
begin
    foreach *element* $(e) \in S$ **do**
        $n \leftarrow n + 1$
        if $e \in K$ **then**
            $count[e] \leftarrow count[e] + 1$;
        else
            $K \leftarrow K \cup \{e\}$
            $count[e] \leftarrow 1$
        if $|K| > 1/\phi$ **then**
            foreach *all* $a \in K$ **do**
                $count[a] \leftarrow count[a] - 1$
                if $count[a] == 0$ **then**
                    $K \leftarrow K \setminus \{a\}$
end

ϕ find all nodes in the hierarchy that have a total number of descendants in the data stream no smaller than $\phi \times N$ after discounting the descendant nodes that are also ϕ-HHH. This is of particular interest for network monitoring (IP clustering, denial-of-service attack monitoring), XML summarization, etc. and explores the internal structure of data.

7.3 Mining Frequent Itemsets from Data Streams

Mining Frequent Itemsets from Data Streams poses many new challenges. In addition to the one-scan constraint, the limited memory requirement, the combinatorial explosion of itemsets exacerbates the difficulties. The most difficult problem in mining frequent itemsets from data streams is that infrequent itemsets in the past might become frequent, and frequent itemsets in the past might become infrequent.

We can identify three main approaches. Approaches that do not distinguish recent items from older ones (using landmark windows); approaches that give more importance to recent transactions (using sliding windows or decay factors); and approaches for mining at different time granularities. They are discussed in the following sections.

7.3.1   Landmark Windows

Manku and Motwani (2002) present the `LossyCounting` algorithm, a one-pass algorithm for computing frequency counts exceeding a user-specified threshold over data streams. Although the output is approximate, the error is guaranteed not to exceed a user-specified parameter. `LossyCounting` accepts two user-specified parameters: a support threshold $s \in [0, 1]$, and an error parameter $\epsilon \in [0, 1]$ such that $\epsilon \ll s$. At any point of time, the `LossyCounting` algorithm can produce a list of item(set)s along with their estimated frequencies.

7.3.1.1   The `LossyCounting` Algorithm

Let N denote the current length of the stream. The answers produced will have the following guarantees:

- All item(set)s whose true frequency exceeds $s \times N$ are output. There are *no false negatives*;

- No item(set) whose true frequency is less than $(s - \epsilon) \times N$ is output;

- Estimated frequencies are less than the true frequencies by at most $\epsilon \times N$.

The incoming stream is conceptually divided into buckets of width $w = \lceil \frac{n}{\epsilon} \rceil$ transactions each. Buckets are labeled with bucket ids, starting from 1. Denote the current bucket id by $b_{current}$. For an element e, denote its true frequency in the stream seen so far by f_e. The frequent elements are stored in a data structure T. T contains a set of entries of the form (e, f, Δ), where e is the element, f its estimated frequency, and Δ is the maximum possible error in f.

The pseudo-code of `LossyCounting` is presented in Algorithm 19. It works as follows. Initially, T is empty. Whenever a new element e arrives, if an entry for e already exists, the algorithm increments its counter f. Otherwise, a new entry is created of the form $(e, 1, \lceil \frac{N}{\epsilon} \rceil)$. At bucket boundaries, the set T is pruned. The rule for deletion is: an entry (e, f, Δ) is deleted if $f + \Delta \leq \lceil \frac{N}{\epsilon} \rceil$. When a user requests a list of item with threshold s, `LossyCounting` outputs all the entries in T where $f \geq (s - \epsilon)N$.

7.3.1.2   Frequent Itemsets Using `LossyCounting`

Depending on the application, the `LossyCounting` algorithm might treat a tuple as a single item or as a set of items. In the latter case, the input stream is not processed transaction by transaction. Instead, the available main memory is filled in with as many transactions as possible. After that, they process such a batch of transactions together. Let β denote the number of buckets in memory.

As for items, `LossyCounting` maintains a data structure T, as a set of entries of the form (set, f, Δ), where set is a subset of items, f is an integer

---

Algorithm 19: The `LossyCounting` Algorithm.

---

input: S: A Sequence of Examples; ϵ: Error margin;
begin

    $n \leftarrow 0; \Delta \leftarrow 0; T \leftarrow 0;$

    foreach *example* $(e) \in S$ **do**

        $n \leftarrow n + 1$

        if e *is monitored* **then**

            Increment $Count_e$;

        else

            $T \leftarrow T \cup \{e, 1 + \Delta\}$

        if $\lceil \frac{n}{\epsilon} \rceil \neq \Delta$ **then**

            $\Delta \leftarrow \frac{n}{\epsilon}$

            foreach *all* $j \in T$ **do**

                if $Count_j < \Delta$ **then**

                    $T \leftarrow T \backslash \{j\}$

end

---

representing its approximate frequency, and Δ is the maximum possible error in f. D is updated as follows:

- **Update itemset:** For each entry (set, f, Δ), update by counting the occurrences of set in the current batch. Delete any entry such that $f + \Delta \leq b_{current}$;

- **New itemset:** If a set set has frequency $f \geq \beta$ in the current batch and does not occur in T, create a new entry $(set, f, b_{current} - \beta)$.

Every set whose true frequency is $f \geq \epsilon \times N$ has an entry in T. Moreover, for any entry $(set, f, \Delta) \in D$, the true frequency f_{set} satisfies the inequality $f \leq f_{set} \leq f + \Delta$. When a user requests a list of items with threshold s, output those entries in T, where $f \geq (s - \epsilon) \times N$.

Jin and Agrawal (2007) develop the `StreamMining` Algorithm using potential frequent 2-itemsets and the Apriori property to reduce the number of candidate itemsets. They use a memory-resident summary data structure that implements a compact prefix tree using hash tables. Their algorithm is approximate and false-positive, which has deterministic bounds on the accuracy. The window model they adopt is the landmark window.

7.3.2 Mining Recent Frequent Itemsets

7.3.2.1 Maintaining Frequent Itemsets in Sliding Windows

Chang and Lee (2005) propose the `estWin` to maintain frequent itemsets over a sliding window. The itemsets generated by `estWin` are maintained in a prefix tree structure, D. An itemset, X, in D has the following three fields: $freq(X)$, $err(X)$ and $tid(X)$, where $freq(X)$ is the frequency of X in the current window since X was inserted into D, $err(X)$ is an upper bound for the frequency of X in the current window before X was inserted into D, and $tid(X)$ is the ID of the transaction being processed, when X was inserted into D. For each incoming transaction Y with $ID = tid_t$, estWin increments the computed frequency of each subset of Y in D. Let N be the number of transactions in the window and tid_1 be the ID of the first transaction in the current window. We prune an itemset X and all X's supersets if:

1. $tid(X) \leq tid_1$ and $freq(X) < \lceil \epsilon \times N \rceil$;

2. $tid(X) > tid_1$ and $freq(X) < \lceil \epsilon \times (N - (tid(X) - tid1)) \rceil$.

We note that X is not pruned if it is a 1-itemset, since estWin estimates the maximum frequency error of an itemset based on the computed frequency of its subsets and thus the frequency of a 1-itemset cannot be estimated again if it is deleted.

After updating and pruning existing itemsets, estWin inserts new itemsets into D. It first inserts all new 1-itemsets, X, into D with $freq(X) = 1$, $err(X) = 0$ and $tid(X) = tid_t$. For each new itemset, $X \subseteq Y$ ($|X| > 2$), if all X's subsets having $siz(|X| - 1)$ are in D before the arrival of Y, then estWin inserts X into D. estWin assigns $freq(X) = 1$ and $tid(X) = tid_t$ and estimates $err(X)$ as the following equation:

$$err(X) = min(min(\{freq(X') + err(X') || \forall X' \subset X \text{ and } |X'| = |X| - 1\}) - 1,$$
$$\lfloor \epsilon(w - |X|) \rfloor + |X| - 1)$$

For each expiring transaction of the sliding window, the itemsets in D that are subsets of the transaction are traversed. For each itemset, X, being visited, if $tid(X) < tid_1$, $freq(X)$ is decreased by 1; otherwise, no change is made since the itemset is inserted by a transaction that comes later than the expiring transaction. Then, pruning is performed on X as described before. Finally, for each itemset, X, in D, estWin outputs X as an frequent itemset if:

1. $tid(X) < tid_1$ and $freq(X) \geq \sigma \times N$;

2. $tid(X) > tid_1$ and $(freq(X) + err(X)) \geq \sigma \times N$.

Chang and Lee (2003), the same authors of estWin, proposed a decay method for mining the most recent frequent itemsets adaptively. The effect of old transactions is diminished by decaying the old occurrences of each itemset as time goes by.

7.3.2.2 Mining Closed Frequent Itemsets over Sliding Windows

Chi, Wang, Yu, and Muntz (2004) consider the problem of mining *closed frequent itemsets* over a data stream sliding window using limited memory space. Their algorithm, `Moment`, uses an in-memory prefix-tree-based structure, called the *Closed Enumeration Tree (CET)*, to maintain a dynamically selected set of itemsets over a sliding-window. Let v_X be a node representing the itemset X in the CET. The dynamically selected set of itemsets (nodes) are classified into the following four types.

- *Infrequent Gateway Nodes (IGN)*: v_X is an IGN if:

    - X is infrequent,

    - v_Y is the parent of v_X and Y is frequent,

    - if v_Y has a sibling, $v_{Y'}$, such that $X = Y \cup Y'$, then Y' is frequent;

- *Unpromising Gateway Nodes (UGN)*: v_X is a UGN if:

    - X is frequent,

    - $\exists Y$ such that Y is a frequent closed itemset, $Y \supset X$, $freq(Y) = freq(X)$ and Y is before X according to the lexicographical order of the itemsets;

- *Intermediate Nodes (IN)*: v_X is an IN if:

    - X is frequent,

    - v_X is the parent of v_Y such that $freq(Y) = freq(X)$,

    - v_X is not a UGN;

- *Closed Nodes (CN)*: v_X is a CN if X is an frequent closed itemset.

All supersets of an infrequent itemset are not frequent. In the CET, an IGN, v_X has no descendants and there is no node, v_Y, such that $Y \supset X$. If v_X is a UGN, then none of v_Xs descendants is a CN; otherwise v_X is a CN but not a UGN. A UGN, v_X, also has no descendants, since no CNs can be found there. Thus, not all itemsets need to be kept in the CET, even though `Moment` computes the exact mining result.

For each incoming transaction, `Moment` traverses the parts of the CET that are related to the transaction. For each node, v_X, visited, it increments its frequency and performs the following updates to the CET according to the change in v_Xs node type:

- v_X is an IGN: If X now becomes frequent, then:

    - for each left sibling v_Y of v_X, `Moment` checks if new children should be created for v_Y as a join result of X and Y, and

    - checks if new descendants of v_X should be created;

- v_X is a UGN: If v_X now becomes an IN or a CN, then `Moment` checks if new descendants of v_X should be created;

- v_X is an IN: v_X may now become a CN but no other update is made to the CET due to v_X;

- v_X is a CN: v_X will remain a CN and no update is made to the CET due to v_X.

When a transaction expires from the sliding window, Moment traverses the parts of the CET that are related to the transaction. For each node, v_X, visited, it decrements its frequency and performs the following updates to the CET.

- X is infrequent: v_X remains an IGN and no update is made to the CET due to v_X.

- X is frequent:

    – If X now becomes infrequent, then v_X becomes an IGN. Moment first prunes all v_Xs descendants. Then, those children of v_Xs left-sided siblings that are obtained by joining with v_X are updated recursively.

    – If X remains frequent: if v_X now becomes a UGN, then Moment prunes all v_Xs descendants; otherwise, we only need to update the node type of v_X if it changes from a CN to an IN and no other update is made to the CET due to v_X.

The merit of Moment is that it computes the exact set of FCIs over a sliding window and can output the current closed frequent itemsets at any time.

7.3.3 Frequent Itemsets at Multiple Time Granularities

The FP-tree algorithm was used as a building block for mining frequent patterns in data streams at multiple time granularities in Giannella, Han, Pei, Yan, and Yu (2004). The FP-Stream Algorithm was designed to maintain frequent patterns under a tilted-time window framework in order to answer time-sensitive queries. The frequent patterns are compressed and stored using a tree structure similar to FP-tree and updated incrementally with incoming transactions. Quoting Giannella et al. (2004):

> *Using this scenario, we can answer the following queries: (1) what is the frequent pattern set over the period t_2 and t_3? (2) what are the periods when $\{a,b\}$ is frequent? (3) does the support of $\{a\}$ change dramatically in the period from t_3 to t_0? and so on. That is, one can 1) mine frequent patterns in the current window, 2) mine frequent patterns over time ranges with granularity confined by the specification of window size and boundary, 3) put different weights on different windows to mine various kinds of weighted frequent patterns, and 4) mine evolution of frequent patterns based on the changes of their occurrences in a sequence of windows.*

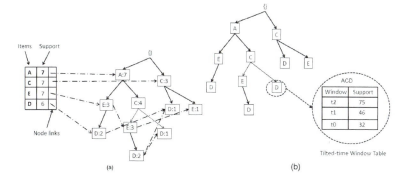

Figure 7.2: The FP-tree generated from the database of Table 7.2 with support set to 4(a). The `FP-stream` structure: the pattern-tree with a tilted-time window embedded (b).

Time windows are a standard approach to deal with evolving data. The frequency of a pattern in different time windows also evolves, that is a pattern that was not frequent in the past might become frequent and vice versa. To ensure the completeness of frequent patterns Giannella et al. consider three categories of patterns: *frequent patterns*, *subfrequent patterns*, and *infrequent patterns*. The frequency of an itemset I over a period of time T is the number of transactions in T in which I occurs. The support of I is the frequency divided by the total number of transactions observed in T. Let the *min_support* be σ and consider a relaxation ratio $\rho = \epsilon/\sigma$, where ϵ is the maximum support error. I is frequent if its support is no less than σ; it is sub-frequent if its support is less than σ but no less than ρ; otherwise, it is infrequent.

The `FP-stream` structure consists of two parts. A global FP-tree held in main memory, and tilted-time windows embedded in this pattern-tree. Incremental updates can be performed on both parts of the `FP-stream`. Incremental updates occur when some infrequent patterns become (sub)frequent, or vice versa. At any moment, the set of frequent patterns over a period can be obtained from FP-stream.

`FP-stream` stores the frequencies for itemset I in a tilted-time window.[2] Assume that the stream of transactions is broken up into batches $B_1, B_2, \ldots, B_n, \ldots$ of fixed sized, where B_n is the most current batch and B_1 the oldest.

As the transactions of the first batch B_1 arrived, the frequencies for all the items are computed, and an ordering *f_list* is created, as in the `FP-tree` Algorithm. This order remains fixed for the subsequent batches. The transactions of B_1 are processed again creating an `FP-tree` pruning all items with frequency less than $\epsilon \times |B_1|$.

---

[2] Giannella et al. (2004) discuss also a more compact structure using logarithmic tilted-time windows.

The maintenance of the tilted-time windows is straightforward. When four quarters are accumulated, they are merged together in one hour bin. After 24 hours, one day is built, and so on. This model allows us to compute the frequent itemsets in the last hour with the precision of a quarter of an hour, the last day frequent itemsets with a precision of an hour, the last month with a precision of a day, etc. For a period of one month we need $4 + 24 + 31 = 59$ units of time. Let $t_1, \ldots, t_n$ be the tilted-time windows which group the batches seen so far. Denote the number of transactions in t_i by w_i. The goal is to mine all frequent itemsets with support larger than σ over period $T = t_k \cup t_{k+1} \cup \ldots \cup t_{k\prime}$, where $1 \leq k \leq k\prime \leq n$. The size of T, denoted by W, is the sum of the sizes of all time-windows considered in T. It is not possible to store all possible itemsets in all periods. FP-stream drops the tail sequences when

$$\forall_i, n \leq i \leq 1, f_I(t_i) < \sigma \times w_i \text{ and } \sum_{j=n}^{i} f_I(t_j) < \epsilon \times \sum_{j=n}^{i} w_j$$

We no longer have the exact frequencies over T. By delivering all frequent itemsets larger than $(\sigma - \epsilon) \times W$ any frequent itemset in T will not miss, although we might get itemsets whose frequency is between $(\sigma - \epsilon) \times W$ and $\sigma \times W$.

Itemsets and their tilted-time window tables are maintained in the FP-stream data structure. When a new batch B arrives, mine the itemsets from B and update the FP-stream structure. For each itemset I mined in B, if I does not appear in the structure, add I if $f_I(B) \geq \epsilon |B|$. Otherwise, add $f_I(B)$ to I's table and then do tail pruning. If all of the windows are dropped, then drop I from the FP-stream data structure. Moreover, any superset of I will also be dropped.

7.4   Sequence Pattern Mining

A *sequence* is an ordered list of itemsets. The problem of mining sequential patterns from large static databases has been widely addressed (Agrawal and Srikant, 1995; Pei, Han, Mortazavi-Asl, Pinto, Chen, Dayal, and Hsu, 2001; Masseglia, Poncelet, and Teisseire, 2003; Marascu and Masseglia, 2006). In recent years, emerging applications such as network traffic analysis, intrusion and fraud detection, web clickstream mining or analysis of sensor data requires mining frequent sequences in the triggered events.

Agrawal and Srikant (1995) define the problem of mining sequential patterns from a static database DB as: Let $I = i_1, i_2, \ldots, i_k$, be a set of k-itemsets. A sequence is an ordered list of itemsets denoted by $\langle s_1, s_2, \ldots, s_n \rangle$ where s_j is an itemset. A sequence $\langle a_1, a_2, \ldots, a_n \rangle$ is a subsequence of another sequence $\langle b_1, b_2, \ldots, b_m \rangle$ if there exist integers $i_1 < i_2 < \ldots < i_n$ such that

$a_1 \subseteq b_{i1}, a_2 \subseteq b_{i2}, \ldots, a_n \subseteq b_{in}$. A sequence is maximal if it is not contained in any other sequence.

For example, let C be a client and $S = \langle (c)(de)(h) \rangle$ be that client's purchases. S means that C bought item c, then he bought d and e at the same moment (i.e., in the same transaction) and finally bought item h.

The *support* of a sequence s, denoted by $supp(s)$, is defined as the fraction of total data-sequences that contain s. If $supp(s) > minsupp$, with a minimum support value $minsupp$ given by the user, s is considered as a *frequent sequential pattern*. The problem of sequential pattern mining is thus to find all the frequent sequential patterns.

There are several algorithms for mining sequential patterns from static databases. The best-known algorithms are GSP (Agrawal and Srikant, 1995) and PrefixSpan (Pei et al., 2001). They represent the two main approaches to the problem: apriori-based and pattern-growth methods. In the next section we present an efficient algorithm for Sequential Pattern Mining over Data Streams.

7.4.1 Reservoir Sampling for Sequential Pattern Mining over Data Streams

Raissi and Poncelet (2007) introduced a novel algorithm in order to efficiently mine sequential patterns over data streams. In their data stream model (see Figure 7.3), on every timestamp, a new data point arrives in the stream and the data point is defined as a couple of sequence *id* and its associated transaction (i.e., itemset). The goal is to mine sequential patterns based on the maintenance of a synopsis of the data stream. Their proposition is motivated by the fact that the volume of data in real-world data streams is usually too huge to be efficiently mined and that an approximate answer for mining tasks is largely acceptable. Their algorithm relies on a biased reservoir sampling (Aggarwal, 2006) technique to build a dynamic sample suitable for sequence mining tasks.

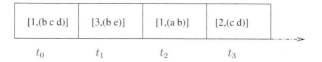

Figure 7.3: Stream model with three different sequence ids with their associated transactions.

The biased reservoir sampling was introduced in (Aggarwal, 2006) and is based on the following fact: overtime, in many cases, the data stream distribution may evolve and the original reservoir sampling results may become irrelevant. A solution is to use a bias function to regulate the sampling from the data stream. In other words, the bias function modulates the sample in order to focus on recent or old behaviors in the stream following application specific constraints. A bias function $f(r, t)$ associated with the rth data point of the stream at the time of arrival of the tth point is proportional to the probability $p(r, t)$ of the rth point belonging to the reservoir at the time of arrival of the tth point. The use of a bias function guarantees that recent points arriving over the stream have higher probabilities to be inserted in the reservoir. However, it is still an open problem to determine if maintenance algorithms can be implemented in one pass but the author in Aggarwal (2006) exploits some properties of a class of memory-less bias functions: the exponential bias function which is defined as follows: $f(r, t) = e^{-\lambda(t-r)}$ with parameter λ being the bias rate. The inclusion of such a bias function enables the use of a simple and efficient replacement algorithm. Furthermore, this special class of bias functions imposes an upper bound on the reservoir size which is independent of the stream length. This is a very interesting property since it means that the reservoir can be maintained in main-memory independently of the stream's length.

In order to efficiently build a biased sample over data streams, the authors started by applying the sampling techniques over a static dataset scenario. The authors introduced several theoretical results concerning the accuracy of the sample and the mined result given a single parameter: the user-defined error threshold.[3] For a random sample $\mathcal{S}_{\mathcal{D}}$ generated from a sequence database $\mathcal{D}$, the authors estimate the probability that the error rate gets higher than the user-defined threshold ϵ, denoted $Pr[e(s, \mathcal{S}_{\mathcal{D}}) > \epsilon]$ by using Hoeffding concentration inequalities (Hoeffding, 1963). Basically, the concentration inequalities are meant to give an accurate prediction of the actual value of a random variable by bounding the error term (from the expected value) with an associated probability.

The same statistical reasoning is applied next for the case of sequential pattern mining over data streams mining. However, the main challenge in this model is that the length of the stream is unknown. Therefore, there is a need to maintain a dynamic sample of the stream. In order to do so, Raissi and Poncelet (2007) proved that a sampling algorithm for sequential pattern mining should respect two conditions:

1. There must be a lower bound on the size of the sample. According to their previous results from the static database model, this is achieved by using an (ϵ, δ)-approximation combined with an exponential biased reservoir sampling method;

2. The insertion and replacement operations, essential for the reservoir updating, must be done at sequence level *and* at transactions level. This is necessary to control the size of the itemsets for each sequence in the reservoir.

---

[3] Notice that a similar approach was used for itemset mining in Toivonen (1996).

The proposed approach is a replacement algorithm using an exponential bias function that regulates the sampling of customers and their transactions over a stream. The algorithm starts with an empty reservoir of capacity $\frac{1}{\lambda}$ (where λ is the bias rate of our exponential bias function) and each data point arriving from the stream is deterministically added to the reservoir by flipping a coin, either as:

- A simple insertion into the reservoir;

- A replacement of a whole sequence and all its related itemsets.

Note that this simple replacement is enough to sample sequences; however, the list of transactions belonging to each sequence in the reservoir needs to be bounded. In order to do so, the approach uses a sliding window mechanism. A sliding window can be defined as a *sequence-based window of size k* consisting of the k most recent data elements that arrived on the stream or as a *timestamp-based window of duration t* containing all the data points whose arrival timestamp is within a time interval t of the current time.

The approach uses a sequence-based window to retain the latest and most recent transactions for a given sequence in the sample (with a black list used in order to respect some consistency properties over the sequences present in the sample). This is useful to get accurate mining tasks over recent horizons of the stream. Besides, the exponential biased function that is used enables the final user to select the desired size of the reservoir (with some constraints on the (ϵ, δ)-approximation) and thus a relevant sample may be maintained in main memory, depending on the application needs.

The merit of the approach is that at any desired moment, it is always possible to obtain accurate and fast results for sequential pattern mining based only on a small dynamic sample residing in main memory. Furthermore, the authors highlight the potential of further works on sampling for sequential pattern mining and especially in the new challenging data streams model.

7.5   Notes

Cheng, Ke, and Ng (2008) present a detailed survey on algorithms for mining frequent itemsets over data streams. Wang and Yang (2005) discuss several models of sequential pattern mining from large datasets.

Raissi, Poncelet, and Teisseire (2007) proposed the system FIDS (*frequent itemsets mining on data streams*). One interesting feature of this system is that each item is associated with a unique prime number. Each transaction is represented by the product of the corresponding prime numbers of individual items into the transaction. As the product of the prime number is unique we can easily check the inclusion of two itemsets (e.g., $X \subseteq Y$) by performing a modulo division on itemsets $(Y \text{ MOD } X)$. If the remainder is 0 then $X \subseteq Y$, otherwise X is not included in Y. FIDS uses a novel data structure to maintain frequent itemsets coupled with a fast pruning strategy. At any time, users can issue requests for frequent sequences over an arbitrary time interval.

Li, Shan, and Lee (2008) proposed an in-memory summary data structure, SFI-forest (*summary frequent itemset forest*), to maintain an approximated set of frequent itemsets. Each transaction of the stream is projected into a set of sub-transactions, and these sub-transactions are inserted into the SFI-forest. The set of all frequent itemsets is determined from the current SFI-forest.

Distributed algorithms for association rule learning were presented in Schuster, Wolff, and Trock (2005).

In the context of Data Stream Management Systems, frequent pattern mining is used to solve iceberg queries, and computing iceberg cubes (Fang, Shivakumar, Garcia-Molina, Motwani, and Ullman, 1998).

Chapter 8

Decision Trees from Data Streams

A decision tree uses a divide-and-conquer strategy. It attacks a complex problem by dividing it into simpler problems and recursively applies the same strategy to the sub-problems. Solutions of sub-problems can be combined to yield a solution of the complex problem. The power of this approach comes from the ability to split the instance-space into subspaces and each subspace is fitted with different models. Decision trees are one of the most used algorithms in the data mining community: they are distribution-free, and tree models exhibit a high degree of interpretability. These factors strongly contribute to their increasing popularity in the data mining community.

8.1 Introduction

Formally, a decision tree is a direct acyclic graph in which each node is either a *decision node* with two or more successors or a *leaf node*. In the simplest model, a *leaf node* is labeled with a *class* label and a *decision node* has some *condition* based on attribute values. Decision trees are one of the most used methods in data mining mainly because of their high degree of interpretability. The hypothesis space of decision trees is within the *disjunctive normal form* (DNF) formalism. Classifiers generated by those systems encode a DNF for each class. For each DNF, the conditions along a branch represent conjuncts and the individual branches can be seen as disjuncts. Each branch forms a rule with a conditional part and a conclusion. The conditional part is a conjunction of conditions. Conditions are tests that involve a particular attribute, operator (e.g., $=$, $\geq$, $\in$, etc.) and a value from the domain of that attribute. These kind of tests correspond, in the input space, to a hyper-plane that is orthogonal to the axes of the tested attribute and parallel to all other axis. The regions produced by these classifiers are all hyper-rectangles. Each leaf corresponds to a region. The regions are mutually exclusive and exhaustive (i.e., cover all the instance space).

Learning decision trees from data streams is one of the most challenging problems for the data mining community. A successful example is the VFDT system (Domingos and Hulten, 2000). The base idea comes from the observation that a small number of examples are enough to select the correct splitting test and expand a leaf. The algorithm makes a decision, that is, installs a split-test at a node, only when there is enough statistical evidence in favor of a split test. This is the case of Gratch (1996); Domingos and Hulten (2000); Gama et al. (2003). VFDT-like algorithms can manage millions of examples using few computational resources with a performance similar to a batch decision tree given enough examples.

8.2   The Very Fast Decision Tree Algorithm

8.2.1   VFDT —The Base Algorithm

The Very Fast Decision Tree (VFDT) algorithm was first presented in Domingos and Hulten (2000). In VFDT a decision tree is learned by re-cursively replacing leaves with decision nodes. Each leaf stores the sufficient statistics about attribute-values. The sufficient statistics are those needed by a heuristic evaluation function that evaluates the merit of split-tests based on attribute-values. When an example is available, it traverses the tree from the root to a leaf, evaluating the appropriate attribute at each node, and following the branch corresponding to the attribute's value in the example. When the example reaches a leaf, the sufficient statistics are updated. Then, each possible condition based on attribute-values is evaluated. If there is enough statistical support in favor of one test over all the others, the leaf is transformed to a decision node. The new decision node will have as many descendant leaves as the number of possible values for the chosen test (therefore this tree is not necessarily binary). The decision nodes only maintain the information about the split-test installed in this node.

The main innovation of the VFDT system is the use of Hoeffding bound (see Section 2.2.2) to decide the sample size to observe before installing a split-test at each leaf. Let $H(\cdot)$ be the evaluation function of an attribute. For the information gain, the range R, of $H(\cdot)$ is $log_2(\#classes)$. Suppose that after observing n examples in a given leaf, x_a is the attribute with the highest $H(\cdot)$, and x_b the attribute with second-highest $H(\cdot)$. Let $\overline{\Delta H} = \overline{H}(x_a) - \overline{H}(x_b)$ be the difference between the two better attributes. Then, if $\overline{\Delta H} > \epsilon$ holds, the Hoeffding bound (Hoeffding, 1963) states with probability $1 - \delta$, that x_a is really the attribute with highest value in the evaluation function in the universe, e.g. if seeing an infinite number of examples. In this case the leaf must be transformed into a decision node that splits on x_a. If $\overline{\Delta H} < \epsilon$, the sample size is not enough to take a stable decision. We need to extend the sample by seeing more examples. As the sample size increases, ϵ decreases, and if there is an informative attribute, it will be pushed up. An assumption behind this rationality is that the distribution generating examples is stationary.

Algorithm 20: VFDT: The Hoeffding Tree Algorithm.

---

input : S: Stream of examples

X: Set of nominal Attributes

Y: $Y = \{y_1, \ldots, y_k\}$ Set of class labels

$H(.)$: Split evaluation function

N_min: Minimum number of examples

δ: is one minus the desired probability

of choosing the correct attribute at any node.

τ: Constant to solve ties.

output: HT: is a Decision Tree

begin

$\quad$ Let $HT \leftarrow$ Empty Leaf (Root)

$\quad$ **foreach** *example* $(x, y_k) \in S$ **do**

$\quad\quad$ Traverse the tree HT from the root till a leaf l

$\quad\quad$ **if** $y_k ==$ *?* **then**

$\quad\quad\quad$ Classify the example with the majority class in the leaf l

$\quad\quad$ **else**

$\quad\quad\quad$ Update sufficient statistics

$\quad\quad\quad$ **if** *Number of examples in $l > N_{min}$* **then**

$\quad\quad\quad\quad$ Compute $H_l(X_i)$ for all the attributes

$\quad\quad\quad\quad$ Let X_a be the attribute with highest H_l

$\quad\quad\quad\quad$ Let X_b be the attribute with second highest H_l

$\quad\quad\quad\quad$ Compute $\epsilon = \sqrt{\frac{R^2 ln(2/\delta)}{2n}}$ (Hoeffding bound)

$\quad\quad\quad\quad$ **if** $(H(X_a) - H(X_b) > \epsilon)$ **then**

$\quad\quad\quad\quad\quad$ Replace l with a splitting test based on attribute X_a

$\quad\quad\quad\quad\quad$ Add a new empty leaf for each branch of the split

$\quad\quad\quad\quad$ **else**

$\quad\quad\quad\quad\quad$ **if** $\epsilon < \tau$ **then**

$\quad\quad\quad\quad\quad\quad$ Replace l with a splitting test based on attribute X_a

$\quad\quad\quad\quad\quad\quad$ Add a new empty leaf for each branch of the split

end

The evaluation of the merit function for each example could be very expensive. It turns out that it is not efficient to compute $H(\cdot)$ every time that an example arrives. VFDT only computes the attribute evaluation function $H(\cdot)$ when a minimum number of examples has been observed since the last evaluation. This minimum number of examples is a user-defined parameter.

When two or more attributes continuously exhibit very similar values of $H(\cdot)$, even with a large number of examples, the Hoeffding bound will not decide between them. This situation can happen even for two or more equally informative attributes. To solve this problem VFDT uses a constant τ introduced by the user for run-off. Taking into account that ϵ decreases when n increases, if $\overline{\Delta H} < \epsilon < \tau$ then the leaf is transformed into a decision node. The split test is based on the best attribute.

8.2.2 Analysis of the VFDT Algorithm

VFDT has the ingredients to process high-speed data streams: using limited computational resources in terms of space, processing a single example each time, and answers or models are available at any time.

There are several important characteristics of VFDT like algorithms that differentiate from the standard greedy-search used by C4.5 (Quinlan, 1993) or Cart (Breiman et al., 1984) like algorithms. One is that VFDT decision models exhibit a low variance profile. Any decision in VFDT, e.g., decision to expand a node, has statistical support. While in C4.5 (or in Cart) the number of examples that support a decision decreases as the tree grows, in VFDT all nodes receive the number of examples needed to make informed decisions. This is possible because of the abundance of data in open-ended streams. The second difference is a direct consequence of the first one: there is no room for pruning, e.g., control overfitting.

A comparative summary between batch decision tree learners and VFDT is presented in the following table:

Decision Processes	Batch Learning	Hoeffding Trees
Decide to expand	Choose the best split from all data in a given node	Accumulate data till there is statistical evidence in favor to a particular splitting test
Pruning	Mandatory	No need
Drift Detection	Assumes data is stationary	Smooth adaptation to the most recent concepts

In Hoeffding trees, the stream of examples traverse the tree till a leaf. The examples that fall in each leaf corresponds to a sort of a time-window over the most recent examples. Figure 8.1 illustrates the correspondence between the nodes and the time-windows over the stream. Note that VFDT still assume that examples are independent.

Domingos and Hulten (2000) proved, under realistic assumptions, that the decision tree generated by the Hoeffding Tree Algorithm is asymptotically close to the one produced by a standard batch algorithm (that is an algorithm that uses all the examples to select the splitting attribute). They use the concept of *intentional disagreement* between two decision trees, defined as the probability that one example follows different paths in both trees. They show that this probability is proportional to δ.

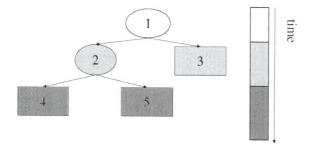

Figure 8.1: Illustrative example of a decision tree and the time-window associated with each node.

8.3 Extensions to the Basic Algorithm

8.3.1 Processing Continuous Attributes

Most real-world problems are described by numerical attributes. Practical applications of learning algorithms to real-world problems should address this issue. In almost all decision trees, a decision node that contains a split-test based on a continuous attribute has two descendant branches. The split-test is a condition of the form $attr_i \leq cut\_point$. The two descendant branches correspond to the values $TRUE$ and $FALSE$ for the split-test. These split-tests introduce an additional problem: select the cut_point that will minimize (or maximize) some merit criterion. For batch decision tree learners, this problem requires a sort operation that is the most time consuming operation (Catlett, 1991).

In this section we discuss efficient methods to deal with numerical attributes in the context of on-line decision tree learning. All of them avoid the sort operation. There is a trade-off between the space required to store the sufficient-statistics and the ability to identify the true cut_point. We can identify two extreme solutions. In one extreme, all possible cut_points are stored in memory, with guarantees to find the exact cut_point given the set of observed data points. In the other extreme, an analytical solution based on discriminant analysis, only two quantities are stored for each class: the mean and standard deviation.

8.3.1.1 Exhaustive Search

In VFDTc (Gama et al., 2003) the cut_point is chosen from all the observed values for that attribute in the sample at a leaf. In order to evaluate the quality of a split, we need to compute the class distribution of the examples

x	71	69	80	83	70	65	64	72	75	68	81	85	72	75
C	+	-	+	-	-	+	-	-	-	-	-	+	+	-

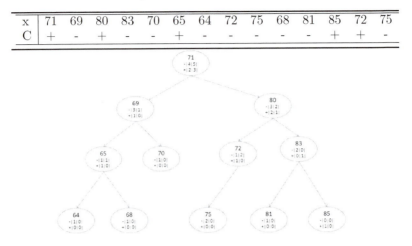

Figure 8.2: Illustrative example of the Btree to store sufficient statistics of a continuous attribute at a leaf.

at which the attribute-value is less than or greater than the *cut_point*. These counts are the sufficient statistics for almost all splitting criteria. They are computed with the use of the two data structures maintained in each leaf of the decision tree. The first data structure is a vector of the classes distribution over the attribute-values for the examples that reach the leaf.

For each continuous attribute j, the system maintains a binary tree structure. A node in the binary tree is identified with a value i (that is the value of the attribute j seen in an example), and two vectors (of dimension k) used to count the values that go through that node. These vectors, *VE* and *VH*, contain the counts of values respectively $\leq i$ and $> i$ for the examples labeled with one of the possible class values. When an example reaches a leaf, all the binary trees are updated. Algorithm 21 presents the algorithm to insert a value in the binary tree. Insertion of a new value in this structure is $O(\log n)$ where n represents the number of distinct values for the attribute seen so far.

To compute the information gain of a given attribute we use an exhaustive method to evaluate the merit of all possible *cut_point*s. In our case, any value observed in the examples so far can be used as *cut_point*. For each possible cut_point, we compute the information of the two partitions using Equation 8.1.

$$info(A_j(i)) = P(A_j \leq i) * iLow(A_j(i)) + P(A_j > i) * iHigh(A_j(i)) \quad (8.1)$$

where i is the split point, $iLow(A_j(i))$ the information of $A_j \leq i$ (Equation 8.2) and $iHigh(A_j(i))$ (Equation 8.3) the information of $A_j > i$. So we choose

---

Algorithm 21: The InsertValueBtree(x_j, y, Btree) Algorithm.

---

input : x_j: Attribute-value
  y: Index of the class label
  Btree: the Btree for the attribute.

output: *Btree*: the Btree for the attribute after inserting value x_j of
  an example from class y.

begin
  if *(x_j == Btree.i)* **then**
    Btree.VE[y] = Btree.VE[y] + 1
  else if *(x_j < Btree.i)* **then**
    Btree.VE[y] = Btree.VE[y] + 1
    InsertValueBtree(x_j, y, Btree.Left)
  else
    Btree.VH[y] = Btree.VH[y] +1
    InsertValueBtree(x_j, y, Btree.Right)

end

---

the split point that minimizes (8.1).

$$iLow(A_j(i)) = -\sum_K P(K = k|A_j \leq i) * log_2(P(K = k|A_j \leq i)) \qquad (8.2)$$

$$iHigh(A_j(i)) = -\sum_K P(K = k|A_j > i) * log_2(P(K = k|A_j > i)) \qquad (8.3)$$

These statistics are easily computed using the counts in the *Btree*, and using the algorithm presented in Algorithm 22. For each attribute, it is possible to compute the merit of all possible *cut_points* traversing the binary tree only once.

When learning decision trees from streaming data, continuous attribute processing is a must. Jin and Agrawal (2003) present a method for numerical interval pruning,

8.3.1.2 Discriminant Analysis

A fast and space efficient analytical method for determining the *cut_point* of a continuous attribute in VFDT-like algorithms was presented in Gama et al. (2004). The method is based on discriminant analysis. It was first presented in Loh and Shih (1997) in the context of off-line decision tree induction. The method is very efficient in terms of space and speed. The sufficient statistics required are the mean and variance per class of each numerical attribute. This is a major advantage over other approaches, like the exhaustive method used in C4.5 (Quinlan, 1993) and in VFDTc (Gama et al., 2003), because all the necessary statistics are computed on the fly, a desirable property when

---

Algorithm 22: The LessThan(i, k, BTree) Algorithm.

---

input : i: Reference value for Attribute A_j.
$\quad\quad\quad$ k: Class label.
$\quad\quad\quad$ *Btree*: the Btree for the attribute A_j.

output: $\#(A_j \leq i)$ for the attribute A_j and class k

begin
$\quad$ **if** *(BTree == NULL)* **then return** (0)
$\quad$ **if** *(BTree.i == i)* **then return** $Btree.VE[k]$
$\quad$ **if** *(BTree.i < i)* **then**
$\quad\quad$ **return** $Btree.VE[k] + LessThan(i, k, BTree.Right)$
$\quad$ **else**
$\quad\quad$ **return** $LessThan(i,k,BTree.Left)$

end

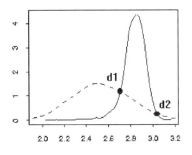

Figure 8.3: Illustrative example of the solutions of Equation 8.4.

Table 8.1: Contingency table to compute the entropy of a splitting test.

	$Att_i \leq d_i$	$Att_i > d_i$
Class +	p_1^+	p_2^+
Class −	p_1^-	p_2^-

processing huge data streams. It guarantees constant time and space to process each example.

The method is restricted to two class problems.[1] It uses a modified form of quadratic discriminant analysis to include different variances on the two classes. The analysis assumes that the distribution of the values of an attribute follows a normal distribution for both classes.

---

[1] To solve multi-class problems, Loh and Shih (1997) use a clustering algorithm to form two super-classes. This strategy is not applicable in the streaming setting. Gama et al. (2004) decompose a k-class problem into $k \times (k-1)/2$ two-class problems, generating a forest of trees (described in Section 10.4.2).

Let $N(\bar{x}, \sigma) = \frac{1}{\sigma\sqrt{2\pi}} \exp\left(-\frac{(x-\bar{x})^2}{2\sigma^2}\right)$ be the normal density function, where $\bar{x}$ and σ^2 are the sample mean and variance of the class. The class mean and variance are estimated from the sample set of examples at each leaf. The best cut-point is the solution of:

$$P(+)N(\bar{x}_+, \sigma_+) = P(-)N(\bar{x}_-, \sigma_-) \qquad (8.4)$$

The quadratic discriminant splits the X-axis into three intervals $(-\infty, d_1)$, (d_1, d_2), (d_2, ∞) where d_1 and d_2 are the possible roots of the Equation 8.4 where $p(i)$ denotes the estimated probability than an example belongs to class i (see Figure 8.3). We prefer a binary split, so we use the root closer to the sample means of both classes. Let d be that root. The splitting test candidate for each numeric attribute i will use the form $Att_i \leq d_i$. To choose the best splitting test from the candidate list we use a heuristic method. We use the information gain to choose, from all the splitting point candidates (one for each attribute), the best splitting test. The information kept by the tree is not sufficient to compute the exact number of examples for each entry in the contingency table. Doing that would require maintaining information about all the examples at each leaf. With the assumption of normality, we can compute the probability of observing a value less or greater than d_i (See Table 8.1). From these probabilities and the distribution of examples per class at the leaf we populate the contingency table. The splitting test with the maximum information gain is chosen. This method only requires that we maintain the mean and standard deviation for each class per attribute. Both quantities are easily maintained incrementally.

8.3.2 Functional Tree Leaves

To classify a test example, the example traverses the tree from the root to a leaf. The example is classified with the most representative class, e.g., the mode, of the training examples that fall at that leaf. A promising alternative, presented in Gama et al. (2003, 2004) and Kirkby (2008), consists of using naive Bayes classifiers at tree leaves. That is, a test example is classified with the class that maximizes the posterior probability given by Bayes rule assuming the independence of the attributes given the class.

There is a simple motivation for this option. VFDT-like algorithms only change a leaf to a decision node when there is a sufficient number of examples to support the change. Usually hundreds or even thousands of examples are required. To classify a test example, the majority class strategy uses information only about class distributions and does not look for the attribute-values. It uses only a small part of the available information, a crude approximation to the distribution of the examples. On the other hand, naive Bayes takes into account not only the prior distribution of the classes, but also the conditional probabilities of the attribute-values given the class. This way, there is a much better exploitation of the available information at each leaf. Moreover, naive

Bayes is naturally incremental. It deals with heterogeneous data and missing values. It has been observed (Domingos and Pazzani, 1997) that for small datasets naive Bayes is a very competitive algorithm.

Assuming that the attributes are independent given the class, the Bayes rule will classify an example $\vec{x}$, in the class that maximizes the *a posterior* conditional probability, given by:

$$P(C_k|\vec{x}) \propto P(C_k) \prod P(x_j|C_k)$$

or equivalently, by applying logarithms:

$$P(C_k|\vec{x}) \propto log(P(C_k)) + \sum log(P(x_j|C_k)).$$

To compute the conditional probabilities $P(x_j|C_k)$ we should distinguish between nominal attributes and continuous ones. In the former the problem is trivial using the sufficient statistics used to compute information gain. In the latter, there are two usual approaches: either assuming that each attribute follows a *normal distribution* or discretizing the attributes. If assuming a normal distribution, the sufficient statistics, the mean and variance for each class, can be computed on the fly. For example, Gama et al. (2004) take advantage of the sufficient statistics to estimate *cut_points* using the discriminant analysis described in Section 8.3.1.2. A discretization method to compute $P(x_j|C_k)$ appears in Gama et al. (2003). The required counts are derived from the binary-tree structure stored at each leaf before it becomes a decision node. Any numerical attribute is discretized into 10 intervals. To count the number of examples per class that fall at each interval we use the algorithm described in Algorithm 23. This algorithm is computed only once in each leaf for each discretization bin. Those counts are used to estimate $P(x_j|C_k)$.

We should note that the use of naive Bayes classifiers at tree leaves does not introduce any overhead in the training phase. In the application phase and for nominal attributes, the sufficient statistics contain all the information for the naive Bayes tables. For continuous attributes, the naive Bayes contingency tables are efficiently derived from the Btree's used to store the numeric attribute-values. The overhead introduced is proportional to depth of the Btree, that is at most $log(n)$, where n is the number of different values observed for a given attribute in a leaf.

8.3.3 Concept Drift

Nodes in a decision tree correspond to hyper-rectangles in particular regions of the instance space. The whole decision tree divides the instance space into nested regions. The root node covers all the instance space, and subsequent nodes in the structure cover sub-regions of the upper nodes. Using the tree structure we can have views of the instance space at different levels of granularity.

Algorithm 23: The algorithm to compute $P(x_j|C_k)$ for numeric attribute x_j and class k at a given leaf.

---

input : BTree: Binary Tree for attribute x_j
nrExs: Vector of the number of examples per Class
X_h: the highest value of x_j observed at the Leaf
X_l: the lowest value of x_j observed at the Leaf
N_j: the number different values of x_j observed at the Leaf
output: *Counts* The vector of size *Nintervals* with the percentage of examples per interval
begin
   if $BTree == NULL$ **then** return 0
   /* number of intervals   */
   $Nintervals \leftarrow min(10, |BTree|)$
   /* interval range   */
   $inc \leftarrow \frac{X_h - X_l}{Nintervals}$
   for $i = 1$ **to** $Nintervals$ **do**
      $Counts[i] \leftarrow LessThan(x_l + inc * i, k, BTree)$
      if $i > 1$ **then**
         $Counts[i] \leftarrow Counts[i] - Counts[i-1]$
         if $x_j \leq X_l + inc * i$ **then**
            return $\frac{Counts}{nrExs[k]}$
         else if $i == Nintervals$ **then**
            return $\frac{Counts}{nrExs[k]}$
end

This is of great interest in time-changing environments because a change or a concept drift may affect only some region of the instance space, and not the instance space as a whole. When drift occurs, it does not have impact in the whole instance space, but in particular regions. Adaptation of global models (like naive Bayes, discriminant functions, SVM) requires reconstruction of the decision model. Granular decision models (like decision rules and decision trees) can adapt parts of the decision model. They need to adapt only those parts that cover the region of the instance space affected by drift. In decision models that fit different functions to regions of the instance space, like Decision Trees and Rule Learners, we can use the granularity of the model to detect regions of the instance space where change occurs and adapt the local model, with advantages of fast adaptation. Nodes near the root should be able to detect abrupt changes in the distribution of the examples, while deeper nodes should detect localized, smoothed and gradual changes.

We should distinguish between the task of *detect a change* from the task of *reacting to a change*. In this section we discuss methods that exploit the tree structure to detect and react to changes.

8.3.3.1   Detecting Changes

The observation that Hoeffding trees define time-windows over the stream leads to a straightforward change detection method: compare the distribution of the target attribute between a node and the sum of distribution in all leaves of the sub-tree rooted at that node. The techniques presented in Kifer et al. (2004) for comparing two distributions can be used for this purpose. We should note that maintaining appropriate sufficient statistics at each node enables the test to be performed on the fly whenever a new labeled example is available. This strategy was used in Gama et al. (2006).

Figure 8.4 presents the path of an example traversing a tree. Error distributions can be estimated in the descending path or in the ascending path. In the descending path, the example is classified at each node, as if that node was a leaf. In the ascending path, the class assigned to the example is propagated upwards.

Comparing the distributions is appealing but might lead to a relatively high time delay in detection. A somewhat different strategy, used in Gama and Medas (2005), exhibits faster detection rates. The system maintains a naive-Bayes classifier at each node of the decision tree. The drift detection algorithm described in Section 3.3 monitors the evolution of the naive-Bayes error rate. It signals a drift whenever the performance goes to an *out-of-control* state.

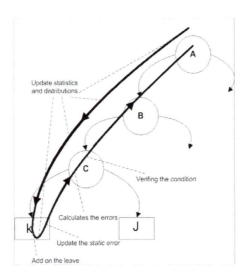

Figure 8.4: Illustrative example of an example traversing the tree: error statistics can be estimated both in the descending path (from the root to a leaf) and in the ascending path (from the leaf to the root).

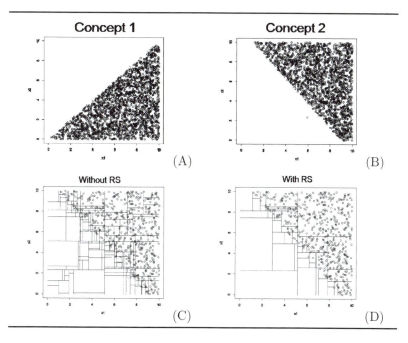

Figure 8.5: The Hyper-plane problem: two classes and by two continuous attributes. The dataset is composed by a sequence of points first from concept-1 (A) followed by points from concept 2 (B). The second row presents the projection of the final decision tree over the instance space. Figure C is the tree without adaptation; Figure D is the pruned tree after detection of a change. Although both have similar holdout performance, the pruned tree better represents the current concept.

8.3.3.2 Reacting to Changes

After detecting a change, we need to update the decision model. Several adaptation methods have been proposed. A first observation is that Hoeffding trees self-adapt to the most recent data. Suppose an abrupt change at a certain point in time. The leaves start receiving examples from a different distribution. Whenever a leaf is expanded the newly generated leaves receive examples from the most recent distribution. The degradation in performance is not so high as one can expect. The most relevant problem is that the decision model becomes much more complex (in terms of number of leaves) than necessary. Figure 8.5 illustrates this aspect.

A natural method to adapt the decision model is to prune the subtree rooted at the node that detects a change. This strategy favors decision models more consistent with the current state of the nature. It can be somewhat drastic, for example if change is detected by the root. It means that changes occur in all the instance space. Pruning can lead to a decrease in performance while the tree does not fully recover from the surgery.

To avoid this last problem, Hulten et al. (2001) presented the CVFDT algorithm. CVFDT is an extension to VFDT designed for time-changing data streams. CVFDT generates alternate decision trees at nodes where there is evidence that the splitting test is no longer appropriate. The system replaces the old tree with the new one when the latter becomes more accurate.

8.3.4   Final Comments

The basic algorithm can include features like the ability to initialize a VFDT tree with a tree produced by a conventional algorithm, or the ability to deactivate all less promising leaves in the case when the maximum of the available memory is reached. Moreover, the memory usage is also minimized, by ignoring attributes that are less promising.

In general, functional leaves have been shown to improve performance of decision trees. In VFDT-like algorithms, all the statistics required by the splitting criteria can be computed incrementally. Moreover, we can directly derive naive Bayes classifiers from the sufficient statistics. Naive Bayes classifiers can be used in leaves to classify test examples, and in inner decision nodes to detect drift.

Very Fast Decision Tree based algorithms share all the properties of standard univariate trees:

- *Interpretability.* Global and complex decisions can be approximated by a series of simpler and local decisions. All decisions are based on the values of the attributes used to describe the problem. Both aspects contribute to the popularity of decision trees.

- *Robustness.* Univariate trees are invariant under all (strictly) monotone transformations of the individual input variables. For example using x_j, $log\ x_j$, or e^{x_j} as the jth input variable yields the same structural result. There is no need to consider input variable transformations. As a consequence of this invariance, sensitivity to long tail distributions and outliers are also reduced (Friedman, 1999).

They have other desirable properties that are specific to this algorithm:

- *Stability.* Stability refers to the ability of an algorithm to generate similar decision models when trained with similar training sets. This is a key characteristic of VFDT-like algorithms that makes them different from the usual greedy hill-climbing decision tree algorithm. The decision which test to install at each splitting node must satisfy statistical criterion: the Hoeffding bound. This feature ensures model stability for permuted data and low variance. On the other hand, methods like *bagging* which are very efficient in reducing variance are no more effective with Hoeffding trees.

- *Any-time classifiers.* The standard top-down induction of decision tree algorithms expands a tree using a depth strategy (Quinlan, 1993; Breiman et al., 1984). The side effect of this strategy is that trees are highly unbalanced during the growing process. Decision trees can be used as classifiers only at the end of the growing process. VFDT expands a leaf when there is strong evidence in favor of a particular splitting-test. The tree growing process is more balanced. This characteristic favors the any-time classifier.

- *Convergence.* Domingos and Hulten (2000) show that the trees produced by the VFDT algorithm are asymptotically close to the ones generated by a batch learner.

8.4 OLIN: Info-Fuzzy Algorithms

Many batch and online learning methods use the information theory to induce classification models. One of the batch information-theoretic methods, developed by Last (2002), is the Info-Fuzzy Network algorithm (also known as Information Network - IFN). IFN is an oblivious decision-tree classification model designed to minimize the total number of predicting attributes. The underlying principle of the IN-based methodology is to construct a multi-layered network in order to maximize the Mutual Information (MI) between the input and the target attributes. Each hidden layer is uniquely associated with a specific predictive attribute (feature) and represents an interaction between that feature and features represented by preceding layers. Unlike popular decision-tree algorithms such as CART and C4.5, the IFN algorithm uses a pre-pruning strategy: a node is split if the split leads to a statistically significant decrease in the conditional entropy of the target attribute (equal to an increase in the conditional mutual information). If none of the remaining candidate input attributes provides a statistically significant increase in the mutual information, the network construction stops. The output of the IFN algorithm is a classification network, which can be used as a decision tree to predict the value (class) of the target attribute. For continuous target attributes, each prediction refers to a discretization interval rather than a specific class.

The OLIN algorithm extends the IFN algorithm for mining continuous and dynamic data streams (Cohen et al., 2008). The system repeatedly applies the IFN algorithm to a sliding window of training examples and changes the size of the training window (and thus the re-construction frequency) according to the current rate of concept drift. The purpose of the system is to predict, at any time, the correct class for the next arriving example. The architecture of the OLIN-based system is presented in Figure 8.7.

The online learning system contains three main parts: the Learning Module

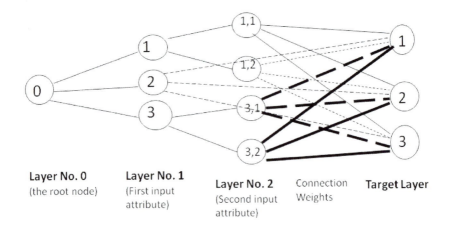

Figure 8.6: An illustrative example of a two-layered info-fuzzy network structure.

is responsible for applying the IN algorithm to the current sliding window of examples; the Classification Module is responsible for classifying the incoming examples using the current network; and the Meta Learning Module controls the operation of the Learning Module. As shown in Figure 8.7, the system builds a network from T_0 training examples; afterwards, the next V_0 examples are classified according to the induced network. According to the regenerative approach of OLIN, when more examples arrive, a completely new network is built from the most recent T_1 examples, where the last example belonging to T_1 is also the last example of V_0. In order to ensure that each example in the data stream will be classified only once, the validation intervals have to be disjoint and consecutive. After constructing a new network, the set V_1 is classified using that network. This regenerative process continues indefinitely if the data stream never stops. The Meta Learning module gets as input the error rates of the training and the validation examples classified by the current IN model. Those error rates are denoted as E_{tr} and E_{val} respectively. In addition, it gets the description of the model itself (selected attributes, entropy information, etc.). Using all these inputs, the module re-calculates the size of the next training window (interval) and the number of validation examples to be classified by the next model. The OLIN system is based on the assumption that if the concept is stable, the training and the validation examples should conform to the same distribution. Thus, the error rates in classifying those examples using the current model should not be significantly different. On the other hand, a statistically significant difference may indicate a possible concept drift. The variance of the differences between the error rates is calculated by the following formula based on a Normal Approximation to

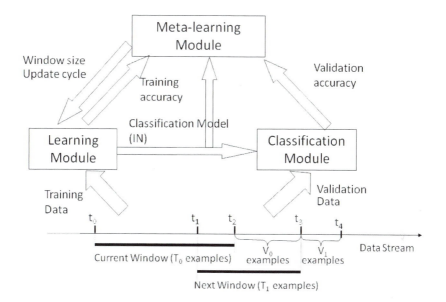

Figure 8.7: OLIN-based system architecture.

the Binominal distribution:

$$Var\_Diff = \frac{E_{tr}(1 - E_{tr})}{W} + \frac{E_{val}(1 - E_{val})}{Add\_Count}$$

where W is the size of the training window and Add_Count is the number of validation examples. The algorithm tests the null hypothesis that the concept is stable, in which case the maximum difference between the training and validation error rates, at the 99% confidence level is:

$$Max\_Diff = Z_{0.99}\sqrt{Var\_Diff} = 2.326\sqrt{Var\_Diff}$$

A concept drift is detected by the algorithm when the difference between the error rates is greater than Max_Diff implying that the null hypothesis can be rejected. In that case, the algorithm re-calculates the size of the next training window using the following formula:

$$W = \frac{\chi^2_\alpha(NI_i - 1)(NT - 1)}{2ln2(H(T) - H(E_{tr}) - E_{tr}log_2(NT - 1))}$$

where α is the significance level sign used by the network construction algorithm (default: $\alpha = 0.1\%$), NI_i is the number of values (or discretized intervals) for the first input attribute A_i in the info-fuzzy network, NT is the number of target values, $H(T)$ is the entropy of the target, and E_{tr} is the training error of the current model. In addition, the number of examples in the next validation interval is reduced by *Red_Add_Count*. Otherwise, the concept is considered stable and both the training window and the validation interval are increased by *Add_Count* examples up to their maximum sizes of *Max_Add_Count* and *Max_Win*, respectively.

8.5   Notes

Decision trees are one of the most studied methods in Machine Learning. The ability to induce decision trees incrementally appears in the Machine Learning community under several designations: *incremental learning, online learning, sequential learning, theory revision,* etc. In systems like ID4 (Van de Velde, 1990), ITI (Utgoff et al., 1997), or ID5R (Kalles and Morris, 1996), a tree is constructed using a greedy search. Incorporation of new information involves re-structuring the actual tree. The re-structuring procedure requires maintaining examples at leaves.

A somewhat related work in scalable algorithms for decision trees appears in (Mehta et al., 1996; Shafer et al., 1996; Gehrke et al., 1999; Dobra and Gehrke, 2002; Gehrke et al., 2000). In the 1990s, the SLIQ (Mehta et al., 1996) and SPRINT (Shafer et al., 1996) algorithms avoided re-sorting attributes using vertical partitioning and maintenance of sort orders. Later on, Rainforest (Gehrke et al., 2000) and Boat (Dobra and Gehrke, 2002) developed strategies that do not require all data to fit in main memory. Nevertheless, both Rainforest and Boat require scanning the data more than once.

Few incremental regression trees have been presented in the literature. A notable exception is the work of Potts and Sammut (2005). Ikonomovska and Gama (2008) present a VFDT-like algorithm for regression, extended later, in Ikonomovska et al. (2009), to deal with non-stationary streams.

Unlike decision trees, rule learners do not need to model all the instance space. Ferrer-Troyano, Aguilar-Ruiz, and Riquelme (2005, 2006) present an incremental rule learning from numerical data streams. Their system FACIL learns decision rules from numerical data streams. Rules may store up-to-date border examples to avoid unnecessary revisions. The system uses a forgetting heuristic that removes border examples and also removes rules based on how old they are.

Chapter 9

Novelty Detection in Data Streams

Novelty detection is a learning task that consists of the identification of new or unknown concepts that the learning system is not aware of during training. This is one of the fundamental requirements of a good classification or identification system, since sometimes the test data contain information about concepts that were not known at the time of training the model. In time-dependent applications, novelty detection represents an important challenge, since concepts are hardly ever constant. This chapter surveys the major approaches for the detection of novelty in data streams.[1]

9.1 Introduction

Novelty detection makes it possible to recognize novel profiles (concepts) in unlabeled data, which may indicate the appearance of a new concept, a change occurred in known concepts or the presence of noise. The discovery of new concepts has increasingly attracted the attention of the knowledge discovery community, usually under the terms *novelty* (Marsland, 2003) or *anomaly detection*. It is a research field somewhat related to statistical *outlier detection* (Barnett and Lewis, 1995). Since to be able to detect novelty the ML technique must allow the learning of a single target or normal concept, the terms *one-class* (Tax, 2001) or *single-class classification* are also frequently used. The absence of negative examples, which would represent the unknown novelty in this scenario, makes it hard for the induction algorithm to establish adequate decision boundaries and, thus, to avoid the extremes of underfitting and overfitting. This problem has also been studied under the term *learning from positive-only examples*.

Besides recognizing novelty, a learning environment that considers the time variable also imposes that the ML technique be able to identify changes occurred in the known or normal concept, which has been addressed under the term *concept drift* (see Section 3.3).

This chapter reviews the major approaches for the detection of novelty in data streams.

---

[1] Based on joint work with Eduardo Spinosa and Andre de Carvalho.

9.2 Learning and Novelty

Learning and novelty are two intrinsically linked concepts. In general, a stable state of awareness, characterized by the resurgence of known stimuli leading to known responses, does not motivate learning. It is incompatible with most real applications, in which concepts are hardly ever permanent. Only a disturbance, i.e., something new that introduces unknown characteristics, may be capable of motivating reasoning for explanations in a search that is itself a learning process. Therefore, the ability to identify novelty is a key to continuous learning. And such ability relies on two basic components: firstly, a description of the current state of awareness, i.e., a representation of the *normal* behavior; and secondly, a constant action of verifying the compatibility between the characteristics of new stimuli and those of the *normal* state.

Informally, the word *novelty* indicates something new or unknown. However, a proper definition of novelty in the context of data mining requires attention to some details in order to avoid confusion with other related concepts. Firstly, novelty should be regarded as a *concept*, i.e., an abstraction of instances that share characteristics. A concise group of examples should be required as an evidence of the appearance of a novel concept, or novelty. On the other hand, sparse independent examples whose characteristics differ greatly from those that define what is *normal*, should be regarded simply as *outliers*, since there is no guarantee that they represent concepts. They might simply be the consequence of noise, for instance. Examples that do not fit the current definition of *normal* are designated *unknown*. This allows us to distinguish between two different areas of research known as *outlier detection* (Barnett and Lewis, 1995) and *novelty detection* (Marsland, 2003).

Given that perspective, novel concepts emerge from the set of examples not currently explained by the normal model, here designated unknown. Thus, the complement of *normal* is *unknown*, not *novelty*. Novelty emerges from what is still unknown, but being unknown is not a sufficient condition for the identification of a novel concept. Hence, a possible definition of Novelty Detection from the inductive machine learning perspective would be: the algorithm's ability to identify data profiles that emerge from the universe of examples that are not explained by the current representation of the normal behavior.

Anomaly is another term sometimes associated with novelty. It usually indicates that the novel concept we wish to identify represents an abnormal event in a specific domain or application, such as a machine fault, for instance. Even though it is often the case, we shall avoid making that assumption and regard anomaly detection as a specialization of novelty detection. Keeping *novelty* a general concept allows us to incorporate other occurrences under novelty detection which are also relevant in the context of online learning, such as the appearance of a new class or subclass.

These techniques are useful in applications such as fault detection (King et al., 2002), radar target detection (Carpenter et al., 1997), statistical process control (Guh et al., 1999), etc. Terms such as *surprising events* or *bursts* (Vlachos et al., 2005) are also used to indicate novelty.

9.2.1 Desiderata for Novelty Detection

Markou and Singh (2003) identify important issues related to novelty detection and enumerate desirable properties for novelty detection methods:

- **Principle of robustness and trade-off**: A novelty detection method must be capable of robust performance on test data that maximizes the exclusion of novel samples while minimizing the exclusion of known samples.

- **Principle of generalization**: The system should be able to generalize without confusing generalized information as novel (Tax, 2001).

- **Principle of independence**: The novelty detection method should be independent of the number of features, and classes available. It should also show reasonable performance in the context of imbalanced dataset, and noise.

- **Principle of adaptability**: A system that recognizes novel samples during test should be able to use this information for learning new concepts (Saunders and Grace, 2008).

- **Principle of computational complexity**: A number of novelty detection applications are online and, therefore, the computational complexity of a novelty detection mechanism should be as low as possible.

We can identify two main lines where novelty detection concepts are used:

- The decision model act as a detector. The requirement is to detect whether an observation is part of the data that the classifier was trained on or it is in fact unknown.

- The decision model is able to learn new characteristic descriptions of the new concepts that appear in the test examples.

9.3 Novelty Detection as a One-Class Classification Problem

In most approaches to novelty detection the objective is to define whether an unseen example represents the *normal* behavior or not. The decision model has knowledge about a single concept, the *normal* behavior of the system. New

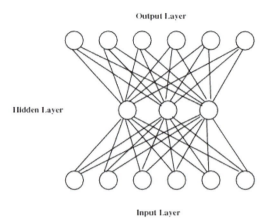

Figure 9.1: Architecture of a neural network for one-class classification. The network is trained, using the backpropagation algorithm, to reproduce the input at the output layer.

unlabeled examples may be identified as members of that profile or not. This context lies in the fact that examples of abnormal behaviors are usually scarce or not available, since in most applications it is hard and expensive to simulate abnormal scenarios. Besides that, it would be infeasible to simulate all possible abnormal situations. For that reason, novelty detectors can rely only on examples of a single profile that represents the normal behavior, hence the terms *one-class*, *single-class classification*, or *learning from positive-only examples*.

Several machine learning techniques have been adapted to work in a one-class scenario. One-class classification techniques are learning methods that proceed by recognizing positive instances of a concept rather than discriminating between its positive and negative instances. This restriction makes it a more difficult challenge to obtain an adequate level of generalization, since counter-examples play an important role in that task. A general method consists of estimating the probability density function of a normal class, for example using Parzen windows, and a rejection threshold.

9.3.1   Autoassociator Networks

Japkowicz et al. (1995) present an approach that consists of training a neural-network trained to reconstruct positive input instances at the output layer (see Figure 9.1). Classification is possible, after training, because positive instances are expected to be reconstructed accurately while negative instances are not.

The base idea explores the ability of the backpropagation algorithm to discover useful intermediate representations at the hidden unit layers inside the network. Japkowicz et al. (1995) proposal consists of training a three layer network, where the number of neurons in the output layer is equal to the input layer. Using the backpropagation algorithm, the network is trained to learn the simple target function $f(\vec{x}) = \vec{x}$, in other words, the network is trained to reproduce the input at the output layer.

Assume an autoassociator network trained from positive instances only. Classification is possible because positive instances are expected to be reconstructed accurately while negative instances are not.

To classify an unlabeled example $\vec{x}$, the example is propagated through the network. Let $\vec{y}$ be the corresponding output. The square error, $\sum_i^k (x_i - y_i)^2$, for positive examples should be low, while negative examples should have high squared error. The decision rule to reject an example is:

If $\sum_i^k (x_i - y_i)^2 < Threshold$ Then the example is considered from the *positive* class. Otherwise, $\vec{x}$ is a counter-example of the *positive* class.

The threshold might be defined by a user and controls the trade-off between fast detection and false alarms rate. As an alternative, it can be learned from a set of independent positive and negative examples.

9.3.2   The Positive Naive-Bayes

The positive naive Bayes (Denis et al., 2005) is an adaptation of the naive Bayes induction algorithm to the positive unlabeled learning context. This algorithm estimates the parameters of a naive Bayes model from positive and unlabeled examples.

Given the Bayes rule, and under the assumption of conditional independence between all the predicting variables given the class, we have that, for a given instance x

$$P(C = c|X) \propto P(C = c) \prod_{i=1}^{n} P(X_i = x_i|C = c)$$

The parameters required to define a two-class naive Bayes model are $p = P(C = 1)$, $P(x_{ij}|1) = P(X_i = j|C = 1)$ and $P(x_{ij}|0) = P(X_i = j|C = 0)$ for all $i = 1, \ldots, n$ and $j = 1, \ldots, r_i$. In the classical naive Bayes algorithm these parameters are estimated from the data by maximum likelihood estimators, but in the positive unlabeled learning context the absence of negative examples makes it unfeasible to estimate $P(x_{ij}|0)$ and p from the data. However, if we take into account that

$$P(x_{ij}|0) = \frac{P(x_{ij}) - P(x_{ij}|1) \times p}{1 - p}$$

where $P(x_{ij})$ stands for $P(X_i = j)$.

Assuming that p is known, we can estimate $P(x_{ij}|0)$ as:

$$\frac{U_{ij} - P(x_{ij}|1) \times p \times U}{(1-p)U}$$

where U_{ij} is the number of unlabeled examples with $X_i = j$ and U the cardinality of the unlabeled examples.

The problem with this estimator is that it can be negative. Calvo et al. (2007) solve the problem by replacing the negative estimations by 0, and then normalizing all the probabilities such that, for each variable X_i, they sum to 1: $\sum_{j=1}^{n} P(x_{ij}|0) = 1$.

$$P(x_{ij}|0) = \frac{1 + max(0; U_{ij} - P(x_{ij}|1) \times p \times U)}{2 + (1-p)U}. \tag{9.1}$$

To summarize, the positive naive Bayes estimates $P(x_{ij}|1)$ from the positive examples by means of a maximum likelihood estimator, p is a parameter set by the user, and $P(x_{ij}|0)$ is estimated by means of Equation 9.1.

Calvo et al. (2007) extend this approach to more complex networks, including Tree Augmented naive Bayes classifiers.

9.3.3   Decision Trees for One-Class Classification

Denis, Gilleron, and Letouzey (2005) extend the ideas of the previous section to estimate the information gain in decision tree learning from positive and unlabeled examples. Let POS be the set of positive examples, and denote by UNL the set of unlabeled examples. At a node n, the set of positive examples is POS_n and the set of unlabeled examples is UNL_n. Assuming that the frequency of positive examples in the unlabeled set is $PosLevel$, the entropy of a particion is computed as:

$$\begin{cases} p_1 = \frac{|POS_n|}{|POS|} \times \frac{|UNL|}{|UNL_n|} \times PosLevel \\ p_0 = 1 - p_1 \\ H(n) = -p_0 \times log_2(p_0) - p_1 \times log_2(p_1) \\ G(n,s) = H(n) - \sum_i \frac{|UNL_{ni}|}{|UNL_n|} \times H(n,i) \end{cases}$$

Li, Zhang, and Li (2009) present a VFDT-like algorithm for one-class classification, using these equations. Given that the $PosLevel$ is unknown, the authors enumerate nine possible values of $PosLevel$, from 0.1 to 0.9, and learn nine different trees. The best tree is chosen by estimating the classification performance of the trees with a set of validating samples.

9.3.4   The One-Class SVM

Let the set of training examples be $\{(x_i, y_i)\}^n$, where x_i is an input vector and $y_i \in \{-1, +1\}$ is its class label. Assume that the first $k-1$ examples are

Table 9.1: Confusion matrix to evaluate one-class classifiers.

		Actual	
		Pos	Neg
	Pos	TP	FP
Predict			
	Neg	FN	TN

positive examples (labeled +1), while the rest are unlabeled examples, which we label −1. If the sample size is large enough, minimizing the number of unlabeled examples classified as positive while constraining the positive examples to be correctly classified will give a good classifier. The following soft margin version of the Biased-SVM (Liu et al., 2003) formulation uses two parameters C_+ and C_- to weight positive errors and negative errors differently:

$$\text{Minimize: } \frac{1}{2}w^t w + C_+ \sum_{i=1}^{k-1} \xi_i + C_- \sum_{i=k}^{n} \xi_i$$

Subject to: $y_i(w^T x_i + b) \geq 1 - \xi_i, \ i = 1, 2, \ldots, n$ and $\xi_i \geq 0, i = 1, 2, \ldots, n$

Intuitively, we give a big value for C_+ and a small value for C_- because the unlabeled set, which is assumed to be negative, also contains positive data.

9.3.5 Evaluation of One-Class Classification Algorithms

The most straightforward evaluation of a novelty detection technique can be done by the analysis of a pair of error rates: one due to examples of the normal concept which have been wrongfully identified as members of an unknown profile, which may be called *false-unknown error rate*, and another due to examples of unknown profiles which have been wrongfully identified as members of the normal concept, which may be called *false-normal error rate*.

Consider the confusion matrix given in Table 9.1, where:

- True positive (TP): Positive examples correctly classified as positive;

- False positive (FP): Negative examples wrongly classified as positive;

- False negative (FN): Positive examples wrongly classified as negative.

- True negative (TN): Negative examples correctly classified as negative;

The relevant performance statistics are:

- $Precision = \frac{TP}{TP+FP}$

- $Recall = \frac{TP}{TP+FN}$ (or Sensitivity)

- $Specificity = \frac{TN}{TN+FP}$

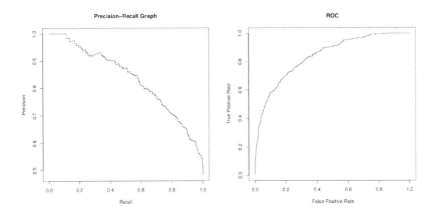

Figure 9.2: Illustrative examples of Precision-Recall and ROC graphs.

Precision can be seen as a measure of exactness; Recall is a measure of completeness. In a classification task, a Precision score of 1.0 for a class C means that every item labeled as belonging to class C does indeed belong to class C (but says nothing about the number of items from class C that were not labeled correctly) whereas a Recall of 1.0 means that every item from class C was labeled as belonging to class C (but says nothing about how many other items were incorrectly also labeled as belonging to class C). The best possible prediction method would yield a point in the upper right corner or coordinate (1,1), representing 100% Precision and 100% Recall.

Usually, Precision and Recall scores are not discussed in isolation. Instead, both are combined into a single measure, such as the F-measure, which is the weighted harmonic mean of precision and recall:

$$F\ measure = \frac{(w+1) \times Recall \times Precision}{Recall + w \times Precision}$$

a weight of 1, leads to the F1 measure:

$$F1 = \frac{2 \times Precision \times Recall}{Precision + Recall}$$

The *receiver operating characteristic* (ROC curve), is a graphical plot of the sensitivity vs. specificity for a binary classifier system as its discrimination threshold is varied. The ROC is obtained by plotting the fraction of true positives vs. the fraction of false positives as the criterion threshold changes (Hand and Till, 2001). The best possible prediction method would yield a point in the upper left corner or coordinate $(0, 1)$ of the ROC space, representing 100% sensitivity (no false negatives) and 100% specificity (no false positives).

9.4   Learning New Concepts

The fact that data is intrinsically time-dependent imposes the use of a flexible model and a learning strategy that enables both the updating of old concepts and the inclusion of new ones. Biologic brains possess an extraordinary capability for molding their structure to change and to incorporate knowledge. For machines, however, this is a more complicated task, and it possibly represents the most important challenge currently faced by Machine Learning researchers.

The central problem of novelty detection lies in the definition of unknown or surprising profiles. The decision of whether a new example should or should not be considered normal depends fundamentally on the domain, which makes it hard to develop a general approach that performs well in different applications. Furthermore, such a decision may depend on even less tangible aspects, i.e., what one considers normal may not be for someone else.

The challenge of designing novelty detectors that adequately identify novel scenarios, while still reliably recognizing the normal condition, may be tackled in different ways. This section describes the major approaches and trends in data streams. Even though our main focus is on *online learning* from data streams, some techniques involving, for instance, time series and large databases, were also included. Even though not all of them may perform *online* detection and updating of the model which represents the normal concept, the similar nature of the data imposes limitations whose investigation may contribute to the study of data streams.

9.4.1   Approaches Based on Extreme Values

The detection of *bursts* in time series is an important research topic, since it may indicate abnormal conditions in various applications, such as the detection of network intrusions or disease outbreaks. Given a time series, the simplest way to identify an outlier is to compare its value to a predefined threshold that acts as a limit between what is expected and what represents surprise.

This strategy has been applied for the identification of correlated burst patterns in multiple time series (Vlachos et al., 2005). The fact that abnormal conditions are correlated reinforces the evidence of an unexpected event at a certain time interval. In this approach, different values for the threshold τ that determines bursts are calculated for each portion of the series, considering that the data in each portion maintains an exponential distribution, characteristic of the financial data used in that work. Once several burst intervals have been identified, the work proceeds to the discovery of overlapping burst regions. For that task, an efficient index structure is adapted from the notion of containment encoded intervals (CEI). In CEI-based indexing, almost all operations can be performed using integer additions and logical shifts, making it both faster and more cost-effective than other alternatives (Wu et al., 2004).

9.4.2   Approaches Based on the Decision Structure

The problem of change detection in data streams may also be faced by considering that, in a standard multiple-class classification problem, the contribution of each decision unit in the classifier is likely to remain stable if no changes are observed in the process which is being monitored. A shift that occurs in the statistics of decision units indicates that the current model might be undergoing a conceptual change.

Fan, Huang, Wang, and Yu (2004) evaluate the use of two observable statistics in a decision tree classifier, obtained on the leaves, to detect potential changes in data streams. The first statistic, PS, computes the number of examples classified by each leaf and compares these values to the respective ones obtained on the training phase. Assume that dt is a decision tree constructed from a training set $\mathcal{D}$. The examples in the data stream $\mathcal{S}$ are classified by a unique path from the root to a leaf node. Assume that n_l is the number of instances classified by leaf l and the size of the data stream is N. Define the statistics at leaf l as:

$$P(l) = \frac{n_l}{N}$$

The sum over all leafs in the tree is $\sum_{l \in dt} P(l) = 1$. $P(l)$ describes how the instance space of the data stream $\mathcal{S}$ is shattered among the leaf nodes solely based on attribute test results of a given decision tree dt. It does not consider either the true class labels or attributes that are not tested by dt. If the combination of attributes values in the data stream $\mathcal{S}$ is different from the training set, it will be reflected in $P(l)$. The change of leaf statistics on a data stream is defined as:

$$PS = \frac{\sum_{l \in dt} |P_S(l) - P_D(l)|}{2}$$

The increase in $P(l)$ of one leaf is contributed by decrease in at least one other leaf. This fact is taken into account by dividing the sum by 2. When there are significant changes in the data stream, particularly distribution drifts, the PS statistic is likely to be high.

A second statistic, LS, is obtained by comparing the error rate obtained in a validation set L_a, to the sum of the expected error rate at every leaf L_e, considering the proportion of examples classified by each of them:

$$LS = |L_a - L_e|$$

Experimental evaluation on a credit card fraud dataset demonstrates that both PS and LS are well correlated with the amount of change in the data stream. The fact that these statistics do not require labeled data is pointed to by the author as an advantage over previous related works.

9.4.3 Approaches Based on Frequency

One way to concretize the notion of *surprise* in the search for unusual patterns is to associate it to its frequency. In that sense, a pattern would be considered surprising or anomalous if *"the frequency of its occurrence differs substantially from that expected by chance, given some previously seen data"* (Keogh et al., 2002). This definition should not be confused with that of *motifs*, which are patterns that appear very frequently, i.e., are overrepresented.

Given that perspective, the TARZAN algorithm (Keogh et al., 2002) was developed to discover surprising patterns in time series in linear space and time. Given a test series X, TARZAN identifies subsequences of X whose frequency of occurrence exceeds what is expected, given a reference series R. Initially, both series are discretized using a process known as the *Symbolic Aggregate approXimation (SAX)* (Lin et al., 2003),[2] resulting in two strings x and r. Then, for each string, subsequences are identified, and their respective frequencies are calculated and stored in two suffix trees T_x and T_r, which can be efficiently accessed. By directly comparing these trees, a surprise value $z(w)$ is obtained for each substring w in T_x, by subtracting its expected number of occurrences from the observed number of occurrences. The expected frequencies are either obtained in T_r, if the w exists in T_r, or estimated by Markov models. Finally, TARZAN identifies the substrings whose $z(w)$ exceeds a threshold defined by the user.

Experimental evaluation of TARZAN was performed in terms of sensitivity and selectivity, using synthetic data consisting of a noisy sine wave, and real data representing the power demand of a research facility for the period of one year. In terms of sensitivity, TARZAN was compared to *i)* IMM, a novelty detection strategy based on negative selection that takes place in natural immune systems (Dasgupta and Forrest, 1996) and *ii)* TSA-tree (Shahabi et al., 2000), a wavelet-based system developed to address surprise and trend queries on time series. Considering the proposed problem of finding an irregular week in terms of power consumption, TARZAN was successful while IMM and TSA-tree failed.

TARZAN was developed in the context of static time series databases, requiring whole time series to be loaded prior to processing. In an online data stream scenario, where the time series could potentially be infinite, several restrictions would apply, as described in Section 5.2.

VizTree (Lin et al., 2004) uses the approach of TARZAN, but aims mainly at the visualization of non-trivial patterns. It also applies SAX for the discretization and representation, stressing the fact that, when compared to other representation schemes, SAX is as good or better at representing *similarities*, which is an important feature in *anomaly* detection. VizTree displays the tree of subsequences using the thickness of branches to represent the frequency of each pattern. With that, the user can identify anomalies in a single time series, by visually exploring less frequent branches, or in two time series, by

---

[2]SAX is described in Section 11.4.

visualizing the difference tree as obtained by TARZAN. VizTree was tested on a time series obtained from images of yoga postures, power consumption and ECG data.

9.4.4   Approaches Based on Distances

By observing the distribution of examples on the feature space, several conclusions can be taken regarding the data. It is possible, for instance, to identify groups or *clusters* of examples and, if labels are available, examine if their grouping and positioning has any semantical significance. A variety of measures based on the positions of examples can be used to, among other tasks, generate models to represent the data and make decisions regarding new examples. This section focuses on the measures that can be used to identify novelty and similar situations.

With the expansion of computer networks, mining streams of text emerged as an important research area. In that scenario, the online identification of the earliest report of a novel event, known as *first story detection*, can be addressed using novelty detection techniques. The high cost of comparing each new document to all past documents motivated a two-level approach named topic-conditioned novelty detection (Yang et al., 2002). New documents are initially classified under general topics, using a standard supervised learning algorithm. Novelty detection itself takes place on a second level, where one detector is built for each topic. Upon receiving a new document, the detector of the corresponding topic compares it to all documents in that topic's history, finds its nearest neighbor and computes a cosine similarity score. The threshold is empirically set based on cross validation. The two-level approach offers the advantage of having defining different stop-word lists for each topic, and results show that this approach substantially improved the performance of novelty detection in this domain.

9.5   The *Online Novelty and Drift Detection* Algorithm

The OnLIne Novelty and Drift Detection (OLINDDA) (Spinosa et al., 2008, 2009) is a two-stage algorithm, able to detect new concepts and changes in previously learned concepts from unlabeled examples. In OLINDDA, the decision model is a set of hyperspheres, defined by a centroid, a radius, and a label.

Learning in OLINDDA is divided in two phases. The two phases are described in the following sections. Figure 9.3 provides an overview of the proposed algorithm.

In the initial phase, the system learns a decision model using a labeled training set. The set of labeled examples might be from a single class: the *normal* class. This initial phase is offline. The decision model, a set of hyperspheres labeled as *normal*, is learned using a k-means algorithm.

After learning the initial model, OLINDDA enters an online phase where the system receives a stream of unlabeled examples. Each example is compared to the current model. If any hypersphere covers the example, that is, the distance between the example and the centroid of the hypersphere is lesser than the radius, the example is classified using the label of the covering hypersphere. Otherwise, since the current decision model cannot classify the example, it is declared *unknown* and stored in a *short term memory* for further analysis later. From time to time, the examples stored in the short term memory are analyzed. It happens whenever the number of examples exceeds a user-defined threshold. The analysis employs again a standard clustering algorithm. OLINDDA looks for clusters with a minimum density, and considers three different cases:

- Clusters that satisfy the density criteria and are far from known concepts. They are declared *novelties* and added to the decision model with new labels.

- Clusters that satisfy the density criteria and are close to known concepts. They are declared *extensions* of existing concepts and added to the decision model with the same label of the closest concept.

- Clusters that are sparse and do not satisfy the density criteria. They are considered *noise*, thus, are not added to the decision model.

Three hypersphere-based models are used to store knowledge about (1) the normal concept, (2) extensions to this normal concept and (3) novel concepts. The *normal* model is the only static one, remaining as a reference to the initial learning stage. It corresponds to what is usually employed by most novelty detection techniques. The *extension* and *novelty* models can be continuously updated, allowing OLINDDA to deal with concepts that appear or change over time. Once newly discovered concepts become part of these two models, they will also help to explain future examples, thus reducing the cost of exploring regions of the feature space that have already been explored. Additionally, such an incremental structure allows the algorithm to start with a basic description, weakening the requirement of an initial set that thoroughly describes the normal concept.

OLINDDA makes use of a clustering algorithm. k-means is used by default considering its low computational cost, an important aspect when dealing with a large amount of data. Other algorithms, such as BIRCH (Zhang et al., 1996) (described earlier in Chapter 6), may also be used.

9.5.1   Initial Learning Phase

The algorithm starts by modeling the *normal* or expected condition in the domain under investigation by analyzing a set of normal examples. In the

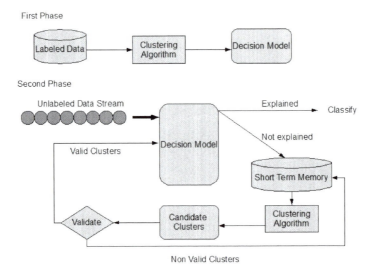

Figure 9.3: Overview of the *Online Novelty and Drift Detection* Algorithm.

problem of intrusion detection in computer networks, for instance, this initial dataset would be built from standard network traffic, without any examples of attacks.

To model the normal concept, k_{ini} clusters are produced using the k-means clustering algorithm. The normal model is composed of k_{ini} hyperspheres, built in feature space, obtained directly from the clusters and represented by their centers and radii. Each hypersphere center is the centroid of its cluster, and its radius is the Euclidean distance from the centroid to the farthest example of the respective cluster.

9.5.2 Continuous Unsupervised Learning Phase

Once the normal model is built, OLINDDA starts to analyze a stream of unlabeled examples.

For each new example, the algorithm first checks whether it can be explained by the knowledge acquired until that point, represented by the models previously described. If the coordinates of the example in feature space lie inside a hypersphere of any of the existing models, it is considered explained by the corresponding model; statistics are updated, and the example is classified and discarded. Otherwise, the example is marked as a member of an *unknown* profile and moved to a short-time memory for further analysis.

Initially, OLINDDA is capable of distinguishing regions that correspond to the normal concept (inside any of the hyperspheres of the normal model) from

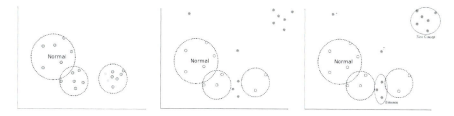

Figure 9.4: Illustrative example of the phases of OLINDDA algorithm. The left figure is the result of the first phase. From labeled data, from the normal class, OLINDDA finds three clusters. The figure in the middle presents the points not classified by the model that are stored in the short-term memory. By applying clustering to the unlabeled examples in short-term memory, OLINDDA finds two valid clusters. One is far away from the normal concept, so it is declared a *new* concept (right figure)

those that have not been explored yet, named *unknown*. In a stable situation, the normal model is expected to explain the majority of the new examples. As new concepts emerge and are added to the *extension* and *novelty* models, it will also be able to explain examples of such concepts.

9.5.2.1 Identifying Novel Concepts

The proposed technique learns concepts initially as clusters formed by examples previously considered *unknown*, that comply with certain restrictions. In order to discover these clusters, each time a new *unknown* example is found, and the number of examples in the *short-term-memory* exceeds a user-defined parameter, k *candidate* clusters are generated from the examples currently available at the short-term memory of unknown profiles. These candidate clusters are then evaluated to determine if any of them indicate the appearance of a new concept, represented by a so-called *valid* cluster.

The validation criterion considers two basic characteristics: cohesiveness and representativeness. Cohesiveness evaluates the degree of similarity between examples of a cluster. Three possible cohesiveness measures can be used.

- **Density**. The density, *dens*, of a cluster c_i is defined by:

$$dens(c_i) = \frac{n(c_i)}{vol(c_i, m)} \tag{9.2}$$

where $n(c_i)$ is the number of examples that belong to c_i and $vol(c_i, m)$ is the volume of the hypersphere whose radius r is the distance from the centroid to the farthest example of c_i. The volume $vol(c_i, m)$ in an

m-dimensional space is given by:

$$vol\,(c_i, m) = \frac{\pi^{\frac{m}{2}} r^m}{\Gamma\left(\frac{m}{2} + 1\right)} \tag{9.3}$$

where Γ is the gamma function:

$$\Gamma\left(\frac{m}{2} + 1\right) = \begin{cases} \left(\frac{m}{2}\right)!, & for\ even\ m; \\ \sqrt{\pi}\frac{m!!}{2^{(m+1)/2}}, & for\ odd\ m. \end{cases} \tag{9.4}$$

This criterion may not be applicable to datasets with a large number of attributes, once as m increases, $vol\,(c_i, m)$ tends to zero (Stibor et al., 2006).

- **Sum of squares of distances between examples and centroid divided by the number of examples**. The sum of squares of distances between examples belonging to c_i and the centroid μ_i is given by:

$$d\,(x_j, \mu_i) = \sum_{x_j \in c_i} (x_j - \mu_i)^2 \tag{9.5}$$

Dividing it by the number of examples that belong to cluster c_i, we obtain a comparable measure $d1$:

$$d1\,(x_j, \mu_i) = \frac{d\,(x_j, \mu_i)}{n\,(c_i)} \tag{9.6}$$

When k-means is chosen as the clustering algorithm, the use of this measure is advantageous from the computational cost point of view, since $\mathrm{d}(x_j, \mu_i)$ is already calculated in the clustering process.

- **Average distance between examples and centroid**. A simpler option is to use the average distance between examples and centroid, $d2$:

$$d2\,(x_j, \mu_i) = \frac{\sum\limits_{x_j \in c_i} |x_j - \mu_i|}{n\,(c_i)} \tag{9.7}$$

The cohesiveness threshold, which establishes the minimum cohesiveness degree required of a candidate cluster, is defined by the normal model. If density is chosen as the cohesiveness measure, a cluster is considered sufficiently cohesive if its density is equal to or higher than the minimum density of the clusters of the normal model. If the cohesiveness measure is either the sum of squares of distances between examples and centroid divided by the number of examples, or the average distance between examples and centroid, the cluster is considered sufficiently cohesive if the value of this measure is equal to or lower than the maximum value of the same measure for the clusters of the normal model.

The second aspect of the validation criterion concerns representativeness. A small cluster may be very cohesive, but not representative enough to indicate the appearance of a novel concept. In order to prevent that, candidate clusters are required to have at least a minimum number of examples, *minexcl*, defined as a parameter. A value between 3 and 5 has been empirically determined as adequate in most cases.

A candidate cluster that complies with both cohesiveness and representativeness restrictions is considered a valid cluster. Initially, all concepts consist of a valid cluster. With time, as concepts can be merged, a concept may be represented by a set of clusters. The merging of concepts will be discussed in Section 9.5.2.3.

9.5.2.2 Attempting to Determine the Nature of New Concepts

Once a valid cluster is identified, OLINDDA proceeds to assess its similarity to the normal concept. We consider that an *extension* of the normal concept should naturally present some similarity to it, which in terms of distances in feature space, means that the new concept should be located in the vicinity of the region associated to the normal concept. Contrary to that, a new concept which is dissimilar to *normal* may represent a novel concept, or *novelty*.

To materialize this notion of vicinity of the normal concept, the proposed technique considers a hypersphere centered at the centroid of the centroids of the clusters of the normal model, and whose radius is the distance to the farthest centroid. If the centroid of the new valid cluster is located inside this hypersphere, the new concept is labeled *extension*. Otherwise, it is considered *novelty*.

As previously mentioned, newly discovered concepts update their corresponding models, which facilitates the classification of future examples. As models are composed mainly of the coordinates of centroids and radii besides a few other distances and statistics, model updating is fast and performed incrementally, which is an important issue in applications involving, for instance, data streams, where time and space constraints apply.

9.5.2.3 Merging Similar Concepts

A new valid cluster may itself represent a new concept. However, depending on the data distribution, a concept may be more adequately described by a set of clusters. For that reason, the similarity between the new valid cluster and known concepts of the corresponding model is also evaluated. OLINDDA does that by checking if the new cluster intercepts any of the existing clusters. If it does not, the cluster is considered a new concept on its own and receives a new label. However, if the new valid cluster intercepts one or more existing clusters, they are grouped under the same label and their statistics are merged. A single cluster may trigger a sequence of mergers, and this process tends to produce a smaller number of concepts (labels) that are usually easier to analyze.

A typical experiment would be to present examples of a single class (representing the normal concept) in the initial phase, and allow OLINDDA to discover the remaining classes as novel concepts. In that scenario, our final goal would be to have produced a class structure as similar as possible to the real one, and the merging of concepts helps directing the algorithm toward that.

9.5.2.4 Automatically Adapting the Number of Clusters

The number of clusters k is an intrinsic parameter of the clustering algorithm. It is used to create the initial normal model, as described in Section 9.5.1, and to periodically generate candidate clusters in the online phase, as described in Section 9.5.2.1.

In the initial model, k is fixed and defined as a parameter (k_{ini}), since it depends on the data distribution. For the generation of candidate clusters in the online phase, however, k is automatically adapted to optimize the chance of discovering a valid cluster. This is done by increasing or decreasing k according to certain conditions. If the value of k is lesser than the optimum, the algorithm will generate clusters whose densities are lesser than the required threshold for cluster validation. Opposed to that, if the value of k is greater than the optimum, the candidate clusters will tend to have fewer examples than the required minimum.

The automatic adaptation of k takes place after each iteration in which candidate clusters were generated. If at least one candidate cluster is considered valid, the value of k is maintained. Otherwise, OLINDDA checks what prevented each cluster from being accepted: too low density or too few examples. Then, considering the most frequent cause of failure for all candidate clusters, it decides how to adapt the value of k. If the majority of failures is due to low density, k is increased. If too few examples is the most frequent cause of failure, k is decreased. After a few iterations, k tends to stabilize around the optimum value that generates valid clusters.

9.5.3 Computational Cost

OLINDDA's computational cost is influenced by several factors. Initially, the cost of verifying whether a new example is explained by one of the existing concepts depends on the total number of concepts of all models. For generating candidate clusters, the cost depends on:

1. The number of examples identified as members of an unknown profile, given that candidate clusters are only generated whenever an example is identified as unknown;

2. The number of examples in the short-time memory of unknown profiles;

3. The cost of the clustering algorithm.

Finally, for checking if a newly discovered concept intercepts one of the existing concepts, while updating models, the computational cost depends on the total number of concepts of the extension and novelty models.

9.6 Notes

Novelty detection is a young and active research line. Traditional approaches to classification require labeled examples to train classifiers'. Classifiers predictions are restricted to the set of class-labels they have been trained. In a data stream, when a new concept emerges, all instances belonging to this new class will be misclassified until a human expert recognizes the new class and manually labels examples and trains a new classifier. To empower machines with the abilities to change and to incorporate knowledge is one of the greatest challenges currently faced by Machine Learning researchers. We believe that a way to confront such defiance is by approaching the detection of both novelty and concept drift by means of a single strategy.

The relation and the frontiers between novelty detection and clustering are still unclear. As in clustering, novelty detection learns new concepts from unlabeled examples. Nevertheless, in contrast to clustering, novelty detection systems has a supervised phase.

Fan et al. (2004) use *active mining* techniques in conjunction with a classifier equipped with a novelty detection mechanism. The examples rejected by the novelty detection system are requested to be labeled by an expert. This approach is useful in the context of data streams where the target label is not *immediately* available but change detection needs to be done immediately, and model reconstruction needs to be done whenever the estimated loss is higher than a tolerable maximum.

Chapter 10

Ensembles of Classifiers

The term *multiple models* or *ensemble of classifiers* is used to identify a set of classifiers for which individual decisions are in some way combined (typically by voting) to classify new examples (Dietterich, 1997). The main idea behind any multiple model system is based on the observation that different learning algorithms explore different representation languages, search spaces, and evaluation functions of the hypothesis. How can we explore these differences? Is it possible to design a set of classifiers that working together can obtain a better performance than each individual classifier? Multiple models are also used in the context of dynamic streams, where the target concept may change over time.

10.1 Introduction

Hansen and Salamon (1990) first introduced the hypothesis that an ensemble of models is most useful when its member models make errors independently with respect to one another. They proved that when all the models have the same error rate, the error rate is less than 0.5, and they make errors completely independently, then the expected ensemble error must decrease monotonically with the number of models.

Figure 10.1 presents an example that clearly illustrates *how* and *why* an ensemble of classifiers works. Figure 10.1(a) shows the variation of the error rate obtained by varying the number of classifiers in an ensemble. This is a simulation study, in a two-class problem. The probability of observing each class is 50%. A varying number of classifiers, from 3 to 24, are used to classify, by uniform vote, each example. The classifiers have the same probability of making an error, but errors are independent of one another.

We consider three scenarios:

- When it is equal to 50% (random choice) the error rate of the ensemble stays constant;

- When it is 55% the error rate monotonically increases;

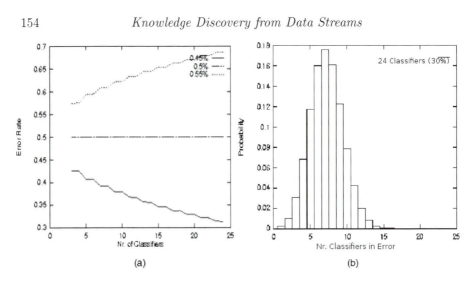

Figure 10.1: (a) Error rate versus number of classifiers in an ensemble. (b) Probability that exactly n of 24 classifiers will make an error.

- When this probability is 45%, the error rate of the ensemble monotonically decreases.

This study illustrates a necessary condition:

> The error of the ensemble decreases, respective to each individual classifier, if and only if each individual classifier has a performance better than a random choice.

In Figure 10.1(b) each bar represents the probability that exactly i classifiers are in error. In that case we use an ensemble of 24 classifiers, each one having an error of 30%. Using uniform voting the ensemble is in error, if and only if 12 or more classifiers are in error. If the error rates of n classifiers are all equal to p ($p < 0.5$) and if the errors are independent, then the probability that the majority vote is wrong can be calculated using the area under the curve of a binomial distribution. We can estimate the probability that more than $n/2$ classifiers are wrong (Dietterich, 1997). Figure 10.1(b) shows this area for the simulation of 24 classifiers. The area under the curve for more than 12 classifiers is 2%, which is much less than the error rate of the individual classifiers (30%).

Two models are said to make a *correlated error* when they *both* classify an example of class i as belonging to class j, $i \neq j$. The degree to which the errors of two classifiers are correlated might be quantified using the *error correlation* metric. We define the *error correlation* between pairs of classifiers as the conditional probability that the two classifiers make the same error given that one of them make an error. This definition of *error correlation* lies in the interval $[0 : 1]$ and the correlation between one classifier and itself is 1. The formal definition is:

$$\phi_{ij} = p(\hat{f}_i(x) = \hat{f}_j(x) | \hat{f}_i(x) \neq f(x) \vee \hat{f}_j(x) \neq f(x)).$$

The error correlation measures the diversity between the predictions of two algorithms:

- High values of ϕ: low diversity, redundant classifiers: the same type of errors;

- Low Values of ϕ: high diversity: different errors.

10.2 Linear Combination of Ensembles

The roots of online learning ensembles can be founded in the `WinNow` algorithm (Littlestone, 1988). `WinNow` is an online algorithm that combines the predictions of several *experts* by majority weighted voting. Each expert is associated with a weight. When the weighted vote misclassifies an example, the weight of the experts in error is updated. `WinNow` uses a multiplicative weight-update scheme, that is, the weight is multiplied by a constant $\beta < 1$. It is restricted to binary decision problems, and exhibits a very good performance when many dimensions are irrelevant.

Littlestone (1988) wrote:

> *A primary advantage of the* `WinNow` *algorithm is that the number of mistakes grows only logarithmically with the number of irrelevant attributes in the examples. At the same time, the algorithm is computationally efficient in both time and space.*

Later on, the same author presented the Weighted-Majority Algorithm (Littlestone and Warmuth, 1994) to combine predictions from a set of base classifiers. The main advantage of this algorithm is that we can bound the error of the ensemble with respect to the best expert in the ensemble. The Weighted-Majority Algorithm (WMA) (Algorithm 24) receives as input a set of predictors and a sequence of examples. Predictors can be experts, learned models, attributes, etc; the only thing that is required for the learning algorithm is that it makes a prediction. Each predictor is associated with a weight, set to 1 in the initial phase.

The examples can be labeled or unlabeled. For each example in the sequence, the algorithm makes predictions by taking a weighted vote among the pool of predictors. Each predictor classifies the example. The algorithm sums the weight of the predictors that vote for the same class, and classifies the example in the most weighted voted class. For the labeled examples, WMA updates the weight associated to each predictor. This is the sequential learning step. The weight attached to wrong predictions is multiplied by a factor β (for example 1/2). The vote of these predictors has less weight in the following predictions.

Algorithm 24: The Weighted-Majority Algorithm.

input: h_i: Set of m learned models $\{h_1, \ldots, h_m\}$
w_i: Set of m weights
(x, y): Training example

begin
    Initial Conditions: $w_i \leftarrow 1$
    foreach *model $h_k \in h$* **do**
        $y_i \leftarrow h_k(x)$
    if $\sum_{i:y_1=1} w_i \geq \sum_{i:y_1=0} w_i$ **then**
        $\hat{y} \leftarrow 1$
    else
        $\hat{y} \leftarrow 0$
    if *y is known* **then**
        for $i = 1$ **to** m **do**
            if $y_i \neq y$ **then**
                $w_i \leftarrow w_i * \beta$

end

The MWA has an interesting property:

Theorem 10.2.1 *Let D be any sequence of examples, A be a set of n predictors, and k be the minimum number of mistakes made by any algorithm in A for the set of examples in D. The number of mistakes made by the weighted-majority algorithm using $\beta = 1/2$, is at most: $2.4 \times (k + log_2(n))$.*

The sequence of values of the weight of any expert in WMA, as it was defined here, always decreases. The weight cannot increase. This is a disadvantage in time-changing streams. A simple adaptation strategy in drifting domains consists of normalizing the weights after each update.

The MWA is quite simple with bounds on the ensemble error. It might be applicable in the cases where the user has reason to believe that one of some pool of known algorithms will perform well, but the user does not know which one. The MWA was further developed in Herbster and Warmuth (1995, 1998) and Cesa-Bianchi et al. (1996).

10.3 Sampling from a Training Set

In this section we analyze methods that combine models generated by a single algorithm. *Diversity* is one of the requirements when using multiple models. Various strategies have been proposed for generation of different

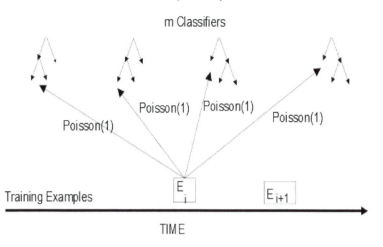

Figure 10.2: Illustrative example of online bagging.

classifiers using the same learning algorithm. Most of them manipulate the training set to generate multiple hypotheses. In the training phase, the learning algorithm runs several times, each time using a different distribution of the training examples. To classify query examples, all learned models classify the example, and predictions are aggregated using some form of voting. This technique works especially well for *unstable* learning algorithms - algorithms whose output classifier undergoes major changes in response to small changes in the training data.

10.3.1 Online Bagging

Bagging is one of the most effective methods for variance reduction. It was introduced by Breiman (1996). The basic idea consists of producing replications of the training set by sampling with replacement. Each replication of the training set has the same size as the original data. Some examples do not appear in it while others may appear more than once. Such a training set is called a *bootstrap replicate* of the original training set, and the technique is called *bootstrap aggregation* (from which the term *bagging* is derived). For a training set with m examples, the probability of an example being selected is $1 - (1 - 1/m)^m$. For a large m, this is about $1 - 1/e$. Each bootstrap replicate contains, on the average, 36.8% ($1/e$) of duplicated examples. From each replication of the training set a classifier is generated. All classifiers are used to classify each example in the test set, usually using a uniform vote scheme.

Bagging seems to require that the entire training set be available at all times because, for each base model, sampling with replacement is done by performing random draws over the entire training set. Oza (2001) proposed a

---

Algorithm 25: The Online Bagging Algorithm.

---

input: L_o: online base Learning Algorithm
h: Set of learned models $\{h_1, \ldots, h_m\}$
(x,y): Latest training example to arrive

begin
    foreach *base model* $h_m \in h$ **do**
        Set k according to Poisson(1)
        for $i = 1$ **to** k **do**
            $h_m \leftarrow L_o(h_m, (x, y))$

end

---

method able to avoid this requirement. Each original training example may be replicated zero, one, or more times in each bootstrap training set because the sampling is done with replacement. Each base model is trained with k copies of each of the original training examples where:

$$P(k) = \frac{exp(-1)}{k!} \tag{10.1}$$

As each training example is available, and for each base model, we choose $k \sim Poisson(1)$ and update the base model k times. Equation 10.1 comes from the fact that as the number of examples tends to infinity, the binomial distribution of k tends to a $Poisson(1)$ distribution. This way, we remove the dependence from the number of examples, and design a bagging algorithm for open-ended data streams.

The algorithm is presented in Algorithm 25 and illustrated in Figure 10.2. Unlabeled examples are classified in the same way as in bagging: uniform voting over the M decision models. Online bagging provides a good approximation to batch bagging given that their sampling methods generate similar distributions of bootstrap training sets.

10.3.2 Online Boosting

Schapire (1990) first proposed a general method to convert a *weak learner* into one that achieves arbitrarily high accuracy. The algorithm originally developed was based on a theoretical model known as the *weak learning model*. This model assumes that there exist *weak* learning algorithms that can do slightly better than random guessing regardless of the underlying probability distribution D used in generating the examples. The work of Schapire shows how to *boost* these weak learners to achieve arbitrarily high accuracy.

The main idea behind the *boosting* algorithm consists of maintaining a weight for each example in the training set that reflects its importance. Adjusting the weights causes the learner to focus on different examples leading

---

Algorithm 26: The Online Boosting Algorithm.

---

input: L_o: online base Learning Algorithm

h: Set of models $\{h_1, \ldots, h_M\}$ learned so far

λ^c: vector (1...M) sum of weights of correct classified examples

λ^w: vector (1...M) sum of weights of incorrect classified examples

(x,y): Latest training example to arrive

begin

    Set the example weight $\lambda \leftarrow 1$

    foreach *base model* $h_m \in h$ **do**

        Set k according to $Poisson(\lambda_d)$

        for $i \in \{1, \ldots, k\}$ **do**

            $h_m \leftarrow L_o(h_m, (x, y))$

        if $y = h_m(x)$ **then**

            $\lambda_m^{sc} \leftarrow \lambda_m^{sc} + \lambda$

            $\epsilon_m \leftarrow \frac{\lambda_m^{sw}}{\lambda_m^{sc} + \lambda_m^{sw}}$

            $\lambda \leftarrow \lambda(\frac{1}{2(1-\epsilon_m)})$

        else

            $\lambda_m^{sw} \leftarrow \lambda_m^{sw} + \lambda$

            $\epsilon_m \leftarrow \frac{\lambda_m^{sw}}{\lambda_m^{sc} + \lambda_m^{sw}}$

            $\lambda \leftarrow \lambda(\frac{1}{2\epsilon_m})$

end

---

to different classifiers. Boosting is an iterative algorithm. At each iteration the weights are adjusted in accordance with the performance of the corresponding classifier. The weight of the misclassified examples is increased. The final classifier aggregates the learned classifiers at each iteration by weighted voting. The weight of each classifier is a function of its accuracy.

Oza (2001) proposes an online version for boosting. The main algorithm is detailed in Algorithm 26 and illustrated in Figure 10.3. Assume an online weak learner L_o. Online boosting receives as inputs: the current set of base models $\{h_1, \ldots, h_M\}$, and the associated parameters $\lambda^c = \{\lambda_1^c, \ldots, \lambda_M^c\}$ and $\lambda^w = \{\lambda_1^w, \ldots, \lambda_M^w\}$, that are the sum of the weights of the correct and incorrectly classified examples per each individual model, respectively. The output of the algorithm is a new classification function that is composed of updated base models h and associated parameters λ_w and λ_c.

Suppose a new example $(\vec{x}, y)$ is available. The algorithm starts by assigning the weight $\lambda = 1$ to the training example. Then the algorithm goes into a loop through the base models. For the first iteration, $k = Poisson(\lambda)$, and the learning algorithm updates h_1 k times using $(\vec{x}, y)$. Now, if h_1 correctly classifies the example, increment λ_{c1}, and compute ϵ_1 that is the weighted fraction of examples correctly classified by h_1. The weight of the example is multiplied

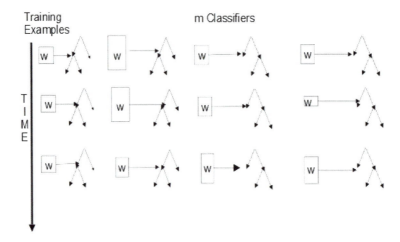

Figure 10.3: Illustrative example of online boosting. The weight of the examples are represented by boxes, the height of which denotes the increase (decrease) of the weight.

by $1/2(1 - \epsilon_1)$. If h_1 misclassifies the example, increment λ_{w1}, compute ϵ_1, and multiply the weight by $1/2\epsilon_1$. The process is repeated for all M models.

Polikar et al. (2001) presents **Learn++** an algorithm, for incremental training ensembles of neural network classifiers. **Learn++** is inspired by boosting, in the sense that each classifier is trained on a strategically updated distribution of the training data that focus on instances previously not seen or learned. The proposed algorithm accommodates new data, including examples that correspond to previously unseen classes. Furthermore, the algorithm does not require access to previously used data during subsequent incremental learning sessions.

10.4 Ensembles of Trees

10.4.1 Option Trees

Option decision trees were introduced by Buntine (1990) as a generalization of decision trees. Option trees can include *option nodes*, which replace a single decision by a set of decisions. An option node is like an *or* node in and/or trees. Instead of selecting the 'best' attribute, all the promising attributes are selected. For each selected attribute a decision tree is constructed. Note that an option tree can have three types of nodes: Nodes with only one test attribute - *decision nodes*; nodes with disjunctions of test attributes - *option nodes*; and leaf nodes.

Classification of an instance x using an option tree is a recursive procedure:

- For a leaf node, return the class label predicted by the leaf.

- For a decision node the example follows the unique child that matches the test outcome for instance x at the node.

- For an option node the instance follows all the subtrees linked to the test attributes. The predictions of the disjunctive test are aggregated by a voting schema.

Option trees is a deterministic algorithm known to be efficient as a variance reduction method. The main disadvantage of *option trees* is that they require much more memory and disk space than ordinary trees. Kohavi and Kunz (1997) claim that it is possible to achieve significant reduction of the error rates (in comparison with regular trees) using *option trees* restricted to two levels of option nodes at the top of the tree.

In the context of streaming data, Kirkby (2008) first propose *option trees*, an extension to the VFDT algorithm, as a method to solve ties. After processing a minimum number of examples, VFDT computes the merit of each attribute. If the difference between the merits of the two best attributes satisfies the Hoeffding bound, VFDT expands the decision tree by expanding the node and generating new leaves. Otherwise, the two attributes are in a *tie*. VFDT reads more examples and the process is repeated. Processing more examples implies a decrease of ϵ (see Equation 2.1). Suppose that there are two equal discriminative attributes. VFDT will require too many examples till ϵ becomes small enough to choose one of them. The original VFDT uses a user-defined constant τ to solve ties. The node is expanded whenever $\epsilon < \tau$ (see Section 8.2). A better solution is to generate an option node, containing tests in all the attributes, such that the difference in merit with respect to the best attribute is less than ϵ.

10.4.2   Forest of Trees

The Ultra Fast Forest of Trees (UFFT) (Gama and Medas, 2005) is an incremental algorithm, that learns a forest of trees from data streams. Each tree in UFFT is a Hoeffding tree, similar to VFDT, but designed for fast processing continuous attributes. For continuous attributes, a splitting test has the form $attribute_i < value_j$. UFFT uses the analytical method for split point selection presented by Loh and Shih (1997), and described in Section 8.3.1.2. For a given attribute, UFFT uses univariate discriminant analysis to choose the most promising $value_j$. The only sufficient statistics required are the mean and variance per class of each numerical attribute. The process is described in section 8.3.1.2. This is a major advantage over other approaches, like the exhaustive method used in C4.5 (Quinlan, 1993) and in VFDTc (Gama et al., 2003) (described in Section 8.3), because all the necessary statistics are computed on the fly using reduced space. This is a desirable property in the treatment of huge data streams because it guarantees constant time and memory to process each example.

10.4.2.1   Generating Forest of Trees

The splitting criteria only apply to two class problems. Most of real-world problems are multi-class. In the original paper (Loh and Shih, 1997) and for a batch-learning scenario, this problem was solved using, at each decision node, a 2-means cluster algorithm to group the classes into two super-classes. UFFT uses another methodology based on round-robin classification (Fürnkranz, 2002). The round-robin classification technique decomposes a multi-class problem into k binary problems, that is, each pair of classes defines a two-classes problem. Fürnkranz (2002) shows the advantages of this method to solve n-class problems. The UFFT algorithm builds a binary tree for each possible pair of classes. For example, in a three-class problem where the set of classes is the set $\{A, B, C\}$, the algorithm grows a forest of binary trees, one tree for each pair: $\{A, B\}$, $\{B, C\}$, and $\{A, C\}$. In the general case of n classes, the algorithm grows a forest of $\frac{n(n-1)}{2}$ binary trees. When a new example is received during the tree growing phase each tree will receive the example if the class attached to it is one of the two classes in the tree label.

10.4.2.2   Classifying Test Examples

When doing classification of a test example, the algorithm sends the example to all trees in the forest. Each tree in the forest makes a prediction, that takes the form of a probability class distribution. Taking into account the classes that each tree discriminates, these probabilities are aggregated using the *sum rule*: for each class c_i, sum the probabilities $P(c_i|\vec{x})$ given by the trees that consider c_i. The class that maximizes the sum is used to classify the example.

10.5   Adapting to Drift Using Ensembles of Classifiers

Ensembles of classifiers are a natural method to deal with time-changing streams. The base assumption is that during change, data is generated from a mixture distribution, which can be seen as a weighted combination of distributions characterizing the target concepts (Scholz and Klinkenberg, 2007). This idea justifies multiple model approaches, where each based classifier has an associated weight that reflects its performance in the most recent data.

The SEA algorithm (Street and Kim, 2001) is one of the first approaches to address the problem of concept drift in learning ensembles of classifiers from data streams. The method builds separate classifiers from sequential batches of training examples. These classifiers are combined into a fixed-size ensemble using a heuristic replacement strategy.

In a similar way, Wang, Fan, Yu, and Han (2003) propose a general framework for mining concept-drifting data streams using weighted ensemble classifiers. They train an ensemble of classification models, such as C4.5, RIPPER, naive Bayes, etc., from sequential batches of the data stream. The classifiers in the ensemble are judiciously weighted based on their expected classification accuracy on the test data under the time-evolving environment. Thus, the ensemble approach improves both the efficiency in learning the model and the accuracy in performing classification.

Assume a training set $\mathcal{D}$, and a classifier $\mathcal{M}$. Let $M_c(x)$ be the probability that example x belongs to class c given by $\mathcal{M}$. The mean square error of a classifier can be expressed by:

$$MSE = \frac{1}{|D|} \sum_{x \in D} (1 - M_c(x))^2$$

The weight of classifier $\mathcal{M}$ should be reversely proportional to its MSE. The weight of a classifier is the advantage of using that model in comparison to a random classifier. The MSE of a random classifier is:

$$MSE_r = \sum_c p(c) \times (1 - p(c))^2$$

where $p(c)$ is the probability of observing class c. The weight w_i of a classifier is given by: $w_i = MSE_r - MSE_i$.

Kolter and Maloof (2003, 2007) present the *Dynamic Weighted Majority* algorithm, an ensemble method for tracking concept drift. This is a general method based on the Weighted Majority algorithm (Littlestone, 1988) and can be used with any online learner in time-changing problems with unknown dynamics. The Dynamic Weighted Majority (DWM) maintains an ensemble of predictive models, referred to as *experts*, each with an associated weight. Experts can be generated by the same base learning algorithm, but are generated at different time steps so they use a different training set of examples. DWM makes predictions using a weighted-majority vote of these *experts*. It dynamically creates and deletes experts in response to changes in performance. Whenever an example is available, each expert is consulted, making a prediction. The final prediction is obtained as a weighted vote of all the experts. For each class, DWM sums the weights of all the experts predicting that class, and predicts the class with greatest weight. The learning element of DWM first predicts the classification of the training example. The weights of all the experts that misclassified the example are decreased by a multiplicative constant β. If the overall prediction was incorrect, a new expert is added to the ensemble with weight equal to the total weight of the ensemble. Finally, all the experts are trained on the example.

Algorithm 27: The `Add Expert` Algorithm for Discrete Classes.

---

input: x, y^T A Training Set with class $y \in Y$
$\qquad \beta \in [0, 1]$: factor for decreasing weights
$\qquad \tau \in [0, 1]$: loss required to add a new expert
begin
$\quad$ Set the initial number of experts: $N_1 \longleftarrow 1$;
$\quad$ Set the initial expert weight: $w_{1,1} \longleftarrow 1$;
$\quad$ **for** $t \leftarrow 1$ **to** T **do**
$\quad\quad$ Get expert predictions: $\epsilon_{t,1}, \ldots, \epsilon_{t,N_t} \in Y$;
$\quad\quad$ Compute prediction: $\hat{y}_t = argmax_{c \in Y} \sum_{i=1}^{N_t} w_{t,i}[c = \epsilon_{t,i}]$;
$\quad\quad$ Update experts weights: $w_{t+1,i} \longleftarrow w_{t,i} \beta^{[y_t = \epsilon_{t,i}]}$;
$\quad\quad$ **if** $\hat{y}_t \neq y_t$ **then**
$\quad\quad\quad$ Add a New Expert;
$\quad\quad\quad$ $N_{t+1} \longleftarrow N_t + 1$;
$\quad\quad\quad$ $w_{t+1,N_{t+1}} \longleftarrow \gamma \sum_{i=1}^{N_t} w_{t,i}$;
$\quad\quad$ Train each expert on example x_t, y_t;
end

Algorithm 28: The `Add Expert` Algorithm for Continuous Classes.

---

input: x, y^T A Training Set with class $y \in [0 : 1]$
$\qquad \beta \in [0, 1]$: factor for decreasing weights
$\qquad \gamma \in [0, 1]$: factor for new expert weight
$\qquad \tau \in [0, 1]$: loss required to add a new expert
begin
$\quad$ Set the initial number of experts: $N_1 \longleftarrow 1$;
$\quad$ Set the initial expert weight: $w_{1,1} \longleftarrow 1$;
$\quad$ **for** $t \leftarrow 1$ **to** T **do**
$\quad\quad$ Get expert predictions: $\epsilon_{t,1}, \ldots, \epsilon_{t,N_t} \in [0, 1]$;
$\quad\quad$ Compute prediction: $\hat{y}_t = \frac{\sum_{i=1}^{N_t} w_{t,i} \epsilon_{t,i}}{\sum_{i=1}^{N_t} w_{t,i}}$;
$\quad\quad$ Suffer loss $\|\hat{y}_t - y_t\|$;
$\quad\quad$ Update experts weights: $w_{t+1,i} \longleftarrow w_{t,i} \beta^{\|\epsilon_{t,i} - y_t\|}$;
$\quad\quad$ **if** $\|\hat{y}_t - y_t\| \geq \tau$ **then**
$\quad\quad\quad$ Add a New Expert;
$\quad\quad\quad$ $N_{t+1} \longleftarrow N_t + 1$;
$\quad\quad\quad$ $w_{t+1,N_{t+1}} \longleftarrow \gamma \sum_{i=1}^{N_t} w_{t,i} \|\epsilon_{t,i} - y_t\|$;
$\quad\quad$ Train each expert on example x_t, y_t;
end

If trained on a large amount of data, DWM has the potential to create a large amount of experts. Ideally, we should be able to remove, and prune the oldest experts while keeping the best experts. Doing this, the accuracy will not decrease. A possible pruning rule removes the oldest expert when the number of experts is greater than a constant k. Other pruning rules might be used. For example, when a new expert is added to the ensemble, if the number of experts is greater than a constant K, remove the expert with the lowest weight before adding the new member. Afterward, the same authors present AddExp algorithm (Kolter and Maloof, 2005), a variant of DWM extended for classification (Algorithm 27) and regression (Algorithm 28). A similar approach, but using a weight schema similar to boosting and explicit change detection, appears in Chu and Zaniolo (2004).

10.6 Mining Skewed Data Streams with Ensembles

Skewed distributions appear in many data stream applications. In these cases, the positive examples are much less popular than the negative ones. Also, misclassifying a positive example usually invokes a much higher loss compared to that of misclassifying a negative example. Network intrusion and fraud detection are examples of such applications. Assume the incoming data stream arrives in sequential chunks, $S_1, S_2, \ldots, S_m$. S_m is the most up-to-date chunk. Moreover, assume that the data comes from two classes, positive and negative classes, and the number of examples in the negative class is much greater than the number of positive examples. In other words, $P(+) \ll P(-)$. The data chunk that arrives next is S_{m+1}. Our goal is to train a classifier based on the data arrived so far to classify the examples in S_{m+1}. We could learn a decision using the most recent data chunk. This works for examples in the negative class since these examples dominate the data chunk and are sufficient for training an accurate model. However, the positive examples are far from sufficient. Most inductive learners built on one chunk will perform poorly on the positive class.

Gao, Fan, Han, and Yu (2007) split each chunk S_i into two parts: P_i, which contains positive examples in S_i, and N_i, which contains negative examples in S_i. The size of P_i is much smaller than that of N_i. To enhance the set of positive examples, the authors propose to collect all positive examples and keep them in the training set. Specifically, the positive examples in the training set are $\{P_1, P_2, \ldots, P_m\}$. The negative examples are randomly undersampled from the last data chunk N_m to make the class distribution balanced. The sampling procedure is repeated k times (see Algorithm 29). Though the strategy is quite simple, it is effective in skewed classification.

Algorithm 29: The Skewed Ensemble Algorithm.

---

input: S_m: current data chunk; S_{m+1}: Test data;
        AP: set of positive examples seen so far; k: number of models in
the ensemble
begin
   | Split S_m into P_m and N_m
   | $AP = \{AP \cup P_m\}$
   | **for** $i = 1$ *to* k **do**
   | | S = Sample $|AP|$ examples from N_m
   | | C_i = Train Classifier using $\{S \cup AP\}$
   | Classify S_{m+1} using the Ensemble $C = \bigcup_{i=1}^{k} C_i$
end

10.7 Notes

The study of voting systems, as a subfield of political science, economics
or mathematics, began formally in the 18th century and many proposals have
been made. The seminal forecasting paper by Granger and Newbold (1976)
stimulated a flurry of articles in the economics literature of the 1970s about
combining predictions from different forecasting models. Hansen and Salamon (1990) showed the variance reduction property of an ensemble system.
Bayesian model averaging has been pointed out as an optimal method (Hoeting et al., 1999) for combining classifiers. It provides a coherent mechanism
for accounting model uncertainty. Schapire (1990) work put the ensemble systems at the center of machine learning research, as he proved that a strong
classifier in probably approximately correct in the sense that it can be generated by combining weak classifiers through a boosting procedure. Lee and
Clyde (2004) introduce an online Bayesian version of bagging. Fern and Givan (2000) show empirical results for both boosting and bagging-style online
ensemble of decision trees in a branch prediction domain. In addition, they
show that, given tight space constraints, ensembles of depth-bounded trees are
often better than single deeper trees. Ensembles of semi-random decision trees
for data streams appear in (Hu et al., 2007). In a similar line, Abdulsalam
et al. (2007) present the *Streaming Random Forests* algorithm, an online and
incremental stream classification algorithm that extends the *Random Forests*
algorithm (Breiman, 2001) to streaming setting.

Chapter 11

Time Series Data Streams

Time series are sequences of measurements that follow non-random orders. The analysis of time series is based on the assumption that successive values of a random variable represent consecutive measurements taken at spaced time intervals. A common notation specifies a time series X indexed by the natural numbers:

$$x_1, x_2, \ldots, x_{t-1}, x_t, \ldots.$$

Time Series Analysis refers to applying different data analysis techniques to model dependencies in the sequence of measurements. The focus of classical time series analysis was on forecasting and pattern identification. Data analysis techniques recently applied to time series include clustering, classification, indexing, and association rules. In this chapter we review techniques able to deal with high-speed time series.

11.1 Introduction to Time Series Analysis

Most time series patterns can be described in terms of two basic classes of components: *trend* and *seasonality*. The former represents a general systematic linear or (most often) nonlinear component that changes over time; the latter repeats itself in systematic intervals over time. Figure 11.1 plots the time series of the electricity load demand in Portugal. It clearly shows seasonal patterns: week patterns, working days, and weekends.

11.1.1 Trend

A moving average is commonly used in time series data to smooth out short-term fluctuations and highlight longer-term trends or cycles. These *smoothing* techniques reveal more clearly the underlying trend, seasonal and cyclic components of a time-series.

We can distinguish *averaging methods* where all data points have the same *relevance* and *weighted averaging methods* where data points are associated with a weight that strengthens their relevance. Relevant statistics in the first group are:

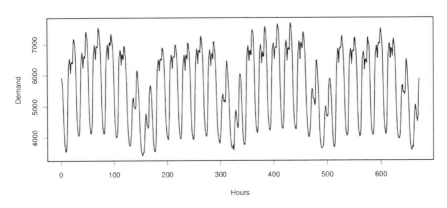

Figure 11.1: Plot of the electricity load demand in Portugal in January 2008. The time-series exhibits seasonality: it clearly shows week patterns, working days, and weekends.

- **Moving average**
  The mean of the previous n data points:

  $$MA_t = MA_{t-1} - \frac{x_{t-n+1}}{n} + \frac{x_{t+1}}{n}$$

- **Cumulative moving average**
  The average of all of the data up until the current data point:

  $$CA_t = CA_{t-1} + \frac{x_t - CA_{t-1}}{t}$$

The second group, weighted moving averages, includes:

- **Weighted moving average**
  has multiplying factors to give different weights to different data points. The most recent data points are more *"important"*:

  $$WMA_t = \frac{nx_t + (n-1)x_{t-1} + \cdots + 2x_{t-n+2} + x_{t-n+1}}{n + (n-1) + \cdots + 2 + 1}$$

- **Exponential moving average**
  The weighting for each older data point decreases exponentially, giving more importance to recent observations while still not discarding older observations entirely.

  $$EMA_t = \alpha \times x_t + (1 - \alpha) \times EMA_{t-1}$$

The idea behind the exponential moving average is to produce an estimate that gives more weight to recent measurements, on the assumption that recent measurements are more likely to be relevant. It does not require maintaining in memory all the points inside the window. Nevertheless, choosing an adequate α is a difficult problem, and it is not trivial.

11.1.2 Seasonality

Autocorrelation and autocovariance are useful statistics to detect periodic signals. Since autocovariance depend on the units of the measurements and is unbounded, it is more convenient to consider autocorrelation that is independent of the units of the measurements, and is in the interval $[-1; 1]$.

Autocorrelation is the cross-correlation of a time-series with itself. It is used as a tool for finding repeating patterns, such as the presence of a periodic signal. Autocorrelation is measured as the correlation between x and $x + l$ where l represents the time lag, and can be computed using Equation 11.1.

$$r(x, l) = \frac{\sum_{i=1}^{n-l}(x_i - \bar{x})(x_{i+l} - \bar{x})}{\sum_{i=1}^{n}(x_i - \bar{x})^2} \tag{11.1}$$

Figure 11.2 plots the autocorrelation of the time-series presented in Figure 11.1, varying the time-lag in the interval [1 hour, 2 weeks]. The plot, denoted as *correlogram*, shows high values for time lag of 1 hour, and multiples of 24 hours. Time-lags of one week (168 hours) are even more autocorrelated in the electrical demand data.

11.1.3 Stationarity

We should point out that a common assumption in many time-series techniques is that the data are stationary. A stationary process has the property that the mean, variance and autocorrelation structure do not change over time.

A usual strategy to transform a given time-series to a stationary one consists of differentiating the data. That is, given the series z_t, we create the new series $y_i = z_i - z_{i-1}$. Nevertheless, information about change points is of great importance for any analysis task.

11.2 Time-Series Prediction

Time-series analysis exploits dependences between time-points. A simple way to model dependence over time is with the *autoregressive* models. The

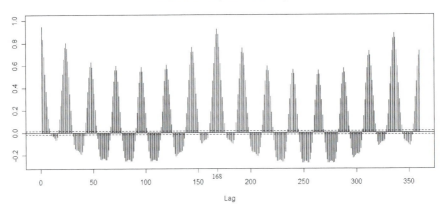

Figure 11.2: A study on the autocorrelation for the electricity load demand in Portugal. In the plot, the x-axis represents the x time horizon [1 hour, 2 weeks], while the y-axis presents the autocorrelation between current time t and time $t-l$. The plot shows high values for time lags of 1 hour, and multiples of 24 hours. Weekly horizons (168 hours) are even more autocorrelated in the electrical network.

simplest autoregressive model of order 1 is:

$$AR(1) : z_t = \beta_0 + \beta_1 \times z_{t-1} + \epsilon_t$$

The simplest method to learn the parameters of the AR(1) model is regress Z on lagged Z. If the model successfully captures the dependence structure in the data then the residuals should look *iid*. There should be no dependence in the residuals.

The case of $\beta_1 = 1$ deserves special attention because of its relevance in economic data series. Many economic and business time series display a *random walk* characteristic. A random walk is an AR(1) model with $\beta_1 = 1$ is:

$$AR(1) : z_t = \beta_0 + z_{t-1} + \epsilon_t$$

A random walker is someone who has an equal chance of taking a step forward or a step backward. The size of the steps is random as well. In statistics (Dillon and Goldstein, 1984) much more sophisticated techniques are used. Most of them are out of the scope of this book.

11.2.1 The Kalman Filter

The Kalman filter (Kalman, 1960) is a recursive filter that estimates the state of a dynamic system from a series of noisy measurements. It is used in problems where we want to estimate the state $x \in \Re^n$ of a dynamic system described by a linear stochastic equation:

$$x_k = Ax_{k-1} + w_{k-1} \tag{11.2}$$

The state of the system is unobservable. Nevertheless we have access to observable noisy measurements $z \in \Re^m$ assumed to be:

$$z_k = Hx_k + v_k \tag{11.3}$$

The variables w_k and v_k represent the process and the measurement noises respectively. It is assumed that both are independent normally distributed centered in 0 and with covariance matrices given by Q and R, respectively. The matrix A in Equation 11.2 relates the state of the system in time $k-1$, with the current state at time k; H in Equation 11.3 relates the current state of the system with the measurement. At a given timestep t, the filter uses the state estimate from the previous timestep to produce an estimate of the state at the current timestep: $\hat{x}_t^-$. This predicted state estimate is also known as the *a priori* state estimate because it does not include observation information from the current timestep. Later, whenever z_t is observed, the current a priori prediction is combined with current observation information to refine the state estimate. This improved estimate, $\hat{x}_t$, is termed the *a posteriori* state estimate.

We have two error estimates. The *a priori* error, $e_k^- \equiv x_k - \hat{x}_k^-$, and the *a posteriori* error, $\hat{e}_k \equiv x_k - \hat{x}_k$.

The covariance matrix of the a priori error estimate is:

$$P_k^- = E\left[e_k^- e_k^{-T}\right] \tag{11.4}$$

and the covariance matrix of the a posteriori error estimate is:

$$P_k = E\left[\hat{e}_k \hat{e}_k^T\right] \tag{11.5}$$

The Kalman filter computes $\hat{x}_k$ as a linear combination of $\hat{x}_k^-$ and the difference between z_k and $H\hat{x}_k^-$:

$$\hat{x}_k = \hat{x}_k^- + K_k\left(z_k - H\hat{x}_k^-\right) \tag{11.6}$$

The difference $\left(z_k - H\hat{x}_k^-\right)$ is the innovation measure or residual, and reflects the difference between predict measurement $H\hat{x}_k^-$, and the observed value z_k. The matrix K, from Equation 11.6, is called the *factor gain* and minimizes the covariance matrix of the a posteriori error (Kalman, 1960; Harvey, 1990). K is given by:

$$K_k = \frac{P_k^- H^T}{HP_k^- H^T + R} \tag{11.7}$$

Whenever the covariance matrix R is near 0, the gain factor K gives more weight to the residual. Whenever the covariance matrix P is near 0, the gain factor K gives less weight to the residual.

The Kalman filter estimates the state of the system using a set of recursive equations. These equations are divided into two groups: time update equations and measurement update equations. The time update equations are responsible for projecting forward (in time) the current state and error covariance estimates to obtain the a priori estimates for the next time step.

$$\hat{x}_k^- = A\hat{x}_{k-1} \tag{11.8}$$

$$P_k^- = AP_{k-1}A^T + Q \tag{11.9}$$

The measurement update equations are responsible for the feedback, i.e. for incorporating a new measurement into the a priori estimate to obtain an improved a posteriori estimate.

$$K_k = \frac{P_k^- H^T}{HP_k^- H^T + R} \tag{11.10}$$

$$\hat{x}_k = \hat{x}_k^- + K_k\left(z_k - H\hat{x}_k^-\right) \tag{11.11}$$

$$P_k = (I - K_k H)\, P_k^- \tag{11.12}$$

The true state is assumed to be an unobserved Markov process (see Figure 11.3), and the measurements are the observed states of a hidden Markov model. The Markov assumption justifies that the true state is conditionally independent of all earlier states given the immediately previous state.

Equations 11.8 and 11.9 forecast the current system state, $\hat{x}_{k-1}$, and the error covariance matrix, P_{k-1}, for the next time-stamp k. We obtain the a priori estimates of the system state, $\hat{x}_k^-$ and the error covariance matrix P_k^-. Equations 11.11 and 11.12 incorporate the measurements, z_k, in the estimates

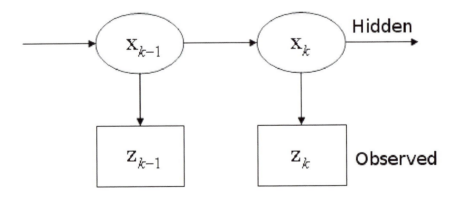

Figure 11.3: Kalman filter as a hidden Markov model.

a priori, producing the estimates a posteriori of the system state, $\hat{x}_k$, and the error covariance matrix, P_k. After computing the a posteriori estimates, all the process is repeated using the a posteriori estimates to compute new estimates a priori. This recursive nature is one of the main advantages of the Kalman filter. It allows easy, fast and computationally efficient implementations (Harvey, 1990).

The performance of the Kalman filter depends on the accuracy of the a priori assumptions:

- Linearity of the difference stochastic equation;

- Estimation of covariances Q and R, assumed to be fixed, known, and follow normal distributions with zero mean.

A clever choice of the parameters is of great importance for a good performance of the filter. Greater values of Q imply that the filter will quickly respond to state changes, at costs of low precision (large variance of P). On the other side, lower values of Q will improve predictions in stationary phases, at costs of slower adaption to changes. Maintaining constant Q and R the covariance matrix, P_k, and the Kalman filter gain, K_k, will converge fast.

11.2.2   Least Mean Squares

One of the most popular adaptive algorithms used today is the Least Mean Squares (LMS) algorithm. Essentially, this algorithm attempts to minimize the error that occurs between the observed signal and the estimated value of the signal, $\hat{y}$. This estimated signal is a linear combination of the inputs: $\hat{y} = w_0 + \sum w_i \times x_i$.

Once the signal and its approximation are found, the error is just the difference between the two at the current point in time: $e = y - \hat{y}$.

Using the error, we can approximate the next set of weights using the delta rule:

$$\Delta_i = (y - \hat{y}) \times x_i$$
$$w_i = w_{i-1} + \mu \times \Delta_i$$

where w_{i-1} is the weight i at previous timestamp, and μ, the learning rate, is a constant.

The main idea behind the least mean squares, or delta rule, is to use gradient descent to search the hypothesis space of possible weight vectors to find the weights that best fit the training examples.

11.2.3   Neural Nets and Data Streams

Neural networks (Bishop, 1995) are a general *function approximation* method. They are widely used in pattern recognition and machine learning in problems that are described by continuous attributes. One interesting property is that a three layer artificial neural network, using for example sigmoides as activation functions, can approximate any continuous function with arbitrary small precision (Mitchell, 1997).

A multi-layer neural network is a directed acyclic graph, where nodes or neurons are organized in layers. Each neuron in one layer is connected with all neurons in the next layer. Associated with each connection there is a weight that strengthens the connection, such that the output signal of a neuron is multiplied by the weight before input to the following neuron.

The most common algorithm to train a neural network is the *backpropagation* algorithm. This is a stochastic steepest gradient descent. It uses several iterations over the training data, and update weights after processing each example or after each iteration. The process ends when a heuristic stop criteria holds or after a user-defined number of epochs. The process used to be offline and the generated model static. The main motivation for this training method is the reduced number of examples with respect to its representation capacity, which may lead to overfitting of the data. The only reason for multiple scans of training data is lack of data – small training sets.

In a seminal book, Bishop (1995, page 304) wrote:

> *However, if the generator of the data itself evolves with time, then this [static] approach is inappropriate and it becomes necessary for the network model to adapt to the data continuously so that "track" the time variation. This requires on-line learning techniques, and raises a number of important issues, many of which are at present largely unresolved and lie beyond the scope of this book.*

The streaming setting, mainly due to the abundance of data, is an advantage that can full exploit the potentialities of neural network based algorithms. Craven and Shavlik (1997) argue that the inductive bias of neural networks is the most appropriate for sequential and temporal prediction tasks.

11.2.3.1   Stochastic Sequential Learning of Neural Networks

Natural and intuitive, this approach consists of propagating each training example and backpropagating the error through the network only once, as data is abundant and continuously flow. The stochastic sequential learning of the MLP is as follows. At each moment t, the system receives an example $\langle \vec{x}_t, y_t \rangle$ and executes two actions. The first consists of propagating $\vec{x}_t$ through the network, and computing the output of the network $\hat{y}_t$. $\hat{y}_t$ is compared with the observed value y_t, and the error is backpropagated while updating the weights. The example can be discarded, and the process continues with the next example.

The main advantage of the stochastic sequential learning method used to train the neural network is the ability to process an infinite number of examples at high speed. Both operations of propagating the example and backpropagating the error through the network are very efficient and can follow high-speed data streams. This training procedure is robust to overfitting, because each example is propagated through the network and the error backpropagated only once. Another advantage is the smooth adaptation in dynamic data streams where the target function gradually evolves over time.

11.2.3.2 Illustrative Example: Load Forecast in Data Streams

Consider the illustrative example described in Section 1.2, where sensors distributed all around electrical-power distribution networks produce streams of data at high-speed. The goal of the system we briefly describe in the following sections[1] is to continuously maintain a predictive model, in each sensor, for three time horizons: next hour, one day ahead, and one week ahead. Remember that at time t our predictive model made a prediction $\hat{y}_{t+k}$, for the time $t + k$, where k is the desired horizon forecast. Later on, at time $t + k$ the sensor measures the quantity of interest y_{t+k}, and we can then estimate the loss of our prediction $L(\hat{y}_{t+k}, y_{t+k})$.

Each sensor is equipped with a feed-forward neural network. The networks may have different topologies for each sensor and are trained with different inputs depending on the horizon forecast. The topology of the neural networks uses 10 inputs, 4 hidden neurons ($tanh$-activated) and a linear output. As usual (Khotanzad et al., 1997), besides the historical values, we consider also four cyclic variables, for hourly and weekly periods (sin and cos). The choice of the networks topology and inputs was mainly motivated by experts' suggestions, autocorrelation analysis and previous work with batch approaches (Hippert et al., 2001). One implication of the chosen inputs is that we no longer maintain the property of processing each observation once. The training of neural networks requires the use of some historical values of each variable to predict. Thus, we introduce a buffer (window with the most recent values) strategy. The size of the buffer depends on the horizon forecast and data granularity and is at most two weeks. Figure 11.4 presents a general description of the procedure executed at each new example.

Overfitting and Variance Reduction. The flexibility of the representational power of neural networks implies error variance. In stationary data streams the variance shrinks when the number of examples go to infinity. In dynamic environments where the target functions smoothly change and even abrupt changes can occur, the variance of predictions is problematic. An efficient variance reduction method is the *dual perturb and combine* (Geurts, 2001) approach. It consists of perturbing each test example several times, adding white noise to the attribute-values, and predicting each perturbed version of the test example. The final prediction is obtained by aggregating (usually by averaging) the different predictions. The method is directly applicable in the stream setting because multiple predictions only involve test examples, which is an advantage over other variance reduction methods like

---

[1]Gama and Rodrigues (2007) present a detailed description of the system.

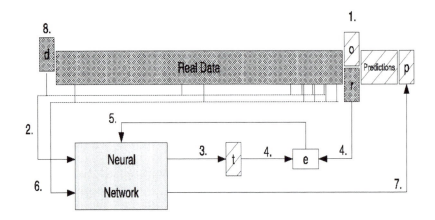

Figure 11.4: Buffered online predictions: 1. new real data arrives (r) at time stamp i, substituting previously made prediction (o); 2. define the input vector to predict time stamp i; 3. execute prediction (t) for time stamp i; 4. compute error using predicted (t) and real (r) values; 5. back-propagate the error one single time; 6. define input vector to predict time stamp i plus the requested horizon; 7. execute prediction of the horizon (p); 8. discard oldest real data (d).

bagging (Breiman, 1996). We can use the *dual perturb and combine* method with three goals: as a method to reduce the variance exhibited by neural networks; as a method to estimate a confidence for predictions (users seem more comfortable with both a prediction and a confidence estimate on the prediction), which is a very relevant point in industrial applications; and as a robust prevention of the uncertainty in information provided by sensors in noisy environments. For example, if a sensor reads 100, most of the time the real-value is around 100: it could be 99 or 101. Perturbing the test example and aggregating predictions also reduce the uncertainty associated with the measurement sent by the sensor.

Improving Predictive Accuracy using Kalman Filters. Our target function is a continuous and derivable function over time. For these types of time series, one simple prediction strategy, reported elsewhere to work well, consists of predicting for time t the value observed at time $t - k$. A study on the autocorrelation (Figure 11.2) in the time series used to train the neural network reveals that for the next hour forecasts, $k = 1$ is the most autocorrelated value, while for the next day and next week the most autocorrelated one is the corresponding value one week before ($k = 168$). This very simple predictive strategy is used as a *default* rule and as a baseline for comparisons. Any predictive model should improve over this naive estimation.

We use this characteristic of the time series to improve neural nets forecasts, by coupling both using a Kalman filter (Kalman, 1960). The Kalman filter is widely used in engineering for two main purposes: for combining measurements of the same variables but from different sensors, and for combining an inexact forecast of a system's state with an inexact measurement of the state. We use a Kalman filter to combine the neural network forecast with the observed value at time $t - k$, where k depends on the horizon forecast as defined above. The one-dimensional Kalman filter works by considering:

$\hat{y}_i = \hat{y}_{i-1} + K(y_i - \hat{y}_{i-1})$ where $\sigma_i^2 = (1 - K)\sigma_{i-1}^2$ and $K = \frac{\sigma_{i-1}^2}{\sigma_{i-1}^2 + \sigma_r^2}$.

11.3 Similarity between Time-Series

Most of time-series analysis techniques (clustering, classification, novelty detection, etc.) require similarity matching between time-series. Similarity is used to solve problems like: Given a query time series Q and a similarity measure $D(Q, S)$ find the most similar time series in a time-series database D. This is usually known as *Indexing* or *Query by Content*

Similarity measures the degree of resemblance between two or more concepts or objects. Similarity measures over time series data represent the main step in time series analysis. A common measure for similarity consists of measuring some form of *distance* between the time-series. Two usual distances are: The **Euclidean** distance and **dynamic time warping**. They are discussed in the next sections.

11.3.1 Euclidean Distance

The Euclidean distance between two time series is the square-root of the sum of the squared distances from each nth point in one time series to the nth point in the other. Given two time series, $Q = q_1, q_2, \ldots, q_n$ and $C = c_1, c_2, \ldots, c_n$, the Euclidean distance between them is defined as:

$$D(Q, C) = \sqrt{\sum_{i=1}^{n}(q_i - c_i)^2}.$$

Geometrically, the Euclidean distance corresponds to the area delimited by the two time-series (see Figure 11.5). The Euclidean distance satisfies the four properties of a distance:

1. identity: $D(Q, Q) = 0$;

2. is always non-negative: $D(Q, C) \geq 0$;

3. is symmetric: $D(Q, C) = D(C, Q)$;

4. satisfies the triangular inequality: $D(Q, C) + D(C, T) \geq D(Q, T)$.

Figure 11.5: Euclidean Distance between time-series Q and C.

Table 11.1:   The two time-series used in the example of dynamic time-warping.

time-stamp	1	2	3	4	5	6	7	8	9	10	11	12
Query	1.0	0.8	0.8	1.4	1.2	1.0	1.5	1.9	1.5	1.5	1.5	1.6
Reference	0.9	0.8	0.8	1.3	1.4	1.2	1.7	1.8	1.6	1.5	1.5	2.0
time-stamp	13	14	15	16	17	18	19					
Query	1.8	2.8	2.5									
Reference	2.5	2.7	2.9	2.5	3.1	2.4	2.9					

The two time-series must have the same number of elements. It is quite efficient as a distance, but not as a measure of similarity. For example, consider two identical time-series, one slightly shifted along the time axis. Euclidean distance will consider them to be very different from each other.

11.3.2   Dynamic Time-Warping

The dynamic time warping (DTW) algorithm finds the optimal alignment between two time series. It is often used to measure time series similarity, classification, and to find corresponding regions between two time series.

Dynamic time warping (DTW) is an algorithm for measuring similarity between two sequences which may vary in time or speed. DTW is a method to find an optimal match between two given sequences (e.g., time series) with certain restrictions. DTW is optimal in the sense that it minimizes the Euclidean distance between the two time series. The optimization process is performed using dynamic programming. The problem for one-dimensional time series can be solved in polynomial time.

Problem Formulation. The warp path must start at the beginning of each time series at $w_1 = (1,1)$ and finish at the end of both time series at $w_K = (n, p)$. This ensures that every index of both time series is used in the warp path. Another constraint on the warp path forces i and j to be monotonically increasing in the warp path.

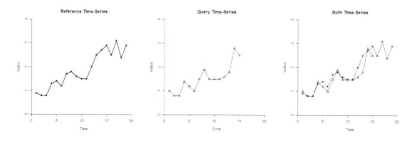

Figure 11.6: The two times-series. The right panel plots the reference time-series; the middle panel plots the query time-series; and the left panel plots both.

Between all possible warp paths, we are interested in the *minimum-distance* warp path. The distance of a warp path W is:

$$Dist(W) = \sum_{k=1}^{k=K} dist(w_{ki}, w_{kj})$$

where $dist(w_{ki}, w_{kj})$ is the Euclidean distance between the two data point indexes (one from X and one from Y) in the kth element of the warp path.

Formally, the dynamic time warping problem is stated as follows:

- Given two time series $X = x_1, x_2, \ldots, x_n$, and $Y = y_1, y_2, \ldots, y_p$, of lengths n and p

- construct a warp path $W = w_1, w_2, \ldots, w_K$

- where K is the length of the warp path and

  - $max(n, p) \leq K < n + p$
  - the kth element of the warp path is $w_k = (i, j)$ where
    * i is an index from time-series X,
    * j is an index from time-series Y.

Vertical sections of the warp path means that a single point in time series X is warped to multiple points in time series Y. Horizontal sections means that a single point in Y is warped to multiple points in X. Since a single point may map to multiple points in the other time series, the time series do not need to be of equal length. If X and Y were identical time-series, the warp path through the matrix would be a straight diagonal line.

To find the minimum-distance warp path, every cell of a cost matrix (of size $n \times p$) must be filled. The value of a cell in the cost matrix is: $D(i, j) = Dist(i, j) + min[D(i - 1, j), D(i, j - 1), D(i - 1, j - 1)]$. In practice very good approximations are obtained by limiting the search of neighbor

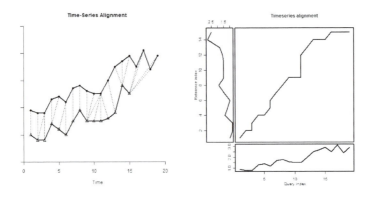

Figure 11.7: Alignment between the two time series. The reference time-series was pushed-up for legibility. The path between the two time series is W={(1,1), (2,2), (3,2), (3,3), (4,4), (5,4), (6,5), (6,6), (7,7), (8,8), (9,9), (10,9), (11,9), (11,10), (11,11), (11,12), (12,13), (13,14), (14,14), (15,14), (16,15), (17,15), (18,15), (19,15)}.

points to a bandwidth. This restriction accelerates all the process and makes it applicable in the streaming setting. Salvador and Chan (2007), among others, resent fast and accurate methods to compute the time warping distance in linear time and space.

11.4   Symbolic Approximation – SAX

Lin, Keogh, Lonardi, and Chiu (2003) present the *Symbolic Approximation – SAX* of time series, allowing a time series with a length n to be transformed into a string with an arbitrary length. The process is linear in time, making it attractive for stream processing. SAX changes the numeric representation of a time series to a string that is a sequence of symbols.

11.4.1   The SAX Transform

SAX is a generic transform and could be applied to any time series analysis technique. It takes linear time, so is a fast symbolic approximation of time series. The SAX transform consists of the three following main steps:

- Piecewise Aggregate Approximation (PAA);

- Symbolic Discretization;

- Distance Measure.

Table 11.2: The SAX lookup table that contains the breakpoints that divide a Gaussian distribution in an arbitrary number of equiprobable regions.

a	3	4	5	6	7	8	9	10
β_1	-0.43	-0.67	-0.84	-0.97	-1.07	-1.15	-1.22	-1.28
β_2	0.43	0	-0.25	-0.43	-0.57	-0.67	-0.76	-0.84
β_3		0.67	0.25	0	-0.18	-0.32	-0.43	-0.52
β_4			0.84	0.43	0.18	0	-0.14	-0.25
β_5				0.97	0.57	0.32	0.14	0
β_6					1.07	0.67	0.43	0.25
β_7						1.15	0.76	0.52
β_8							1.22	0.84
β_9								1.28

11.4.1.1 Piecewise Aggregate Approximation (PAA)

The first step consists of a dimensionality reduction approximation of the original time series. A time series with size n is approximated using PAA to a time series with size w using the following equation:

$$\bar{c}_i = \frac{w}{n} \sum_{j=\frac{w}{n}(i-1)+1}^{\frac{w}{n}i} c_j$$

where $\bar{c}_i$ is the ith element in the approximated time series. w is a user defined parameter and represents the number of episodes (intervals) of the transformed time series. If we plot a time series in a Cartesian space, the piecewise aggregate approximation divides the x axis into a set of intervals of the same size.

11.4.1.2 Symbolic Discretization

The second step of SAX transforms the output of PAA into a string of symbols. It is the symbolic discretization phase. It requires another user defined parameter that is the cardinality of the alphabet of symbols. The objective is a mapping from number to symbols, such that all symbols occur with equal probability. In the Cartesian space representation, the symbolic discretization step divides the y axis into intervals. The number of intervals is given by the alphabet of symbols.

Leonardi et al. (2007) observe that normalized time-series have a Gaussian distribution. Under that assumption, we can determine the breakpoints that will produce equal-size areas, from one point to another, under the Gaussian curve. Breakpoints are a sorted list of numbers $\beta = \beta_1, \ldots, \beta_{\alpha-1}$ that the area under a $N(0,1)$ Gaussian curve from β_i to β_{i+1} is $1/\alpha$. β_0 is defined as $-\infty$ and β_α as $+\infty$. These breakpoints are determined by looking in a statistical table. For example, Table 11.2 gives the breakpoints for values of α between 3 and 10.

According to the output of piecewise aggregate approximation, the coding

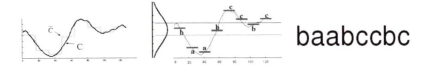

Figure 11.8: The main steps in SAX. a) Piecewise Aggregate Approximation; b) Symbolic Discretization; c) The output SAX string.

schema is: If a point is less than the smallest breakpoint, then it is denoted as a. Otherwise and if the point is greater than the smallest breakpoint and less than the next larger one, then it is denoted as b, etc.

11.4.1.3   Distance Measure

The output of the second step in SAX is a string. How can we work with the string? How can we define a sound metric to work with strings?

The following distance measure is applied when comparing two different SAX strings:

$$MINDIST(\hat{Q}, \hat{C}) = \sqrt{\frac{w}{n} \sum_{1}^{w} dist(\hat{q}_i, \hat{c}_i)^2}$$

where $dist(q, c)$ can be determined using a lookup table (Lin et al., 2003). A relevant property of $MINDIST$ is that it lower bounds the Euclidean distance, that is, for all Q and S, we have $MINDIST(\hat{Q}, \hat{S}) \leq D(Q, S)$.

11.4.1.4   Discussion

SAX provides a symbolic representation for time-series data. Three important properties of SAX are:

- Lower bounding of Euclidean distance;
- Dimensionality and numerosity reduction;
- Compact representation.

Using strings to represent time-series are powerful representations, allowing the use of tools that are difficult or impossible with other representations. SAX has been used for different purposes: Finding motifs in time series (Keogh, Lonardi, and Chiu, 2002; Lin, Keogh, Lonardi, and Chiu, 2003); visualizing massive time series (Lin, Keogh, and Lonardi, 2004; Lin, Keogh, Lonardi, Lankford, and Nystrom, 2004); clustering from streams (Keogh, Lin, and Truppel, 2003); Kolmogorov complexity analysis in data mining (Lin, Keogh, and Lonardi, 2004); and finding *discords* in time series (Keogh, Lin, and Fu, 2005).

11.4.2 Finding *Motifs* Using SAX

Patel, Keogh, Lin, and Lonardi (2002) discuss the problem of identification of previously unknown, frequently occurring patterns in time-series. They call such patterns *motifs*. Motifs are subsequences that repeat in several related sequences. They are useful as a tool for summarizing and visualizing massive time series databases.

Given a positive real number R (called *range*) and a time series T containing a subsequence C beginning at position p and of length n, and a subsequence M beginning at $q > p + n$, if $D(C, M) \leq R$, then M is called a matching subsequence of C. Given a time series T, a subsequence length n and a range R, the most significant motif in T (denoted as *1-Motif*) is the subsequence C_1 that has the highest count of matches. The Kth most significant motif in T (called thereafter *K-Motif*) is the subsequence CK that has the highest count of matches, and satisfies $D(C_K, Ci) > 2R$, for all $1 \leq i < K$.

The *Enumeration of Motifs through Matrix Approximation (*EMMA*)* algorithm begins by sliding a moving window of length n across the time series. The subsequences are normalized, and converted to a symbolic representation with parameters w (word length) and a (alphabet size). A hash function receives as input the SAX string, and computes an integer in the range 1 to w^a: $h(C, w, a) = 1 + \sum_{i=1}^{w}(ord(\hat{c}_i - 1) \times a^{i-1})$ where $ord(\hat{c}_i)$ is the ordinal value of each symbol: $ord(a) = 1$, $ord(b) = 2$ and so forth.

Data is rearranged into a hash table with w^a addresses, and a total of size $O(m)$. This arrangement of the data has the advantage of approximately grouping similar subsequences together. This information is used as a heuristic for motif search. If there is an overrepresented pattern in the time series, we should expect that most copies of it hashed to the same location. The address with the most hits corresponds to the most promising candidate. Nevertheless, it can contain some false positive subsequences. EMMA builds a list of all subsequences that mapped to this address, and uses a brute force algorithm to find the *motifs*.

11.4.3 Finding *Discords* Using SAX

Keogh, Lin, and Fu (2005) extended SAX to the task of discovering the most unusual time series subsequences, called *discords*, in time series. The technique is termed as *Hot* SAX.

Discords are the time series subsequences that are maximally different from the rest of the time series subsequences. Time series discords have many uses for data mining, including data cleaning, and anomaly detection.

A brute force algorithm for finding discords is simple. Given the length of the subsequence, take each possible subsequence of that length and find the distance to the nearest non-self match. The subsequence with the greatest distance is the discord. The brute force technique has complexity n^2, where n is the length of the sequence. The approach based on SAX is 3 to 4 times faster than brute force technique (Keogh et al., 2005). This makes it a candidate for data streaming applications.

Hot-SAX process starts by passing a sliding window of a fixed size over the whole time series. Each window generates one subsequence, which is approximated using SAX. The SAX word is a much lower dimensional representation for the time series. The SAX word is insert in a *trie* and in an array indexed according to its position in the original time series. Leaf nodes in the *trie* contain the array index where the word appears. The index refers to the starting position of the SAX word in the original time-series. The number of occurrences of each SAX word is also inserted in the array. The two data structures (array and trie) complement each other. Both structures can be created in time and space linear to the length of the time-series.

The number of occurrences of each SAX word is used to detect low (or high) frequency patterns. *Discords* are patterns with lower frequency.

11.5 Notes

Time series are a well studied topic in statistics and signal processing. Methods for time series analyses are often divided into two classes: frequency-domain methods and time-domain methods. The reference technique is the ARIMA methodology developed by Box and Jenkins (1976). The analysis of a series of data in the frequency domain includes Fourier transforms and its inverse (Brigham, 1988). More recent techniques, multiresolution techniques, attempt to model time dependence at multiple scales.

Chapter 12

Ubiquitous Data Mining

Over the last few years, a new world of small and heterogeneous devices (mobile phones, PDAs, GPS devices, intelligent meters, etc.) has emerged. They are equipped with limited computational and communication power, and have the ability to sense, to communicate and to interact over some communication infrastructure. These large-scale distributed systems have in many cases to interact in real-time with their users. Ubiquitous Data Mining is an emerging area of research at the intersection of distributed and mobile systems and advanced knowledge discovery systems. In this chapter we discuss some introductory issues related to distributed mining (Section 12.2) and resource-constraint mining (Section 12.4).

12.1   Introduction to Ubiquitous Data Mining

Many important applications require processing data streams originated from or sent to resource-constrained distributed computing environments. The dissemination of personal digital assistants (PDAs), smart phones, and GPS systems users might request sheer amounts of data of interest to be streamed to their mobile devices. Storing, retrieving, and querying these huge amounts of data are infeasible due to resource limitations. Data stream mining can play an important role in helping mobile users in on-the-move decision making. This chapter focuses on techniques for mining distributed streams in resource-aware environments.

The emergence of all kinds of sensor networks, RFIDs, etc. allows remote data collection. The most recent generation of sensors is equipped with computational power and communications devices. Knowledge discovery in these environments has unlimited research opportunities. To be able to act autonomously, sensors must *sense their environment and receive data from other devices*, and make sense of the gathered data. Sensors must *adapt continuously to changing environmental conditions* (including their own condition) and evolving user habits and needs. This touches both short-term and real-time adaptiveness and longer term capability for incremental learning and changes detection. Moreover, they are *resource-aware* because of the real-time constraint of limited memory, computer, and battery power and communication resources.[1]

12.2   Distributed Data Stream Monitoring

Bhaduri and Kargupta (2008) present an overview on distributed mining approaches. The authors consider:

- The *periodic* approach is to simply rebuild the model from time to time;

- The *incremental* approach is to update the model whenever the data changes;

- The *reactive* approach is to monitor the change, and rebuild the model only when it no longer suits the data.

Their analysis of the different approaches is:

> *The* periodic *approach can be highly inefficient since there is the risk of wasting resources even if the data is stationary and also the risk of model inaccuracy if the updating is delayed.* Incremental *algorithms are very efficient; however their major drawback is that a separate algorithm needs to be handcrafted for every problem. Data driven* reactive *algorithms are efficient, simple and can accommodate a wide variety of function computation.*

Reactive approaches in data mining tasks over P2P networks appear in Wolff et al. (2006) for local L2-thresholding; Schuster et al. (2005) for association rule mining; Bhaduri and Kargupta (2008) for multivariate regression; Bhaduri et al. (2008) for learning distributed decision-trees, etc.

Some illustrative examples of real-time distributed stream mining include: The MobiMine (Kargupta et al., 2002) system, a client/server PDA-based distributed data mining application for financial data streams. The server computes the most active stocks in the market, and the client in turn selects a subset of this list to construct the personalized WatchList according to an optimization module. The *EnVironment for On-Board Processing - EVE* (Tanner et al., 2003) is used for astronomical data stream mining. Data streams are generated from measurements of different on-board sensors. Only interesting patterns are sent to the ground stations for further analysis preserving the limited bandwidth.

---

[1]We should point out a step in this direction by the VFDT algorithm, described in Chapter 8. VFDT has the ability to deactivate all less promising leaves in the case where the maximum of available memory is reached. Moreover, the memory usage is also minimized, eliminating attributes that are less promising.

Algorithm 30: The Randomized Distributed Dot Product Algorithm.

---

1 - A sends B a random number generator seed.

2 - A and B cooperatively generate $k \times m$ random matrix R where $k \ll m$. Each entry is generated independently and identically from some fixed distribution with mean zero and finite variance.

3 - A and B compute $\hat{a} = Ra$, $\hat{b} = Rb$, respectively.

4 - A sends $\hat{a}$ to B.

5 - B computes $D = \frac{\hat{a}^T \hat{b}}{k}$

The *MineFleet* system (Kargupta et al., 2007) is a real-time mobile data stream mining environment where the resource-constrained *small* computing devices need to perform various non-trivial data management and mining tasks on-board a vehicle in real-time. MineFleet analyzes and monitors the data generated by the vehicle's on-board diagnostic system and the Global Positioning System (GPS). It continuously monitors data streams generated by a moving vehicle using an on-board computing device, identifies the emerging patterns, and reports these patterns to a remote control center over a low-bandwidth wireless network connection. This involves computing various empirical properties of the data distribution such as correlation, inner-product, and Euclidean distance matrices in a resource-constrained environment.

12.2.1 Distributed Computing of Linear Functions

To illustrate the challenges that emerge from distributed data, consider two sets of measurements $q = (q_1, \ldots, q_m)$ and $s = (s_1, \ldots, s_m)$ at two distributed sites Q and S, respectively. Suppose we want to approximate the Euclidean distance between them.

The problem of computing the Euclidean distance between a pair of data vectors q and s can be represented as:

$$\sum_{i=1}^{m} (q_i - s_i)^2 \Leftrightarrow \sum_{i=1}^{m} (q_i^2 + s_i^2 - 2q_i s_i) \Leftrightarrow \sum_{i=1}^{m} q_i^2 + \sum_{i=1}^{m} s_i^2 - 2 \sum_{i=1}^{m} q_i s_i.$$

Each node has information to compute the sum of squares of its own data points, the main problem is in computing $\sum q_i \times s_i$, that is the dot product $\langle q \cdot s \rangle$, because it requires sharing information between peers. How can we compute the Euclidean distance, minimizing the messages between Q and S?

Randomization is a useful technique in distributed computing. A simple and communication efficient example of randomization techniques for computing the inner product between two vectors observed at two different sites is illustrated by Algorithm 30 (Park and Kargupta, 2002). Instead of sending a m-dimensional vector to the other site, we only need to send a k-dimensional vector where $k \ll m$ (a user-defined parameter) and the dot product can still be estimated accurately. As a matter of fact, it can be shown that the expected value of D is $\langle q \cdot s \rangle$.

12.2.1.1   A General Algorithm for Computing Linear Functions

Wolff, Bhaduri, and Kargupta (2009) present a general algorithm to compute functions of linear combinations of the data in a distributed system.

Consider a set of peers $V = \{p_1, \ldots, p_n\}$ connected to one another via some communication infrastructure. The set of peers with which p_i can directly communicate N_i is known to p_i. Each p_i measures a time varying input vector in $\Re^d$. Peers send sets of input vectors to their neighbors. Denote $X_{i,j}$ the latest set of vectors sent by peer p_i to p_j. Thus, the latest set of input vectors known to p_i is $K_i = \bigcup_{p_j \in N_i} X_{j,i}$, which is designated by the *knowledge of p_i*. The *agreement* between p_i and any neighbor $p_j \in N_i$ is $A_{i,j} = X_{i,j} \cup X_{j,i}$. The *withheld knowledge* of p_i with respect to a neighbor p_j is the difference between agreement and knowledge $W_{i,j} = K_i \setminus A_{i,j}$. The set of all inputs is the *global input*: $G = \bigcup_{p_i \in V} X_{i,i}$. The goal is to induce linear functions F over G. Since G is not available at any peer p_i, Wolff et al. (2009) derive conditions on K_i, $A_{i,j}$ and $W_{i,j}$ which allow to learn F in G. The main result is the theorem:

Theorem 12.2.1 (Convex Stopping Rule) *Let $G(V, E)$ be a spanning tree in which V is a set of peers and let $X_{i,i}$ be the input of peer p_i, K_i be its knowledge and $A_{i,j}$ and $W_{i,j}$ be its agreement and withheld knowledge with respect to a neighbor $P_j \in N_i$. Let $R \subseteq \Re^d$ be any convex region. If at a given time no message traverses the network and for all p_i and $p_j \in N_i$, and $\overline{K_i} \in R$ and $\overline{A_{i,j}} \in R$ and either $W_{i,j} = 0$ or $\overline{W_{i,j}} \in R$, then $\overline{G} \in R$.*

The relevance of Theorem 12.2.1 is that, under the conditions described, $\overline{K_i}$ and $\overline{G}$ reside in the same convex region, so p_i can stop sending messages to its neighbors and output $||\overline{K_i}||$. If the conditions of the theorem hold for every peer, the Theorem 12.2.1 guarantees this is the correct solution; otherwise there must be messages in transit, or some peer p_k for whom the condition does not hold. In this case, p_k must send a message that will change its output, or will receive a message that eventually changes $\overline{K_i}$.

Based on this theorem, the authors present several specific algorithms for specific functions F. Here, we will focus on an interesting function: thresholding the $L2$ norm of the average vector, that is deciding if $||G|| < \epsilon$ (Algorithm 31). In this case, the area where F is true is inside of an ϵ circle and is convex. This area is denoted by R_{in}. The area outside the ϵ-circle can be divided using tangents to random unit vectors $\hat{u}_i$ that define convex half-regions $H_j = \{\vec{x} : \vec{x} \cdot \hat{u}_j \geq \epsilon\}$. They are entirely outside the circle, so F is false. The area between the half-spaces and the circle is a tie area (T). The space is covered by $\{R_{in}, H_1, \ldots, H_l, T\}$ (see Figure 12.1a).

If, for every peer and each of its neighbors, both the agreement and the withheld knowledge are in a convex shape, then so is the global average (see

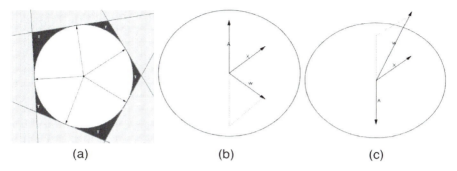

(a)   (b)   (c)

Figure 12.1: The left figure plots the cover of the space: the ϵ-circle is in white, the half-spaces are defined by the tangents to vectors $\vec{u}$ in gray, and the *tie* regions in dark. For peer p_i: $\vec{X}$ is its own estimate of global average, $\vec{A}$ is the agreement with neighbor P_j, and $\vec{W}$ is the withheld knowledge with respect to neighbor P_j ($\vec{W} = \vec{X} - \vec{A}$). In the first figure all the peer estimates are inside the circle. Both the agreement and withheld knowledge are inside too. Hence according to the theorem, the global average is inside the circle.

Figure 12.1b). Each peer p_i checks if its X_i, $A_{i,j}$ and $W_{i,j}$ are inside a circle of radius ϵ (Figure 12.1b), outside the polygon defined by the tangents to d spaced vectors (Figure 12.1c) of length ϵ, or between the circle and the polygon, the *tie* region. In the first case, the peer does not need to send data. In the second case, peers need to communicate to verify if the conditions of the theorem hold. In the third case, the peer has to propagate any data it has to its neighbors.

The Algorithm 31 is event driven. A peer needs to send a message when its local data change, if it receives a message from another peer, or if the set of neighbors changes. In any of these cases, the peer checks if the condition of the theorem holds. First, the peer P_i finds the region R such that $\vec{K}_i \in R$. If $R = T$, then $\vec{K}_i$ is in a tie region and hence P_i has to send all its data. If, for all $P_j \in N_i$, both $\vec{A}_{i,j} \in R$ and $\vec{W}_{i,j} \in R$, P_i does nothing; otherwise it needs to set $X_{i,j}$ and $X_{i,j}$ and send these, such that after the message is sent, the condition of the theorem holds for this peer. Similarly, whenever it receives a message ($\vec{X}$ and $|\vec{X}|$), it sets $\vec{X}_{j,i} \leftarrow \vec{X}$ and $|\vec{X}_{j,i}| \leftarrow |\vec{X}|$. This may trigger another round of communication since its $\vec{K}_i$ can now change. The algorithm is intended for asynchronous systems. This is the justification for the waiting loop to restrict the frequency in which messages are sent.

12.2.2 Computing Sparse Correlation Matrices Efficiently

Sparse correlation matrices are of particular interest because of their use in monitoring applications. As pointed out in Kargupta, Puttagunta, Klein, and Sarkar (2007), such correlation matrices are widely prevalent, since in most

---

Algorithm 31: Local L2 Thresholding.

Input of peer p_i: ϵ, L, $X_{i,i}$, N_i, l

Global constants: A random seed s

Data structure for p_i: For each $p_j \in N_i$ $\overline{X_{i,j}}$, $|X_{i,j}|$, $\overline{X_{j,i}}$, $|X_{j,i}|$, last_message

Output of peer p_i: 0 if $||\overline{K_i}|| < \epsilon$, 1 otherwise

Computation of $\Re_F$:

- Let $R_{in} = \{\vec{x} : ||\vec{x}|| \leq \epsilon\}$
- Let $\hat{u}_1, \ldots, \hat{u}_l$ be pseudo-random unit vectors
- Let $H_j = \{\vec{x} : \vec{x} \cdot \hat{u}_j \geq \epsilon\}$
- Let $\Re_F = \{R_{in}, H_1, \ldots, H_l, T\}$

Computation of $\overline{X_{i,j}}$ **and** $|X_{i,j}|$:

$|X_{i,j}| \leftarrow \frac{|K_i|\overline{K_i} - |X_{j,i}|\overline{X_{j,i}}}{|K_i| - |X_{j,i}|}$

$w \leftarrow |X| \leftarrow |K_i| - |X_{j,i}|$

while $(A_{i,j} \notin R_F(K_i) \text{ or } \overline{W_{i,j}} \notin R_F(\overline{K_i}) \text{ and } |W_{i,j}| \neq 0)$ **do**

    $\lfloor \; w \leftarrow |w/2| \text{ and } \overline{X_{i,j}} \leftarrow |K_i| - |X_{j,i}| - w$

Initialization: $last\_message \leftarrow -\infty, compute R_F$

On receiving a message $\overline{X}, |X|$ **from** p_j:

- $\overline{X_{i,j}} \leftarrow \overline{X}$ and $|X_{i,j}| \leftarrow |X|$

On change in $X_{i,i}$, N_i, $\overline{K_i}$ **or** $|K_i|$: call OnChange()

OnChange():

- **foreach** $p_j \in N_i$: **do**

    if *one of the following conditions occur:*

    - *1* $R_F(\overline{K_i}) = T$ *and either* $\overline{A_{i,j}} \neq \overline{K_i}$ *or* $|A_{i,j}| \neq |K_i|$

    - *2* $|W_{i,j}| = 0$ *and* $|A_{i,j}| \neq |K_i|$

    - *3* $A_{i,j} \notin R_F(\overline{K_i})$ *or* $W_{i,j} \notin R_F(\overline{K_i})$ **then**

        $\lfloor$ call SendMessage(p_j)

SendMessage(p_j):

- **if** $time() - last\_message \geq L$ **then**

    if $R_F(\overline{K_i}) = T$ **then**

        $\lfloor$ $\overline{X_{j,i}} \leftarrow \overline{W_{j,i}}$

        $\lfloor$ $|X_{j,i}| \leftarrow |W_{j,i}|$

    else

        Compute $\overline{X_{j,i}}$ and $|X_{j,i}|$

        $last\_message \leftarrow time()$

        $\lfloor$ Send $\overline{X_{j,i}}$ and $|X_{j,i}|$ to p_j

else

    $\lfloor$ Wait $L - (time() - last\_message)$ time units and call OnChange()

---

real-life high-dimensional applications features are not highly correlated with every other feature. Instead, only a small group of features are usually highly correlated with each other. This results in a sparse correlation matrix. In most stream applications, for example those previously enumerated in this chapter, the difference in the consecutive correlation matrices generated from two subsequent sets of observations is usually small, thereby making the difference matrix a very sparse one.

In the following we present the FMC algorithm, developed by Kargupta et al. (2007), to determine the significant coefficients in a matrix generated from the difference of the correlation matrices obtained at different times. The method is used to:

1. Detect significant correlation coefficients;

2. Detect whether something changed in the correlations matrix;

3. Identify subspaces in the correlation matrix that are likely to contain the significantly changed coefficients.

12.2.2.1 Monitoring Sparse Correlation Matrices

Given a data matrix U with m observations and n features, the correlation matrix is computed by $U^T U$, assuming that the columns of U are normalized to have zero mean and unit length. A straightforward approach to compute the correlation matrix using matrix multiplication takes $O(mn^2)$ number of multiplications. FMC (Kargupta et al., 2007) uses a more efficient technique for computing and monitoring sparse correlation matrices. In order to achieve this, the authors first demonstrate how to estimate the sum of squared values of the elements in the correlation matrix that are above the diagonal. They define this sum as $C = \sum_{1 \leq j_1 < j_2 \leq n} Corr^2(j_1, j_2)$, where $Corr(j_1, j_2) = \sum_{i=1}^{m} u_{i,j_1} u_{i,j_2}$ represents the correlation coefficient between the feature corresponding to the j_1–th and j_2–th columns of the data matrix U. This approach uses a randomized algorithm (Motwani and Raghavan, 1997) to compute C, which will be used to test the existence of significant correlation coefficients. Consider an $m \times n$ data matrix U and an n-dimensional random vector $\sigma = [\sigma_1, \sigma_2, \cdots, \sigma_n]^T$, where each $\sigma_j \in \{-1, 1\}$ is independently and identically distributed. Let v_i be a random projection of the i-th row of the data matrix U using this random vector σ, that is: $v_i = \sum_{j=1}^{n} u_{i,j} \sigma_j$. Define a random variable $Z = (\sum_{i=1}^{m} v_i^2 - n)/2$ and $X = Z^2$. Then,

$$E[X] = C = \sum_{1 \leq j_1 < j_2 \leq n} Corr^2(j_i, j_2) \tag{12.1}$$

and $Var[X] \leq 2C^2$, where $E[X]$ and $Var[X]$ represent the expectation and the variance of the random variable X, respectively.

12.2.2.2 Detecting Significant Correlations

Given a subset $L = \{j_1, j_2, \cdots, j_k\}$ of k–columns from the data matrix U, let U_L be the data matrix with only data column vectors from the set L, i.e. $U_L = [u_{j_1}, u_{j_2}, \cdots u_{j_k}]$. In order to detect if any of these columns are strongly correlated, we first estimate C for U_L using the previous approach. Let C_L be the true value of C over this pruned dataset and Y_L be the estimated value. If any of the correlation coefficients has a magnitude greater than θ, then the true value of C_L must be a value greater than or equal to θ^2 (from Chebyshev inequality). This test is used to determine whether or not there are any significant correlations among the data columns in U_L. If the estimated value Y_L is less than θ^2, we declare that the columns $L = \{j_1, j_2, \cdots, j_k\}$ are not significantly correlated.

This technique can be used to design a divide and conquer strategy that first checks the possible existence of any significant correlation coefficient among a set of data columns before actually checking out every pair-wise coefficient. If the test turns out to be negative, then we discard the corresponding correlation coefficients for further consideration. The algorithm performs a tree-search in the space of all correlation coefficients. Every leaf-node of this tree is associated with a unique coefficient; every internal node a is associated with the set of all coefficients corresponding to the leaf-nodes in the subtree rooted at node a. The algorithm tests to see if the estimated $C_a \geq \theta^2$ at every node starting from the root of the tree. If the test determines that the subtree is not expected to contain any significant coefficient, then the corresponding sub-tree is discarded. Otherwise, the search proceeds in this sub-tree.

12.2.2.3 Dealing with Data Streams

Let $U^{(t)}$ and $U^{(t+1)}$ be the consecutive data blocks at times t and $t + 1$ respectively. Let $Corr(j_1^{(t)}, j_2^{(t)})$ be the correlation coefficients between the j_1–th column and the j_2–th column of $U^{(t)}$ and, similarly, let $Corr(j_1^{(t+1)}, j_2^{(t+1)})$ be the correlation coefficients between j_1–th column and j_2–th column of $U^{(t+1)}$. Along the same lines, let $Z^{(t)}$ and $Z^{(t+1)}$ be the estimated values of Z for the two data blocks at times t and $t+1$, respectively. Let $X^{(t)}$ and $X^{(t+1)}$ be the corresponding estimated values of X. Note that we use the same σs for computing $X^{(t)}$ as well as $X^{(t+1)}$. Let us define,

$$\Delta^{(t+1)} = Z^{(t+1)} - Z^{(t)}$$

Then we can find the expected value of $\left(\Delta^{(t+1)}\right)^2$ in a manner similar to finding $E[X]$ described earlier (Equation 12.1).

$$E\left[\left(\Delta^{(t+1)}\right)^2\right] = \sum_{1 \leq j_1 < j_2 \leq n} \left(Corr(j_i^{(t+1)}, j_2^{(t+1)}) - Corr(j_i^{(t)}, j_2^{(t)})\right)^2$$

This can be used to directly look for significant changes in the correlation matrix using the divide and conquer strategy previously described. This method is used to detect whether something changed in the correlations matrix, and identify subspaces in the correlation matrix that are likely to contain the significantly changed coefficients.

12.3   Distributed Clustering

Consider a sensor network scenario where each sensor produces a continuous stream of data. Suppose we have m distributed sites, and each site i has a data source S_i^t at time t. The goal is to continuously maintain a k-means clustering of the points in $S^t = \cup_i^m S_i^t$.

12.3.1   Conquering the Divide

This problem has been discussed in a seminal paper *Conquering the Divide: Continuous Clustering of Distributed Data Streams* (Cormode et al., 2007), where several distributed algorithms were discussed. The base algorithm is the *Furthest Point* clustering (Gonzalez, 1985), a 2-approximation of the optimal clustering.

12.3.1.1   Furthest Point Clustering

The base idea consists of randomly selecting the first cluster center c_1 among data points. Subsequent $k - 1$ cluster centers are chosen as the points that are more distant from the previous centers $C = \{c_1, c_2, \ldots, c_{i-1}\}$, by maximizing the minimum distance to the centers. This algorithm requires k passes over training points. It has an interesting property. It ensures a 2-approximation of the optimal clustering. A skeleton of the proof is: Suppose that the $k + 1$ iteration produces $k + 1$ points separated by a distance at least D. The optimal k clustering must have a diameter at least D. By the triangular inequality, the chosen clustering has diameter of at most $2 \times D$.

12.3.1.2   The Parallel Guessing Clustering

Based on the *Furthest Point* algorithm, Cormode et al. (2007) developed a one pass clustering algorithm: the *Parallel Guessing Clustering*. The base idea consists in selecting an arbitrary point (p_j) as the first center. The set of centers is initialized as $C = \{p_j\}$. Then, for each incoming point p, compute $r_p = min_{c \in C} d(p, c)$. If $r_p > R$, set $C = C \cup p$. This strategy would be correct if we knew R. However, in unbounded data streams, R is unknown in advance. The solution proposed by Cormode et al. (2007) consists of making multiple guesses for R as $(1+\epsilon/2)$, $(1+\epsilon/2)^2$, $(1+\epsilon/2)^3$, and run the algorithm in parallel. If a guess for the value of R generates more than k centers, this implies that R is smaller than the optimal radius (R_o). When $R \geq 2R_0$ and k or less centers are found, then a valid clustering is generated. Each local site maintains a *Parallel Guessing Algorithm* using its own data source. Whenever it reaches a solution, it sends to the coordinator the k centers and the radius R_i. Each local site only re-sends information when the centers change. The coordinator site maintains a *Furthest Point Algorithm* over the centers sent by local sites.

12.3.2   *DGClust* – Distributed Grid Clustering

Rodrigues et al. (2008) present a distributed grid clustering algorithm for sensor networks. The main intuition behind DGClust is to reduce dimensionality, by monitoring and clustering only frequent states, and communication, by applying online sensor data discretization and controlled transmission to a central server. Each local sensor receives data from a given source, producing a univariate data stream, which is potentially infinite. Data are processed locally, being incrementally discretized into a univariate adaptive grid. Each new data point triggers a cell in this grid, reflecting the current state of the data stream at the local site. Whenever a local site changes its state, that is, the triggered cell changes, the new state is communicated to a central site.

The central site keeps the global state of the entire network where each local site's state is the cell number of each local site's grid. The number of cell combinations to be monitored by the central site can be huge in large sensor networks. However, it is expected that only a small number of these combinations are frequently triggered by the whole network, as observed in the example sketched in Figure 12.2. Thus, the central site keeps only a small list of counters of the most frequent global states. Finally, the current clustering definition is defined and maintained by a simple adaptive partitional clustering algorithm applied on the frequent states central points.

12.3.2.1   Local Adaptive Grid

The incremental discretization at each sensor univariate stream X_i uses the *Partition Incremental Discretization* (*PiD*) algorithm (Gama and Pinto, 2006),[2] which consists of two layers. The first layer simplifies and summarizes the data, while the second layer constructs the final grid. Within the scope of this work, we consider only equal-width discretization. Although equal-frequency discretization may seem better, it implies heavier computation and communication, and its benefits fade out with the frequent state monitoring step.

Each local site i keeps the two-layered discretization of the univariate stream, with p_i intervals in the first layer and w_i intervals in the second layer, where $k < w_i << p_i$ but $w_i \in O(k)$. At each time t, each local sensor produces a value $X_i(t)$ and defines its local discretized state $s_i(t)$, drawn from the set of possible states S_i, the unit cells in the univariate grid ($|S_i| = w_i$). If no value is read, or $s_i(t) = s_i(t-1)$, no information is sent to the central site. The pro-

---

[2]Described in Section 4.3.

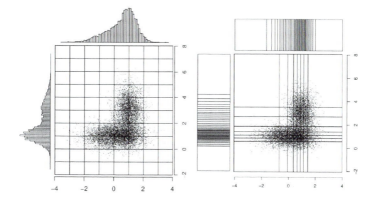

Figure 12.2: Example of a 2-sensor network. Although the number of cells to monitor increases exponentially with the number of sensors (dimensions), and unless data is uniformly distributed in all dimensions (extremely unlikely in usual data) the data occupy much fewer cells. Left plot presents an equal-width discretization, while right plot presents an equal-frequency discretization.

cess of updating the first layer works online, doing a single scan over the data stream, hence being able to process infinite sequences of data, processing each example in constant time and (almost) constant space. The update process of the second layer works online along with the first layer. For each new example $X_i(t)$, the system increments the counter in the second-layer cell where the triggered first-layer cell is included, defining the discretized state $s_i(t)$. The grid represents an approximated histogram of the variable produced at the local site.

The central site monitors the global state of the network at time t by combining each local discretized state $s(t) = \langle s_1(t), s_2(t), ..., s_d(t)\rangle$. Each $s(t)$ is drawn from a finite set of cell combinations $E = \{e_1, e_2, ..., e_{|E|}\}$, with $|E| = \prod_{i=1}^{d} w_i$. Given the exponential size of E, the central site monitors only a subset F of the top-m most frequent elements of E, with $k < |F| << |E|$. Relevant focus is given to size requirements, as $|E| \in O(k^d)$, but $|F| \in O(dk^\beta)$, with small β. Finally, the top-m frequent states central points are used in an online adaptive partitional clustering algorithm, which defines the current k cluster centers, being afterwards continuously adapted.

12.3.2.2 Frequent State Monitoring

DGClust considers synchronous processing of sensor data. The global state is updated at each time stamp as a combination of each local site's state, where each value is the cell number of each local site's grid, $s(t) = \langle s_1(t), s_2(t), ..., s_d(t)\rangle$. If in that period no information arrives from a given local site i, the central site assumes that site i stays in the previous local state ($s_i(t) \leftarrow s_i(t-1)$). Given that common sensor networks usually imply asynchronous communication, this problem could be easily coped with using a time frame where the central server could wait for data from the nodes.

A major issue with our setting is that the number $|E|$ of cell combinations to be monitored by the central site is exponential to the number of sensors, $|E| = O(w^d)$. However, only a small number of these combinations represent states which are frequently visited by the whole network. This way, the central site keeps a small list, F, of counters of the most frequent global states, whose central points will afterwards be used in the final clustering algorithm, with $|F| = O(dk^\beta)$, for small β.

Each seen global state $e \in E$ is a frequent element f_r whose counter $count_r$ currently estimates that it is the rth most frequent state. The system applies the *Space-Saving* algorithm (Metwally et al., 2005) to monitor only the top-m elements.

One important characteristic of this algorithm is that it tends to give more importance to recent examples, enhancing the adaptation of the system to data evolution. This is achieved by assigning to a new state entering the top-m list one plus the count of hits of the evicted state. Hence, even if this is the first time this state has been seen in the data, it will be at least as important to the system as the one being discarded.

12.3.2.3   Centralized Online Clustering

The goal of DGClust is to find and continuously keep a cluster definition, reporting the k cluster centers. Each frequent state f_i represents a multivariate point, defined by the central points of the corresponding unit cells s_i for each local site X_i. As soon as the central site has a top-m set of states, with $m > k$, a simple partitional algorithm can start, applied to the most frequent states.

In the general task of finding k centers given m points, there are two major objectives: minimize the *radius* (maximum distance between a point and its closest cluster center) or minimize the *diameter* (maximum distance between two points assigned to the same cluster) (Cormode et al., 2007). This strategy gives a good initialization of the cluster centers, computed by finding the center k_i of each cluster after attracting the remaining points to the closest center c_i. This algorithm is applied as soon as the system finds a set of $m' > k$ guaranteed top-m states.

It is known that a single iteration is not enough to converge to the actual centers in simple *k-means* strategies. Hence, we consider two different states on the overall system operation: *converged* and *non-converged*. At every new state $s(t)$ that is gathered by the central site, if the system has not yet converged, it adapts the clusters centers using the m' guaranteed top-m states.

If the system has already converged, two different scenarios might occur. If the current state is being monitored as one of the m' top-m states, then the set of points actually used in the final clustering is the same, so the clustering centers remain the same. No update is performed. However, if the current state has just become *guaranteed* top-m, then the clusters may have changed so we

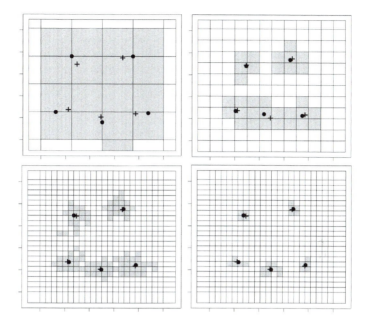

Figure 12.3: Example of final definition for 2 sensors data, with 5 clusters. Each coordinate shows the actual grid for each sensor, with top-m frequent states (shaded cells), gathered (circles) and real (crosses) centers, for different grid resolutions.

move into a non-converged state of the system, updating the cluster centers. Another scenario where the clusters centers require adaptation is when one or more local sites transmit their new grid intervals, which are used to define the central points of each state. In this case, we also update and move to non-converged state.

Figure 12.3 presents an example of a final grid, frequent cells and cluster centers for a specific case with $d = 2$, $k = 5$, for different values of w and m. The flexibility of the system is exposed, as different parameter values yield different levels of results. Moreover, the continuous update keeps track of the most frequent cells, keeping the gathered centers within acceptable bounds. A good characteristic of this system is its ability to adapt to resource-restricted environments: system granularity can be defined given the resources available in the network processing sites.

12.4   Algorithm Granularity

Many important applications require data streams to be originated from or sent to resource-constrained computing environments. Sensing equipments onboard astronomical spacecrafts, for example, generate large streaming data that represent a typical example in this context. Transferring this amount of data to the ground stations for analysis and decision making is infeasible due to bandwidth limitation of the wireless communication (Castano et al., 2003; Srivastava and Stroeve, 2003; Tanner et al., 2003). The applicable solution is for the data analysis to take place onboard the spacecraft. The results are then sent periodically to the ground stations for further analysis by scientists. Another motivating application is analyzing data generated in wireless sensor networks. The same analogy is applied with the additional constraint of having sensor nodes consuming their energy rapidly with data transmission (Bhargava et al., 2003). In-network data analysis onboard sensor nodes are a valid and possible solution to preserve energy consumption.

The last two cases represent the need for onboard data analysis. Data received in resource-constrained environment represent a different category of applications. With the dissemination of personal digital assistants (PDAs) and smart phones, users might request sheer amounts of data of interest to be streamed to their mobile devices. Storing and retrieving these huge amounts of data are also infeasible due to resource limitations. Data stream mining can play an important role in helping mobile users in on-the-move decision making.

The previous cases and others stimulate the need for data stream mining in resource-constrained environments. However, most of the techniques developed so far have addressed the research challenges posed by processing high-speed data streams by applying lightweight techniques without consideration of resource availability (Gaber et al., 2005). There is an obvious need for techniques that can adapt to variations of computational resources. This need is based on the following arguments:

- It has been proven experimentally (Bhargava et al., 2003) that running mining techniques onboard resource-constrained devices consumes less energy than transmitting data streams to a high performance central processing power;

- Extremely large amounts of flowing data streams from 1 Mb/Second for oil drills (Muthukrishnan, 2005) to 1.5 TB/day for astronomical applications (Coughlan, 2004); and

- The resource constraints of data stream sources and processing units in a wide range of stream applications including wireless sensor networks and mobile devices.

The algorithm granularity is the first generic approach to address the issue of adapting the algorithm parameters, and consequently the consumption rate of computational resources dynamically. In the following three sections, details of this approach including an overview, formalization and a generic procedure are presented.

12.4.1 Algorithm Granularity Overview

Resource consumption patterns represent the change in resource consumption over a period of time which we term as time frame. The algorithm granularity settings are the input, output, and processing settings of a mining algorithm that can vary over time to cope with the availability of resources and current data stream arrival rate. The following are definitions of each of these settings:

Algorithm Input Granularity (AIG): represents the process of changing the data stream arrival rates that feed the algorithm. Examples of techniques that could be used include sampling, load shedding, and creating data synopsis.

Algorithm Output Granularity (AOG): is the process of changing the output size of the algorithm in order to preserve the limited memory space. We refer to this output as the number of knowledge structures, for example, number of clusters or association rules.

Algorithm Processing Granularity (APG): is the process of changing the algorithm parameters in order to consume less processing power. Randomization and approximation techniques represent the strategies of *APG*.

It should be noted that there is a collective interaction among the previous three settings. AIG mainly affects the data rate and it is associated with bandwidth consumption and battery. On the other hand, AOG is associated with memory and APG is associated with processing power. However, changes in any of them affect the other resources. The process of enabling resource awareness should be very lightweight in order to be feasible in a streaming environment characterized by its scarcity of resources. Accordingly, the algorithm granularity settings only consider direct interactions, as shown in Figure 12.4.

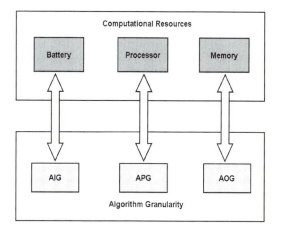

Figure 12.4: The effect of algorithm granularity on computational resources.

12.4.2　Formalization of Algorithm Granularity

The algorithm granularity requires continuous monitoring of the computational resources. This is done over fixed time intervals/frames, here denoted as TF. According to this periodic resource monitoring, the mining algorithm changes its parameters to cope with the current consumption patterns of resources. These parameters are AIG, APG and AOG settings discussed briefly in the previous section. It has to be noted that setting the value of TF is critical for the success of the running technique. The higher the TF is, the lower the adaptation overhead will be, but at the expense of risking a high consumption of resources during the long time frame. The use of algorithm granularity as a general approach for mining data streams will require some formal definitions and notations. The following definitions will be used next:

- R: set of computational resources $R = \{r_1, r_2, \ldots, r_n\}$;

- TF: time interval for resource monitoring and adaptation;

- ALT: application lifetime;

- ALT': time left to last the application lifetime;

- $NoF(r_i)$: number of time frames to consume the resources r_i, assuming that the consumption pattern of r_i will follow the same pattern of the last time frame;

- $AGP(r_i)$: algorithm granularity parameter that affects the resource r_i.

Accordingly, the main rule to be used to use the algorithm granularity approach is as follows:

IF $\frac{ALT'}{TF} > NoF(r_i)$ THEN SET $AGP(r_i)-$ ELSE SET $AGP(r_i)+$

Where $AGP(r_i)+$ achieves higher accuracy at the expense of higher consumption of the resource r_i, and $AGP(r_i)-$ achieves lower accuracy at the advantage of lower consumption of the resource r_i.

This simplified rule could take different forms according to the monitored resource and the algorithm granularity parameter applied to control the consumption of this resource. Interested readers are referred to Gaber and Yu (2007) for applying the above rule in controlling a data stream clustering algorithm termed as *RA-Cluster*.

12.4.2.1　Algorithm Granularity Procedure

Interested practitioners can use the following procedure for enabling resource awareness and adaptation for their data stream mining algorithms. The procedure follows the following steps:

1. Identify the set of resources that mining algorithm will adapt accordingly (R);

2. Set the application lifetime (ALT) and time interval/frame (TF);

3. Define $AGP(r_i)+$ and $AGP(r_i)-$ for every $r_i \in R$;

4. Run the algorithm for TF;

5. Monitor the resource consumption for every $r_i \in R$;

6. Apply $AGP(r_i)+$ or $AGP(r_i)-$ to every $r_i \in R$ according to the ratio $\frac{ALT'}{TF} : NoF(r_i)$ and the rule given in Section 12.4.2;

7. Repeat the last three steps.

Applying the previous procedure is all that is needed to enable resource awareness and adaptation, using the algorithm granularity approach, to stream mining algorithms. Further details on algorithm output granularity are presented in the following sections.

12.4.2.2 Algorithm Output Granularity

The algorithm output granularity is designed in a such way that controls the input/output rate of the mining algorithm taking into account the data stream rate and computational resources availability. AOG operates using three factors to enable the adaptation of the mining algorithm to the available memory:

1. The rate of the incoming data stream;

2. The rate of the algorithm output;

3. From these two, an estimated time to fill the available memory according to the logged history of data rate and algorithm output rate is calculated.

These three factors are used to adjust what we call the algorithm threshold. The algorithm threshold encourages (or not) the creation of new outputs in accordance with the available memory, the data stream rate, and the mining technique. Figure 12.5 shows how the algorithm threshold can control the output rate of a mining algorithm according to the three factors that AOG operates on. The data arrives sequentially and its rate is calculated. The algorithm runs with an initial threshold value, and the rate of the output is calculated. The threshold is adjusted periodically to conserve the available memory according to the relationship among the three factors.

AOG is a three-stage, resource-aware threshold-based data stream mining approach.

1. **Mining Phase**
   In this step, the algorithm threshold that can control the algorithm output rate is determined as an initial value set by the user of the system (or preset to a default initial value).

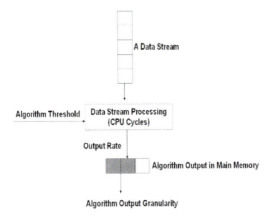

Figure 12.5: The algorithm output granularity approach.

2. **Adaptation Phase**
   In this phase, the threshold value is adjusted to cope with the data rate of the incoming stream, the available memory, and time constraints to fill the available memory with resultant knowledge structures.

3. **Knowledge Integration Phase**
   This phase represents the merging of produced results when the computational device is running out of memory.

AOG has been instantiated for several data mining tasks (Gaber et al., 2004). The approach was implemented for data stream mining in:

- **Clustering**: The threshold is used to specify the minimum distance between the cluster center and the data stream record. Clusters that is within short proximity might be merged.

- **Classification**: In addition to using the threshold in specifying the distance, the class label is checked. If the class label of the stored records and the new item/record that are close (within the accepted distance) is the same, the weight of the stored item is increased and stored along with the weighted average of the other attributes, otherwise the weight is decreased and the new record is ignored.

- **Frequent patterns**: The threshold is used to determine the number of counters for the frequent items and to release the least frequent items from memory.

This integration allows the continuity of the data mining process. Otherwise the computational device would run out of memory even with adapting the algorithm threshold to its highest possible value that results in the lowest

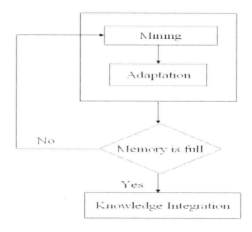

Figure 12.6: Algorithm output granularity stages.

possible generation of knowledge structures Figure 12.6 shows a flowchart of
the AOG-mining process. It shows the sequence of the three stages of AOG.

The algorithm output granularity approach is based on the following rules:

- The algorithm output rate (AR) is a function of the data rate (DR), i.e.,
  $AR = f(DR)$. Thus, the higher the input rate, the higher the output
  rate. For example the number of clusters created over a period of time
  should depend on the number of data records received over this period
  of time.

- The time needed to fill the available memory by the algorithm results
  (knowledge structures namely: clusters, classification models and frequent items) (TM) is a function of (AR), i.e., $TM = f(AR)$. Thus,
  a higher output rate would result in shorter time to fill the available
  memory assigned for the application.

- The algorithm accuracy (AC) is a function of (TM), i.e., $AC = f(TM)$.
  If the time of filling the available memory is considerably short, that
  would result in a higher frequency of knowledge integration such as
  cluster merging. The higher the frequency of knowledge integration, the
  less accurate the results are.

12.5 Notes

Scalable and distributed algorithm for decision tree learning in large and
distributed networks was reported in Bar-Or et al. (2005) and Bhaduri et al.
(2008). Kargupta and Park (2001) present a Fourier analysis-based technique

to analyze and aggregate decision trees in mobile resource-aware environ-ments. Branch et al. (2006) address the problem of unsupervised outlier de-tection in wireless sensor networks. Chen et al. (2004) present distributed algorithms for learning Bayesian networks.

Privacy-preserving data mining (Agrawal and Srikant, 2000) is an emerging research topic, whose goal is to identify and disallow mining patterns that can reveal sensitive information about the data holder. Privacy-preserving is quite relevant in mining sensitive distributed data.

The *gossip* algorithms (Boyd et al., 2006) are a class of distributed asyn-chronous algorithms for computation and information exchange in an arbitrar-ily connected network of nodes. Nodes operate under limited computational, communication and energy resources. These constraints naturally give rise to *gossip* algorithms: schemes which distribute the computational burden and in which a node communicates with a randomly chosen neighbor. Bhaduri and Kargupta (2008) argue that the major drawback of gossip algorithms is their scalability and the slow answer to dynamic data.

Chapter 13

Final Comments

Data mining is faced with new challenges. All of them share common issues: a continuously flow of data generated by evolving distributions, the domains involved (the set of attribute-values) can also be huge, and computation resources (processing power, storage, bandwidth, and battery power) are limited. In this scenario, data mining approaches involving fixed training sets, static models, stationary distributions, and unrestricted computational resources are almost obsolete.

The next generation of data mining implies new requirements to be considered. The algorithms will have to use *limited computational resources* (in terms of computations, space and time). They will have only a *limited direct access to data* and may have to communicate with other agents on *limited bandwidth* resources. In a community of smart devices, answers will have to be ready in an *anytime protocol*. Machine Learning algorithms will have to enter the world of *limited rationality*: they are limited by the information they have, the resources available, and the finite amount of time they have to make decisions. These are the main lessons learned in this book.

13.1 The Next Generation of Knowledge Discovery

Aside from the computational and communication problems inherent to ubiquitous environments, there are issues linked to the nature of the data themselves. As soon as one is contemplating lifelong learning tasks with data originating from various places, new problems arise. Clearly, we can identify three categories of questions. The first one is related to the fact that data are geographically situated. The second is related to the temporal nature of the data generation from which several aspects are important for learning because the underlying regularities may change over time. The third is related with structured (or semi-structured) data available through the Internet, attached with semantic information. In the following, these three categories of problems are examined in turn.

13.1.1   Mining Spatial Data

There are now several data generation environments where the nodes generating the data are spatially spread and interrelated and where these relations are meaningful and important for data mining tasks. Examples include satellite recordings, emergence of mobile phones, GPS and RFID devices, all kind of sensor networks, etc. The spatial information is essential in the discovery of meaningful regularities from data. Work on spatial data mining has been scarce even though applications in satellite remote sensing and geographical databases have spurred a growing interest in methods and techniques to augment databases management and perform data mining with spatial reasoning capabilities.

13.1.2   The Time Situation of Data

The fact that, in ubiquitous environments, data are produced on a real-time basis, or, at least, in a sequential fashion, and that the environment and the task at hand may change over time, profoundly modifies the underlying assumptions (examples are independently and identically distributed) on which most of the existing learning techniques are based, and demands the development of new principles and new algorithms.

When the samples of data are both spatially and time situated, data points can no longer be considered as independently and identically distributed, a fact that is reinforced when the underlying generative process is itself changing over time.

13.1.3   Structured Data

In some challenging applications of data mining, data are better described by sequences (for example DNA data), trees (XML documents), and graphs (chemical components). Tree mining in particular is an important field of research (Bifet and Gavaldà, 2008, 2009). XML patterns are tree patterns, and XML is becoming a standard for information representation and exchange over the Internet; the amount of XML data is growing, and it will soon constitute one of the largest collections of human knowledge.

13.2   Where We Want to Go

What makes current learning problems different from earlier problems is the large volume and continuous flow of distributed data. These characteristics impose new constraints on the design of learning algorithms. Large volumes of data require efficient bias management, while the continuous flow of data requires change detection algorithms to be embedded in the learning process.

But, the main lesson we – researchers in knowledge discovery – can learn from the challenges that ubiquity and flooding data pose is that learning algorithms are limited. Real world is much greater even than a network of computers.

Knowledge discovery from data streams requires the ability of predictive *self-diagnosis*. A significant and useful intelligence characteristic is diagnostics–not only after failure has occurred, but also predictive (before failure) and advisory (providing maintenance instructions). The development of such self-configuring, self-optimizing, and self-repairing systems is a major scientific and engineering challenge. All these aspects require monitoring the evolution of the learning process, taking into account the available resources, and the ability of reasoning and learning about it.

Appendix A

Resources

A.1 Software

Examples of publicly available software for learning from data streams include:

- **VFML:** The VFML (Hulten and Domingos, 2003) toolkit for mining high-speed time-changing data streams.
  Available at http://www.cs.washington.edu/dm/vfml/.

- **MOA:** The MOA (Holmes et al., 2007) system for learning from massive data sets. Available at http://www.cs.waikato.ac.nz/~abifet/MOA/.

- **Rapid-Miner** (Mierswa et al., 2006) is a data mining system with plug-in for stream processing. Available at http://rapid-i.com/.

- **SAX** (Lin et al., 2003) is the first symbolic representation for time series that allows for dimensionality reduction and indexing with a lower-bounding distance measure.
  Available at http://www.cs.ucr.edu/~jessica/sax.htm.

A.2 Datasets

- UCI Knowledge Discovery in Databases Archive, an online repository of large datasets which encompasses a wide variety of data types, analysis tasks, and application areas.
  http://kdd.ics.uci.edu/

- UCR Time-Series Datasets, maintained by Eamonn Keogh, University California at Riverside, US.
  http://www.cs.ucr.edu/~eamonn/time_series_data

- KDD Cup Center, the annual Data Mining and Knowledge Discovery competition organized by ACM Special Interest Group on Knowledge

Discovery and Data Mining.
http://www.sigkdd.org/kddcup/

- Frequent Itemset Mining Dataset Repository.
http://fimi.cs.helsinki.fi/data/

- *Intel Lab Data* contains information about data collected from 54 sensors deployed in the Intel Berkeley Research lab.
http://db.csail.mit.edu/labdata/labdata.html

- Mining Data Streams Bibliography, Maintained by Mohamed Gaber, Monash University, Australia.
http://www.csse.monash.edu.au/~mgaber/WResources.html

- Distributed Data Mining: http://www.umbc.edu/ddm/

- Time Series Data Library: http://www.robjhyndman.com/TSDL/

Some useful datasets information:

- **Led database generator** (available from the UCI repository)
The original problem definition and source is Breiman et al. (1984). This is a simple domain, which contains 7 Boolean attributes and 10 concepts, the set of decimal digits. LED displays contain 7 light-emitting diodes – hence the reason for 7 attributes. Each attribute value has the 10% probability of having its value inverted. The optimal Bayes misclassification rate is 26%.

- **Waveform database generator**(available from the UCI repository)
The original problem definition and source is Breiman et al. (1984). There are two generators available. The first version is defined by 21 numerical attributes. The second one contains 40 attributes. In both versions, each class is generated from a combination of 2 of 3 *base* waves. Each instance is generated with added noise (mean 0, variance 1) in each attribute. It is known that the *optimal Bayes* error is 14%.

- **The *SEA concepts***
The dataset was first described in Street and Kim (2001). It consists of three attributes, where only two are relevant attributes: $x_i \in [0, 10]$, where $i = 1, 2, 3$. The target concept is $x_1 + x_2 \leq \beta$, where $\beta \in \{7, 8, 9, 9.5\}$. The training set has four blocks. For the first block the target concept is with $\beta = 8$. For the second, $\beta = 9$; the third, $\beta = 7$; and the fourth, $\beta = 9.5$. That is, the target concept changes over time.

Bibliography

Abdulsalam, H., D. B. Skillicorn, and P. Martin (2007). Streaming random forests. In *IDEAS '07: Proceedings of the 11th International Database Engineering and Applications Symposium*, Washington, DC, pp. 225–232. IEEE Computer Society.

Aggarwal, C. (2006). On biased reservoir sampling in the presence of stream evolution. In U. Dayal, K.-Y. Whang, D. B. Lomet, G. Alonso, G. M. Lohman, M. L. Kersten, S. K. Cha, and Y.-K. Kim (Eds.), *Proceedings International Conference on Very Large Data Bases*, Seoul, Korea, pp. 607–618. ACM.

Aggarwal, C. (2007). *Data Streams – Models and Algorithms*. Springer.

Aggarwal, C., J. Han, J. Wang, and P. Yu (2003). A framework for clustering evolving data streams. In *Proceedings of the International Conference on Very Large Data Bases*, Berlin, Germany, pp. 81–92. Morgan Kaufmann.

Aggarwal, C., J. Han, J. Wang, and P. Yu (2006). A framework for on-demand classification of evolving data streams. *IEEE Transactions on Knowledge and Data Engineering 18*(5), 577–589.

Agrawal, R., T. Imielinski, and A. Swami (1993, May). Mining association rules between sets of items in large databases. In *Proceedings of the ACM SIGMOD International Conference on Management of Data*, Washington DC, pp. 207–216.

Agrawal, R. and R. Srikant (1994, September). Fast algorithms for mining association rules in large databases. In J. B. Bocca, M. Jarke, and C. Zaniolo (Eds.), *Proceedings of the 20th International Conference on Very Large Data Bases, VLDB*, Santiago, Chile, pp. 487–499. Morgan Kaufmann.

Agrawal, R. and R. Srikant (1995). Mining sequential patterns. In P. S. Yu and A. L. P. Chen (Eds.), *International Conference on Data Engineering*, Taipei, Taiwan, pp. 3–14. IEEE Computer Society.

Agrawal, R. and R. Srikant (2000). Privacy-preserving data mining. In *Proceedings of the ACM SIGMOD International Conference on Management of Data*, Dallas, TX, pp. 439–450. ACM Press.

Akaike, H. (1974). A new look at the statistical model identification. *IEEE Transactions on Automatic Control 19*(6), 716–723.

Asuncion, A. and D. Newman (2007). UCI Machine Learning repository. http://www.ics.uci.edu/~mlearn/MLRepository.html.

Babcock, B., S. Babu, M. Datar, R. Motwani, and J. Widom (2002). Models and issues in data stream systems. In P. G. Kolaitis (Ed.), *Proceedings of the 21nd Symposium on Principles of Database Systems*, Madison, WI, pp. 1–16. ACM Press.

Babcock, B., M. Datar, and R. Motwani (2002). Sampling from a moving window over streaming data. In *Proceedings of the Annual ACM SIAM Symposium on Discrete Algorithms*, San Francisco, CA, pp. 633–634. Society for Industrial and Applied Mathematics.

Babcock, B., M. Datar, R. Motwani, and L. O'Callaghan (2003). Maintaining variance and k-medians over data stream windows. In T. Milo (Ed.) *Proc. of the 22nd Symposium on Principles of Database Systems*, San Diego, CA, ACM Press.

Bar-Or, A., R. Wolff, A. Schuster, and D. Keren (2005). Decision tree induction in high dimensional, hierarchically distributed databases. In *Proceedings SIAM International Data Mining Conference*, Newport Beach, pp. 466–470. SIAM Press.

Barbará, D. (2002, January). Requirements for clustering data streams. *SIGKDD Explorations 3*(2), 23–27.

Barbará, D. and P. Chen (2000). Using the fractal dimension to cluster datasets. In *Proceedings of the ACM International Conference on Knowledge Discovery and Data Mining*, Boston, MA, pp. 260–264. ACM Press.

Barbará, D. and P. Chen (2001). Tracking clusters in evolving data sets. In *Proceedings of the Fourteenth International Florida Artificial Intelligence Research Society Conference*, Key West, FL, pp. 239–243. AAAI Press.

Barnett, V. and T. Lewis (1995). *Outliers in Statistical Data* (3rd ed.). John Wiley & Sons.

Basseville, M. and I. Nikiforov (1993). *Detection of Abrupt Changes: Theory and Applications*. Prentice-Hall Inc.

Bhaduri, K. and H. Kargupta (2008). An efficient local algorithm for distributed multivariate regression in peer-to-peer networks. In *Proceedings SIAM International Conference on Data Mining*, Atlanta, CA, pp. 153–164. SIAM Press.

Bhaduri, K., R. Wolff, C. Giannella, and H. Kargupta (2008). Distributed decision-tree induction in peer-to-peer systems. *Statistical Analysis and Data Mining 1*(2), 85–103.

Bhargava, R., H. Kargupta, and M. Powers (2003). Energy consumption in data analysis for on-board and distributed applications. Technical report, University Maryland.

Bhattacharyya, G. and R. Johnson (1977). *Statistical Concepts and Methods*. New York, John Willey & Sons.

Bifet, A. and R. Gavaldà (2006). Kalman filters and adaptive windows for learning in data streams. In L. Todorovski and N. Lavrac (Eds.), *Proceedings of the 9th Discovery Science*, Volume 4265 of *Lecture Notes on Artificial Intelligence*, Barcelon, Spain, pp. 29–40. Springer.

Bifet, A. and R. Gavaldà (2007). Learning from time-changing data with adaptive windowing. In *Proceedings SIAM International Conference on Data Mining*, Minneapolis, MN, pp. 443–448. SIAM.

Bifet, A. and R. Gavaldà (2008). Mining adaptively frequent closed unlabeled rooted trees in data streams. In *Proceedings of the ACM International Conference on Knowledge Discovery and Data Mining*, Las Vegas, NV, pp. 34–42.

Bifet, A. and R. Gavaldà (2009). Adaptive XML tree classification on evolving data streams. In *Machine Learning and Knowledge Discovery in Databases, European Conference*, Volume 5781 of *Lecture Notes in Computer Science*, Bled, Slovenia, pp. 147–162. Springer.

Birant, D. and A. Kut (2007, January). St-dbscan: An algorithm for clustering spatial-temporal data. *Data Knowledge Engineering 60*(1), 208–221.

Bishop, C. M. (1995). *Neural Networks for Pattern Recognition*. Oxford University Press.

Bock, H. and E. Diday (2000). *Analysis of symbolic data: Exploratory Methods for Extracting Statistical Information from Complex Data*. Springer.

Boulle, M. (2004). Khiops: A statistical discretization method of continuous attributes. *Machine Learning 55*(1), 53–69.

Box, G. and G. Jenkins (1976). *Time series analysis: forecasting and control*. Holden-Day.

Boyd, S., A. Ghosh, B. Prabhakar, and D. Shah (2006). Randomized gossip algorithms. *IEEE Transactions on Information Theory 52*(6), 2508–2530.

Brain, D. and G. Webb (2002). The need for low bias algorithms in classification learning from large data sets. In T.Elomaa, H.Mannila, and H.Toivonen (Eds.), *Principles of Data Mining and Knowledge Discovery PKDD-02*, Volume 2431 of *Lecture Notes in Artificial Intelligence*, Helsinki, Finland, pp. 62–73. Springer.

Branch, J. W., B. K. Szymanski, C. Giannella, R. Wolff, and H. Kargupta (2006). In-network outlier detection in wireless sensor networks. In *IEEE International Conference on Distributed Computing Systems*, pp. 51–60.

Breiman, L. (1996). Bagging predictors. *Machine Learning 24*, 123–140.

Breiman, L. (2001). Random forests. *Machine Learning 45*, 5–32.

Breiman, L., J. Friedman, R. Olshen, and C. Stone (1984). *Classification and Regression Trees*. Wadsworth International Group., USA.

Brigham, E. O. (1988). *The fast Fourier transform and its applications*. Prentice Hall.

Broder, A. Z., M. Charikar, A. M. Frieze, and M. Mitzenmacher (2000). Min-wise independent permutations. *Journal of Computer and System Sciences 60*(3), 630–659.

Buntine, W. (1990). *A Theory of Learning Classification Rules*. Ph.D. thesis, University of Sydney.

Calvo, B., P. Larrañaga, and J. A. Lozano (2007). Learning Bayesian classifiers from positive and unlabeled examples. *Pattern Recognition Letters 28*(16), 2375–2384.

Carpenter, G., M. Rubin, and W. Streilein (1997). ARTMAP-FD: Familiarity discrimination applied to radar target recognition. In *Proceedings of the International Conference on Neural Networks*, Volume III, pp. 1459–1464.

Castano, B., M. Judd, R. C. Anderson, and T. Estlin (2003). Machine learning challenges in Mars rover traverse science. Technical report, NASA.

Castillo, G. and J. Gama (2005). Bias management of Bayesian network classifiers. In A. Hoffmann, H. Motoda, and T. Scheffer (Eds.), *Discovery Science, Proceedings of 8th International Conference*, Volume 3735 of *Lecture Notes in Artificial Intelligence*, Singapore, pp. 70–83. Springer.

Catlett, J. (1991). Megainduction: a test flight. In *Machine Learning: Proceedings of the 8th International Conference*. Chicago, IL, Morgan Kaufmann.

Cauwenberghs, G. and T. Poggio (2000). Incremental and decremental support vector machine learning. In *Proceedings of the Neural Information Processing Systems*.

Cesa-Bianch, N. and G. Lugosi (2006). *Prediction, Learning and Games*. Cambridge University Press.

Cesa-Bianchi, N., Y. Freund, D. P. Helmbold, and M. K. Warmuth (1996). On-line prediction and conversion strategies. *Machine Learning 25*, 71–110.

Chakrabarti, A., K. D. Ba, and S. Muthukrishnan (2006). Estimating entropy and entropy norm on data streams. In *STACS: 23rd Annual Symposium on Theoretical Aspects of Computer Science*, Marseille, France, pp. 196–205.

Chakrabarti, A., G. Cormode, and A. McGregor (2007). A near-optimal algorithm for computing the entropy of a stream. In *Proceedings of ACM-SIAM Symposium on Discrete Algorithms*, Minneapolis, MN, pp. 328–335.

Chakrabarti, K., M. Garofalakis, R. Rastogi, and K. Shim (2001). Approximate query processing using wavelets. *Very Large Data Bases Journal 10*(2–3), 199–223.

Chang, J. H. and W. S. Lee (2003). Finding recent frequent itemsets adaptively over online data streams. In L. Getoor, T. E. Senator, P. Domingos, and C. Faloutsos (Eds.), *Proceedings of the ACM SIGKDD International Conference on Knowledge Discovery and Data Mining*, Washington, DC, pp. 487–492. ACM.

Chang, J. H. and W. S. Lee (2005). estWin: Online data stream mining of recent frequent itemsets by sliding window method. *Journal Information Science 31*(2), 76–90.

Chen, R., K. Sivakumar, and H. Kargupta (2004). Collective mining of Bayesian networks from heterogeneous data. *Knowledge and Information Systems Journal 6*(2), 164–187.

Cheng, J., Y. Ke, and W. Ng (2008). A survey on algorithms for mining frequent itemsets over data streams. *Knowledge and Information Systems 16*(1), 1–27.

Chernoff, H. (1952). A measure of asymptotic efficiency for tests of a hypothesis based on the sums of observations. *Annals of Mathematical Statistics 23*, 493– 507.

Chi, Y., H. Wang, P. S. Yu, and R. R. Muntz (2004). Moment: Maintaining closed frequent itemsets over a stream sliding window. In *Proceedings of the IEEE International Conference on Data Mining*, Brighton, UK, pp. 59–66. IEEE Computer Society.

Chu, F. and C. Zaniolo (2004). Fast and light boosting for adaptive mining of data streams. In H. Dai, R. Srikant, and C. Zhang (Eds.), *PAKDD*, Volume 3056 of *Lecture Notes in Computer Science*, Pisa, Italy, pp. 282–292. Springer.

Cohen, L., G. Avrahami, M. Last, and A. Kandel (2008). Info-fuzzy algorithms for mining dynamic data streams. *Applied Soft Computing 8*(4), 1283–1294.

Cohen, P. (1995). *Empirical Methods for Artificial Intelligence*. MIT Press.

Cormode, G. and M. Hadjieleftheriou (2009). Finding the frequent items in streams of data. *Communications ACM 52*(10), 97–105.

Cormode, G., F. Korn, S. Muthukrishnan, and D. Srivastava (2008). Finding hierarchical heavy hitters in streaming data. *ACM Transactions on Knowledge Discovery from Data 1*(4), 1–48.

Cormode, G. and S. Muthukrishnan (2003). What's hot and what's not: tracking most frequent items dynamically. In *ACM Symposium on Principles of Database Systems 2003*, San Diego, CA, pp. 296–306. ACM Press.

Cormode, G. and S. Muthukrishnan (2005). An improved data stream summary: the count-min sketch and its applications. *Journal of Algorithms 55*(1), 58–75.

Cormode, G., S. Muthukrishnan, and W. Zhuang (2007). Conquering the divide: Continuous clustering of distributed data streams. In *ICDE: Proceedings of the International Conference on Data Engineering*, Istanbul, Turkey, pp. 1036–1045.

Coughlan, J. (2004). Accelerating scientific discovery at NASA. In *Proceedings SIAM International Conference on Data Mining*. FL, SIAM Press.

Craven, M. and J. Shavlik (1997). Using neural networks for data mining. *Future Generation Computer Systems 13*, 211–229.

Dai, B.-R., J.-W. Huang, and M.-Y. Yeh (2006). Adaptive clustering for multiple evolving streams. *IEEE Transactions on Knowledge and Data Engineering 18*(9), 1166–1180.

Dasgupta, D. and S. Forrest (1996). Novelty detection in time series data using ideas from immunology. In *Proceedings of the International Conference on Intelligent Systems*. Cleveland, OH, ISCA Press.

Datar, M., A. Gionis, P. Indyk, and R. Motwani (2002). Maintaining stream statistics over sliding windows. In *Proceedings of Annual ACM-SIAM Symposium on Discrete Algorithms*, San Francisco, CA, pp. 635–644. Society for Industrial and Applied Mathematics.

Dawid, A. P. (1984). Statistical theory: The prequential approach. *Journal of the Royal Statistical Society-A 147*, 278–292.

Demsar, J. (2006). Statistical comparisons of classifiers over multiple data sets. *Journal of Machine Learning Research 7*, 1–30.

Denis, F., R. Gilleron, and F. Letouzey (2005). Learning from positive and unlabeled examples. *Theoretical Computer Science 348*(1), 70–83.

Dietterich, T. (1996). Approximate statistical tests for comparing supervised classification learning algorithms. Corvallis, technical report no. 97.331, Oregon State University.

Dietterich, T. (1997). Machine learning research: four current directions. *AI Magazine 18*(4), 97–136.

Dillon, W. and M. Goldstein (1984). *Multivariate Analysis, Methods and Applications.* J. Wiley & Sons, Inc.

Dobra, A. and J. Gehrke (2002). Secret: a scalable linear regression tree algorithm. In *ACM-SIGKDD Knowledge Discovery and Data Mining*, Edmonton, Canada, pp. 481–487. ACM.

Domingos, P. (1998). Occam's two razor: the sharp and the blunt. In *Proceedings of the 4th International Conference on Knowledge Discovery and Data Mining*, Madison, WI, pp. 37–43. AAAI Press.

Domingos, P. and G. Hulten (2000). Mining High-Speed Data Streams. In I. Parsa, R. Ramakrishnan, and S. Stolfo (Eds.), *Proceedings of the ACM Sixth International Conference on Knowledge Discovery and Data Mining*, Boston, MA, pp. 71–80. ACM Press.

Domingos, P. and G. Hulten (2001). A general method for scaling up machine learning algorithms and its application to clustering. In C. Brodley (Ed.), *Machine Learning, Proceedings of the 18th International Conference*, Walliamstown, PA, pp. 106–113. Morgan Kaufmann.

Domingos, P. and M. Pazzani (1997). On the optimality of the simple Bayesian classifier under zero-one loss. *Machine Learning 29*, 103–129.

Dougherty, J., R. Kohavi, and M. Sahami (1995). Supervised and unsupervised discretization of continuous features. In *Proceedings 12th International Conference on Machine Learning*, Tahoe City, CA, pp. 194–202. Morgan Kaufmann.

Elnekave, S., M. Last, and O. Maimon (2007, April). Incremental clustering of mobile objects. In *International Conference on Data Engineering Workshop*, Istanbul, Turkey, pp. 585–592. IEEE Press.

Faloutsos, C., B. Seeger, A. J. M. Traina, and C. T. Jr. (2000). Spatial join selectivity using power laws. In *SIGMOD Conference*, Dallas, TX, pp. 177–188.

Fan, W. (2004). Systematic data selection to mine concept-drifting data streams. In J. Gehrke and W. DuMouchel (Eds.), *Proceedings of the 10th International Conference on Knowledge Discovery and Data Mining*, Seattle, pp. 128–137. ACM Press.

Fan, W., Y. Huang, H. Wang, and P. S. Yu (2004). Active mining of data streams. In *Proceedings of the SIAM International Conference on Data Mining*, FL, pp. 457–460. SIAM.

Fang, M., N. Shivakumar, H. Garcia-Molina, R. Motwani, and J. D. Ullman (1998). Computing iceberg queries efficiently. In *Proceedings of the International Conference on Very Large Data Bases*, New York, NY, pp. 299–310. Morgan Kaufmann.

Farnstrom, F., J. Lewis, and C. Elkan (2000). Scalability for clustering algorithms revisited. *SIGKDD Explorations 2*(1), 51–57.

Fayyad, U. and K. Irani (1993). Multi-interval discretization of continuous-valued attributes for classification learning. In *13th International Joint Conference of Artificial Intelligence*, Chambéry, France, pp. 1022–1029. Morgan Kaufmann.

Fern, A. and R. Givan (2000). Online ensemble learning: An empirical study. In P. Langley (Ed.), *Machine Learning, Proceedings of the 17th International Conference*, Stanford, CA, pp. 279–186. Morgan Kaufmann.

Ferrer-Troyano, F., J. Aguilar-Ruiz, and J. Riquelme (2005). Incremental rule learning and border examples selection from numerical data streams. *Journal of Universal Computer Science 11*(8), 1426–1439.

Ferrer-Troyano, F., J. S. Aguilar-Ruiz, and J. C. Riquelme (2004). Discovering decision rules from numerical data streams. In *Proceedings of the ACM Symposium on Applied Computing*, Nicosia, Cyprus, pp. 649–653. ACM Press.

Ferrer-Troyano, F. J., J. S. Aguilar-Ruiz, and J. C. Riquelme (2006). Data streams classification by incremental rule learning with parameterized generalization. In *Proceedings of the ACM Symposium on Applied Computing*, Dijon, France, pp. 657–661. ACM.

Fisher, D. H. (1987). Knowledge acquisition via incremental conceptual clustering. *Machine Learning 2*, 139–172.

Flajolet, P. and G. N. Martin (1985). Probabilistic counting algorithms for data base applications. *Journal of Computer and System Sciences 31*(2), 182–209.

Freedman, D. and P. Diaconis (1981). On the histogram as a density estimator: l_2 theory. *Probability Theory 57*(4), 453–476.

Friedman, J. (1999). Greedy function approximation: a gradient boosting machine. Technical report, Statistics Department, Stanford University.

Fürnkranz, J. (2002). Round Robin Classification. *Journal of Machine Learning Research 2*, 721–747.

Fürnkranz, J. and P. A. Flach (2005). Roc 'n' rule learning-towards a better understanding of covering algorithms. *Machine Learning 58*(1), 39–77.

Gaber, M. and P. Yu (2007). A holistic approach for resource-aware adaptive data stream mining. *New Generation Computing 25*(1), 95–115.

Gaber, M., A. Zaslavsky, and S. Krishnaswamy (2005). Mining data streams: A review. *SIGMOD Record 34*(2), 18–26.

Gaber, M. M., A. B. Zaslavsky, and S. Krishnaswamy (2004). Towards an adaptive approach for mining data streams in resource constrained environments. In *International Conference on Data Warehousing and Knowledge Discovery*, Volume 3181 of *Lecture Notes in Computer Science*, Zaragoza, Spain, pp. 189–198. Springer.

Gama, J., R. Fernandes, and R. Rocha (2006). Decision trees for mining data streams. *Intelligent Data Analysis 10*(1), 23–46.

Gama, J. and M. Gaber (2007). *Learning from Data Streams – Processing Techniques in Sensor Networks*. Springer.

Gama, J. and P. Medas (2005). Learning decision trees from dynamic data streams. *Journal of Universal Computer Science 11*(8), 1353–1366.

Gama, J., P. Medas, G. Castillo, and P. Rodrigues (2004, October). Learning with drift detection. In A. L. C. Bazzan and S. Labidi (Eds.), *Advances in Artificial Intelligence - SBIA 2004*, Volume 3171 of *Lecture Notes in Computer Science*, São Luis, Brazil, pp. 286–295. Springer.

Gama, J., P. Medas, and R. Rocha (2004). Forest trees for on-line data. In *Proceedings of the ACM Symposium on Applied Computing*, Nicosia, Cyprus, pp. 632–636. ACM Press.

Gama, J. and C. Pinto (2006). Discretization from data streams: applications to histograms and data mining. In *ACM Symposium on Applied Computing*, Dijou France, pp. 662–667. ACM Press.

Gama, J., R. Rocha, and P. Medas (2003). Accurate decision trees for mining high-speed data streams. In *Proceedings of the ACM SIGKDD International Conference on Knowledge Discovery and Data Mining*, Washington, DC, pp. 523–528. ACM Press.

Gama, J. and P. P. Rodrigues (2007). Stream-based electricity load forecast. In *Proceedings of the European Conference on Principles and Practice of Knowledge Discovery in Databases*, Volume 4702 of *Lecture Notes in Computer Science*, Warsaw, Poland, pp. 446–453. Springer.

Ganti, V., J. Gehrke, and R. Ramakrishnan (2002). Mining data streams under block evolution. *SIGKDD Explorations 3*(2), 1–10.

Gao, J., W. Fan, J. Han, and P. S. Yu (2007). A general framework for mining concept-drifting data streams with skewed distributions. In *SIAM International Conference on Data Mining*, Minneapolis, MN, pp. 3–14. SIAM.

Gehrke, J., V. Ganti, R. Ramakrishnan, and W.-Y. Loh (1999). BOAT-Optimistic Decision Tree Construction. In *Proceedings ACM SIGMOD International Conference on Management of Data*, Philadelphia, PA, pp. 169–180. ACM.

Gehrke, J., R. Ramakrishnan, and V. Ganti (2000). Rainforest - a framework for fast decision tree construction of large datasets. *Data Mining Knowledge Discovery 4*(2/3), 127–162.

Geurts, P. (2001). Dual perturb and combine algorithm. In *Proc. of the Eighth International Workshop on Artificial Intelligence and Statistics*, Key West, FL, pp. 196–201. Springer Verlag.

Ghosh, B. and P. Sen (1991). *Handbook of Sequential Analysis*. Narcel Dekker.

Giannella, C., J. Han, J. Pei, X. Yan, and P. Yu (2004). Mining frequent patterns in data streams at multiple time granularities. In H. Kargupta, A. Joshi, K. Sivakumar, and Y. Yesha (Eds.), *Data Mining: Next Generation Challenges and Future Directions*, pp. 105–124. AAAI/MIT Press.

Gibbons, P. B., Y. Matias, and V. Poosala (1997). Fast incremental maintenance of approximate histograms. In *Proceedings of Very Large Data Bases*, Athens, Greece, pp. 466–475.

Gonzalez, T. F. (1985). Clustering to minimize the maximum intercluster distance. *Theoretical Computer Science 38*(2/3), 293–306.

Granger, C. W. J. and P. Newbold (1976). The use of r2 to determine the appropriate transformation of regression variables. *J. Econometrics 4*, 205–210.

Grant, E. and R. Leavenworth (1996). *Statistical Quality Control*. McGraw-Hill.

Gratch, J. (1996). Sequential inductive learning. In *Proceedings of Thirteenth National Conference on Artificial Intelligence*, Volume 1, Portland, pp. 779–786.

Grünwald, P. (2007). *The Minimum Description Length Principle*. MIT Press.

Guh, R., F. Zorriassatine, and J. Tannock (1999). On-line control chart pattern detection and discrimination - a neural network approach. *Artificial Intelligence Engeneering 13*, 413–425.

Guha, S. and B. Harb (2005). Wavelet synopsis for data streams: minimizing non-euclidean error. In *Proceeding of the 11th ACM SIGKDD International Conference on Knowledge Discovery in Data Mining*, New York, NY, pp. 88–97. ACM Press.

Guha, S., A. Meyerson, N. Mishra, R. Motwani, and L. O'Callaghan (2003). Clustering data streams: Theory and practice. *IEEE Transactions on Knowledge and Data Engineering 15*(3), 515–528.

Guha, S., R. Rastogi, and K. Shim (1998). Cure: an efficient clustering algorithm for large databases. In *Proceedings ACM SIGMOD International Conference on Management of Data*, Seattle, pp. 73–84. ACM Press.

Guha, S., K. Shim, and J. Woo (2004). Rehist: Relative error histogram construction algorithms. In *Proceedings of the 30th International Conference on Very Large Data Bases*, Toronto, Canada, pp. 288–299. Morgan Kaufmann.

Han, J. and M. Kamber (2006). *Data Mining Concepts and Techniques*. Morgan Kaufmann.

Han, J., J. Pei, Y. Yin, and R. Mao (2004). Mining frequent patterns without candidate generation. *Data Mining and Knowledge Discovery 8*, 53–87.

Hand, D. J. and R. J. Till (2001). A simple generalisation of the area under the roc curve for multiple class classification problems. *Machine Learning 45*, 171–186.

Hansen, L. and P. Salamon (1990). Neural networks ensembles. *IEEE Transactions on Pattern Analysis and Machine Intelligence 12*(10), 993–1001.

Harries, M., C. Sammut, and K. Horn (1998). Extracting hidden context. *Machine Learning 32*, 101–126.

Harvey, A. (1990). *Forecasting, Structural Time Series Models and the Kalman Filter*. Cambridge University Press.

Hastie, T., R. Tibshirani, and J. Friedman (2000). *The Elements of Statistical Learning, Data Mining, Inference and Prediction*. Springer.

Herbster, M. and M. Warmuth (1995). Tracking the best expert. In A. Prieditis and S. Russel (Eds.), *Machine Learning, Proceedings of the 12th International Conference*. Tahoe City, CA, Morgan Kaufmann.

Herbster, M. and W. Warmuth (1998). Tracking the best expert. *Machine Learning 32*, 151–178.

Hinneburg, A. and D. A. Keim (1999). Optimal grid-clustering: Towards breaking the curse of dimensionality in high-dimensional clustering. In *Very Large Data Bases*, Edinburgh, Scotland, pp. 506–517. Morgan Kaufmann.

Hippert, H. S., C. E. Pedreira, and R. C. Souza (2001). Neural networks for short-term load forecasting: a review and evaluation. *IEEE Transactions on Power Systems 16*(1), 44–55.

Hoeffding, W. (1963). Probability inequalities for sums of bounded random variables. *Journal of the American Statistical Association 58*(301), 13–30.

Hoeting, J. A., D. Madigan, A. E. Raftery, and C. T. Volinsky (1999). Bayesian model averaging: A tutorial. *Statistical Science 14*(1), 382–401.

Holmes, G., R. Kirkby, and B. Pfahringer (2007). MOA: Massive Online Analysis. Technical report, University of Waikato. http://sourceforge.net/projects/∼moa-datastream.

Hu, X.-G., P. pei Li, X.-D. Wu, and G.-Q. Wu (2007). A semi-random multiple decision-tree algorithm for mining data streams. *J. Computer Science Technology 22*(5), 711–724.

Hulten, G. and P. Domingos (2001). Catching up with the data: research issues in mining data streams. In *Proc. of Workshop on Research Issues in Data Mining and Knowledge Discovery*, Santa Barbara, CA.

Hulten, G. and P. Domingos (2003). VFML – a toolkit for mining high-speed time-changing data streams. Technical report, University of Washington. http://www.cs.washington.edu/dm/vfml/.

Hulten, G., L. Spencer, and P. Domingos (2001). Mining time-changing data streams. In *Proceedings of the 7th ACM SIGKDD International conference on Knowledge Discovery and Data Mining*, San Francisco, CA, pp. 97–106. ACM Press.

Ikonomovska, E. and J. Gama (2008). Learning model trees from data streams. In J.-F. Boulicaut, M. R. Berthold, and T. Horváth (Eds.), *Discovery Science*, Volume 5255 of *Lecture Notes in Computer Science*, Budapest, Hungary, pp. 52–63. Springer.

Ikonomovska, E., J. Gama, R. Sebastião, and D. Gjorgjevik (2009). Regression trees from data streams with drift detection. In *Discovery Science*, Volume 5808 of *Lecture Notes in Computer Science*, Porto, Portugal, pp. 121–135. Springer.

Japkowicz, N., C. Myers, and M. Gluck (1995). A novelty detection approach to classification. In *In Proceedings of the 14th Joint Conference on Artificial Intelligence*, Montréal, Canada, pp. 518–523.

Jawerth, B. and W. Sweldens (1994). An overview of wavelet based multiresolution analyses. *SIAM Review 36*(3), 377–412.

Jin, R. and G. Agrawal (2003). Efficient decision tree construction on streaming data. In P. Domingos and C. Faloutsos (Eds.), *Proceedings of the International Conference on Knowledge Discovery and Data Mining*, Washington, DC, pp. 571–576. ACM Press.

Jin, R. and G. Agrawal (2007). Data streams – models and algorithms. See Aggarwal (2007), Chapter Frequent Pattern Mining in Data Streams, pp. 61–84.

Kalles, D. and T. Morris (1996). Efficient incremental induction of decision trees. *Machine Learning 24*, 231–242.

Kalman, R. (1960). A new approach to linear filtering and prediction problems. *Journal of Basic Engineering 82*(1), 35–45.

Kargupta, H., B. Park, S. Pittie, L. Liu, D. Kushraj, and K. Sarkar (2002). Mobimine: Monitoring the stock market from a PDA. *ACM SIGKDD Explorations 3*(2), 37–46.

Kargupta, H. and B.-H. Park (2001). Mining decision trees from data streams in a mobile environment. In *IEEE International Conference on Data Mining*, San Jose, CA, pp. 281–288. IEEE Computer Society.

Kargupta, H., V. Puttagunta, M. Klein, and K. Sarkar (2007). On-board vehicle data stream monitoring using minefleet and fast resource constrained monitoring of correlation matrices. *New Generation Computing 25*(1), 5–32.

Karp, R., S. Shenker, and C. Papadimitriou (2003, March). A simple algorithm for finding frequent elements in streams and bags. *ACM Transactions on Database Systems 28*(1), 51–55.

Kaski, S. and T. Kohonen (1994). Winner-take-all networks for physiological models of competitive learning. *Neural Networks 7*(6-7), 973–984.

Kearns, M., Y. Mansour, A. Y. Ng, and D. Ron (1997). An experimental and theoretical comparison of model selection methods. *Machine Learning 27*, 7–50.

Keogh, E., S. Lonardi, and B. Y. Chiu (2002). Finding surprising patterns in a time series database in linear time and space. In *Proceedings of the ACM SIGKDD International Conference on Knowledge Discovery and Data Mining*, Edmonton, Canada, pp. 550–556. ACM Press.

Keogh, E. J., J. Lin, and A. W.-C. Fu (2005). HOT SAX: Efficiently finding the most unusual time series subsequence. In *Proceedings of the International Conference on Data Mining*, Houston, TX, pp. 226–233. IEEE Press.

Keogh, E. J., J. Lin, and W. Truppel (2003). Clustering of the time series subsequences is meaningless: Implications for previous and future research. In *Proceedings of the IEEE International Conference on Data Mining*, pp. 115–122. IEEE Computer Society.

Kerber, R. (1992). Chimerge: discretization of numeric attributes. In *Proceedings of the 10th National Conference on Artificial Intelligence*, pp. 388–391. MIT Press.

Khotanzad, A., R. Afkhami-Rohani, T.-L. Lu, A. Abaye, M. Davis, and D. J. Maratukulam (1997, July). ANNSTLF–A neural-network-based electric load forecasting system. *IEEE Transactions on Neural Networks 8*(4), 835–846.

Kifer, D., S. Ben-David, and J. Gehrke (2004). Detecting change in data streams. In *Proceedings of the International Conference on Very Large Data Bases*, Toronto, Canada, pp. 180–191. Morgan Kaufmann.

King, S., D. King, P. Anuzis, K. Astley, L. Tarassenko, P. Hayton, and S. Utete (2002). The use of novelty detection techniques for monitoring high-integrity plant. In *Proceedings of International Conference on Control Applications*, Volume 1, pp. 221–226.

Kirkby, R. (2008). *Improving Hoeffding Trees*. Ph.D. thesis, University of Waikato, New Zealand.

Kleinberg, J. (2004). Bursty and hierarchical structure in streams. *Data Mining and Knowledge Discovery 7*(4), 373–397.

Klinkenberg, R. (2004). Learning drifting concepts: Example selection vs. example weighting. *Intelligent Data Analysis 8*(3), 281–300.

Klinkenberg, R. and T. Joachims (2000). Detecting concept drift with support vector machines. In P. Langley (Ed.), *Proceedings of 17th International Conference on Machine Learning*, Stanford, CA, pp. 487–494. Morgan Kaufmann.

Klinkenberg, R. and I. Renz (1998). Adaptive information filtering: Learning in the presence of concept drifts. In *Learning for Text Categorization*, Madison, WI, pp. 33–40. AAAI Press.

Kohavi, R. and C. Kunz (1997). Option decision trees with majority votes. In D. Fisher (Ed.), *Machine Learning Proc. of 14th International Conference*, Nashville, TN, pp. 161–169. Morgan Kaufmann.

Kolter, J. and M. Maloof (2005). Using additive expert ensembles to cope with concept drift. In L. Raedt and S. Wrobel (Eds.), *Machine Learning, Proceedings of the 22th International Conference*, Bonn, Germany, pp. 449 –456. OmniPress.

Kolter, J. Z. and M. A. Maloof (2003). Dynamic weighted majority: A new ensemble method for tracking concept drift. In *Proceedings of the 3th International IEEE Conference on Data Mining*, FL, pp. 123–130. IEEE Computer Society.

Kolter, J. Z. and M. A. Maloof (2007). Dynamic weighted majority: An ensemble method for drifting concepts. *Jounal of Machine Learning Research 8*, 2755–2790.

Koychev, I. (2000). Gradual forgetting for adaptation to concept drift. In *Proceedings of ECAI 2000 Workshop Current Issues in Spatio-Temporal Reasoning*. Berlin, Germany, pp. 101–106.

Koychev, I. (2002). Tracking changing user interests through prior-learning of context. In *AH '02: Proceedings of the Second International Conference on Adaptive Hypermedia and Adaptive Web-Based Systems*, London, UK, pp. 223–232. Springer.

Kuh, A., T. Petsche, and R. L. Rivest (1990). Learning time-varying concepts. In *Neural Information Processing Systems*, pp. 183–189.

Lanquillon, C. (2001). *Enhancing Text Classification to Improve Information Filtering*. Ph.D. thesis, University of Madgdeburg, Germany.

Last, M. (2002). On-line classification of non-stationary data streams. *Intelligent Data Analysis 6*(2), 129–147.

Lazarescu, M., S. Venkatesh, and H. Bui (2004). Using multiple windows to track concept drift. *Intelligent Data Analysis 8*(1), 29–60.

Lee, H. K. H. and M. A. Clyde (2004). Lossless online Bayesian bagging. *Journal of Machine Learning Research 5*, 143–151.

Leonardi, S., J. Lin, E. Keogh, and B. Chiu (2007). Efficient discovery of unsual patterns in time series. *New Generation Computing 25*(1), 61–116.

Leydesdorff, L. (2005). Similarity measures, author cocitation analysis, and information theory. *Journal of the American Society for Information Science and Technology 56*(7), 769–772.

Li, C., Y. Zhang, and X. Li (2009). OcVFDT: one-class very fast decision tree for one-class classification of data streams. In O. A. Omitaomu, A. R. Ganguly, J. Gama, R. R. Vatsavai, N. V. Chawla, and M. M. Gaber (Eds.), *KDD Workshop on Knowledge Discovery from Sensor Data*, Paris, France, pp. 79–86. ACM.

Li, H.-F., M.-K. Shan, and S.-Y. Lee (2008). DSM-FI: An efficient algorithm for mining frequent itemsets in data streams. *Knowledge and Information Systems 17*(1), 79–97.

Lin, J., E. Keogh, and S. Lonardi (2004). Visualizing and discovering non-trivial patterns in large time series databases. *Information Visualization 4*(2), 61–82.

Lin, J., E. Keogh, S. Lonardi, and B. Chiu (2003). A symbolic representation of time series, with implications for streaming algorithms. In *Proceedings of the ACM SIGMOD Workshop on Research Issues in Data Mining and Knowledge Discovery*, Washington, DC, pp. 2–11.

Lin, J., E. J. Keogh, S. Lonardi, J. P. Lankford, and D. M. Nystrom (2004). Viztree: a tool for visually mining and monitoring massive time series databases. In *Proceedings of the Very Large Data Bases Conference*, Toronto, Canada, pp. 1269–1272. Morgan Kaufmann.

Littlestone, N. (1988). Learning quickly when irrelevant attributes abound: A new linear-threshold algorithm. *Machine Learning 2*, 285–318.

Littlestone, N. and M. K. Warmuth (1994). The weighted majority algorithm. *Information and Computation 108*(2), 212–261.

Liu, B., Y. Dai, X. Li, W. S. Lee, and P. S. Yu (2003). Building text classifiers using positive and unlabeled examples. In *ICDM*, FL, pp. 179–188. IEEE Computer Society.

Loh, W. and Y. Shih (1997). Split selection methods for classification trees. *Statistica Sinica 7*, 815–840.

Maloof, M. and R. Michalski (2000). Selecting examples for partial memory learning. *Machine Learning 41*, 27–52.

Manku, G. S. and R. Motwani (2002). Approximate frequency counts over data streams. In *VLDB*, Hong Kong, pp. 346–357. Morgan Kaufmann.

Marascu, A. and F. Masseglia (2006). Mining sequential patterns from data streams: a centroid approach. *Journal Intelligent Information Systems 27*(3), 291–307.

Marascu, A. and F. Masseglia (2009). Parameterless outlier detection in data streams. In *Proceedings of the 2009 ACM Symposium on Applied Computing*, Honolulu, HI, pp. 1491–1495.

Markou, M. and S. Singh (2003). Novelty detection: A review - part 1: Statistical approaches. *Signal Processing 83*(12), 2481–2497.

Marsland, S. (2003). Novelty detection in learning systems. *Neural Computing Surveys 3*, 157–195.

Masseglia, F., P. Poncelet, and M. Teisseire (2003). Incremental mining of sequential patterns in large databases. *Data Knowledge Engineering 46*(1), 97–121.

Matias, Y., J. S. Vitter, and M. Wang (1998). Wavelet-based histograms for selectivity estimation. In *Proceedings of the 1998 ACM SIGMOD International Conference on Management of Data*, New York, NY, USA, pp. 448–459. ACM Press.

Mehta, M., R. Agrawal, and J. Rissanen (1996). Sliq: A fast scalable classifier for data mining. In *Proceedings International Conference on Extending Database Technology*, Volume 1057 of *Lecture Notes in Computer Science*, Avignon, France, pp. 18–32. Springer.

Metwally, A., D. Agrawal, and A. E. Abbadi (2005). Efficient computation of frequent and top-k elements in data streams. In *10th International Conference Database Theory - ICDT*, Volume 3363 of *Lecture Notes in Computer Science*, Edinburgh, UK, pp. 398–412, Springer.

Mierswa, I., M. Wurst, R. Klinkenberg, M. Scholz, and T. Euler (2006, August). Yale: Rapid prototyping for complex data mining tasks. In L. Ungar, M. Craven, D. Gunopulos, and T. Eliassi-Rad (Eds.), *Proceedings of the 12th ACM SIGKDD International Conference on Knowledge Discovery and Data Mining*, New York, NY, pp. 935–940. ACM.

Misra, J. and D. Gries (1982). Finding repeated elements. Technical report, Cornell University, Ithaca, NY, USA.

Mitchell, T. (1997). *Machine Learning*. MacGraw-Hill Companies, Inc.

Motwani, R. and P. Raghavan (1997). *Randomized Algorithms*. Cambridge University Press.

Mouss, H., D. Mouss, N. Mouss, and L. Sefouhi (2004). Test of Page-Hinkley, an approach for fault detection in an agro-alimentary production system. In *Proceedings of the Asian Control Conference*, Volume 2, pp. 815–818.

Muthukrishnan, S. (2005). *Data Streams: Algorithms and Applications*. Now Publishers.

Oza, N. (2001). *Online Ensemble Learning*. Ph.D. thesis, University of California, Berkeley.

Page, E. S. (1954). Continuous inspection schemes. *Biometrika 41*(1/2), 100–115.

Pang, K. P. and K. M. Ting (2004). Improving the centered CUSUMS statistic for structural break detection in time series. In G. I. Webb and X. Yu (Eds.), *AI 2004: Advances in Artificial Intelligence: 17th Australian Joint Conference on Artificial Intelligence*, Volume 3339 of *Lecture Notes in Computer Science*, pp. 402–413. Springer.

Park, B.-H. and H. Kargupta (2002). Data mining handbook. In N. Ye (Ed.), *Data Mining Handbook*, Chapter Distributed Data Mining: Algorithms, Systems, and Applications, pp. 341–358. Lawrence Erlbaum Associates.

Park, N. H. and W. S. Lee (2004). Statistical grid-based clustering over data streams. *SIGMOD Record 33*(1), 32–37.

Patel, P., E. Keogh, J. Lin, and S. Lonardi (2002). Mining motifs in massive time series databases. In *Proceedings of IEEE International Conference on Data Mining*, Maebashi City, Japan, pp. 370–377. IEEE Computer Society.

Pearson, K. (1896). Regression, heredity and panmixia. *Philosophical Transactions of the Royal Society 187*, 253–318.

Pei, J., J. Han, B. Mortazavi-Asl, H. Pinto, Q. Chen, U. Dayal, and M. Hsu (2001). Prefixspan: Mining sequential patterns by prefix-projected growth. In *Proceedings of the 17th International Conference on Data Engineering*, Heidelberg, Germany, pp. 215–224. IEEE Computer Society.

Peter Kriegel, H., P. Kröger, and I. Gotlibovich (2003). Incremental optics: Efficient computation of updates in a hierarchical cluster ordering. In *International Conference on Data Warehousing and Knowledge Discovery, Lecture Notes on Computer Science*, Prague, Czech Republic, pp. 224–233. Springer.

Pinto, C. and J. Gama (2007). Incremental discretization, application to data with concept drift. In *ACM Symposium on Applied Computing*, Seoul, Korea, pp. 467–468. ACM Press.

Polikar, R., L. Udpa, S. Udpa, and V. Honavar (2001). Learn++: An incremental learning algorithm for supervised neural networks. *IEEE Transactions on Systems, Man, and Cybernetics 31*, 497–508.

Potts, D. and C. Sammut (2005). Incremental learning of linear model trees. *Machine Learning 61*(1-3), 5–48.

Pratt, K. B. and G. Tschapek (2003). Visualizing concept drift. In *Proceedings of the ACM SIGKDD International Conference on Knowledge Discovery and Data Mining*, Washington, DC, pp. 735–740. ACM Press.

Quinlan, R. (1993). *C4.5: Programs for Machine Learning*. Morgan Kaufmann Publishers, Inc. San Mateo, CA.

Raissi, C. and P. Poncelet (2007). Sampling for sequential pattern mining: From static databases to data streams. In *Proceedings of the 7th International Conference on Data Mining (ICDM 07)*, Omaha, NE, pp. 631–636.

Raissi, C., P. Poncelet, and M. Teisseire (2007, February). Towards a new approach for mining maximal frequent itemsets over data stream. *Journal of Intelligent Information Systems 8*(1), 23–36.

Ramakrishnan, R. and J. Gehrke (2003). *Database Management Systems*. McGraw-Hill.

Rodrigues, P. P., J. Gama, and L. M. B. Lopes (2008). Clustering distributed sensor data streams. In *European Conference on Machine Learning and Knowledge Discovery in Databases*, Volume 5212 of *Lecture Notes in Computer Science*, Antwerp, Belgium, pp. 282–297. Springer.

Rodrigues, P. P., J. Gama, and J. P. Pedroso (2008). Hierarchical clustering of time series data streams. *IEEE Transactions on Knowledge and Data Engineering 20*(5), 615–627.

Salvador, S. and P. Chan (2007). FastDTW: Toward accurate dynamic time warping in linear time and space. *Intelligent Data Analysis 11*(5), 561–580.

Salzberg, S. (1997). On comparing classifiers: Pitfalls to avoid and a recommended approach. *Data Mining and Knowledge Discovery 1*(1), 317–327.

Saunders, R. and K. Grace (2008). Towards a computational model of creative cultures. In *AAAI Spring Symposium on Creative Intelligent Systems*, pp. 26–28.

Schaffer, C. (1993). Selecting a classification method by cross-validation. *Machine Learning 13*, 135–143.

Schapire, R. (1990). The strength of weak learnability. *Machine Learning 5*, 197–227.

Schlimmer, J. C. and R. H. Granger (1986). Incremental learning from noisy data. *Machine Learning 1*, 317–354.

Scholz, M. and R. Klinkenberg (2007). Boosting classifiers for drifting concepts. *Intelligent Data Analysis 11*(1), 3–28.

Schön, T., A. Eidehall, and F. Gustafsson (2005, December). Lane departure detection for improved road geometry estimation. Technical Report LiTH-ISY-R-2714, Department of Electrical Engineering, Linköping University, SE-581 83 Linköping, Sweden.

Schroeder, M. (1991). *Fractal, Chaos, Power Laws: Minutes from an Infinite Paradise*. W. H. Freeman and Company.

Schuster, A., R. Wolff, and D. Trock (2005). A high-performance distributed algorithm for mining association rules. *Knowledge and Information Systems 7*(4), 458–475.

Scott, D. (1979). On optimal and data base histograms. *Biometrika 66*, 605–610.

Sebastião, R. and J. Gama (2007). Change detection in learning histograms from data streams. In *Progress in Artificial Intelligence, Portuguese Conference on Artificial Intelligence*, Volume 4874 of *Lecture Notes in Computer Science*, Guimarães, Portugal, pp. 112–123. Springer.

Severo, M. and J. Gama (2006). Change detection with Kalman filter and Cusum. In *Discovery Science*, Volume 4265 of *Lecture Notes in Computer Science*, Barcelona, Spain, pp. 243–254. Springer.

Shafer, J., R. Agrawal, and M. Mehta (1996). Sprint: A scalable parallel classifier for data mining. In *Proceedings of the International Conference on Very Large Data Bases*, Bombay, India, pp. 544–555. Morgan Kaufmann.

Shahabi, C., X. Tian, and W. Zhao (2000). Tsa-tree: a wavelet-based approach to improve the efficiency of multi-level surprise and trend queries on time-series data. In *Proceedings of the 12th International Conference on Scientific and Statistical Database Management*, pp. 55–68.

Sharfman, I., A. Schuster, and D. Keren (2007). A geometric approach to monitoring threshold functions over distributed data streams. *ACM Transactions Database Systems 32*(4), 301–312.

Sheikholeslami, G., S. Chatterjee, and A. Zhang (1998). Wavecluster: A multi-resolution clustering approach for very large spatial databases. In *Proceedings of the 24rd International Conference on Very Large Data Bases*, San Francisco, CA, pp. 428–439. Morgan Kaufmann.

Shewhart, W. (1931). *Economic control of quality of manufactured product.* D. Van Nostrand Company.

Simon, H. (1997). *Models of Bounded Rationality.* MIT Press.

Sousa, E., A. Traina, J. C. Traina, and C. Faloutsos (2007). Evaluating the intrinsic dimension of evolving data streams. *New Generation Computing 25*(1), 33–60.

Spath, H. (1980). *Cluster Analysis Algorithms for Data Reduction and Classification.* Ellis Horwood.

Spiliopoulou, M., I. Ntoutsi, Y. Theodoridis, and R. Schult (2006). Monic: modeling and monitoring cluster transitions. In *Proceedings ACM International Conference on Knowledge Discovery and Data Mining*, Philadelphia, PA, pp. 706–711. ACM Press.

Spinosa, E., J. Gama, and A. Carvalho (2008). Cluster-based novel concept detection in data streams applied to intrusion detection in computer networks. In *Proceedings of the ACM Symposium on Applied Computing*, Fortaleza, Brazil, pp. 976–980. ACM Press.

Spinosa, E. J., A. C. P. de Leon Ferreira de Carvalho, and J. Gama (2009). Novelty detection with application to data streams. *Intelligent Data Analysis 13*(3), 405–422.

Srivastava, A. and J. Stroeve (2003). Onboard detection of snow, ice, clouds and other geophysical processes using kernel methods. Technical report, Research Institute for Advanced Computer Science, NASA Ames Research Center.

Stibor, T., J. Timmis, and C. Eckert (2006). On the use of hyperspheres in artificial immune systems as antibody recognition regions. In *International Conference on Artificial Immune Systems*, Volume 4163 of *Lecture Notes in Computer Science*, pp. 215–228. Springer.

Street, W. N. and Y. Kim (2001). A streaming ensemble algorithm SEA for large-scale classification. In *Proceedings of the 7th ACM SIGKDD International Conference on Knowledge Discovery and Data Mining*, San Francisco, CA, pp. 377–382. ACM Press.

Tanner, S., S. Graves, M. Alshayeb, E. Criswell, A. McDowell, M. McEniry, and K. Regner (2003). Eve: On-board process planning and execution. In *Earth Science Technology Conference*. NASA.

Tatbul, N., U. Cetintemel, S. Zdonik, M. Cherniack, and M. Stonebraker (2003). Load shedding in a data stream manager. In *Proceedings of the International Conference on Very Large Data Bases*, Berlin, Germany, pp. 309–320. VLDB Endowment.

Tax, D. M. J. (2001). *One-Class Classification - Concept-Learning in the Absence of Counter-Examples*. Ph.D. thesis, Delft University of Technology, Faculty of Information Technology and Systems.

Toivonen, H. (1996). Sampling large databases for association rules. In T. M. Vijayaraman, A. P. Buchmann, C. Mohan, and N. L. Sarda (Eds.), *Proceedings International Conference on Very Large Data Bases*, Bombay, India, pp. 134–145. Morgan Kaufmann.

Utgoff, P., N. Berkman, and J. Clouse (1997). Decision tree induction based on efficient tree restructuring. *Machine Learning 29*, 5–44.

Valiant, L. G. (1984). A theory of the learnable. *Communications of ACM 27*(11), 1134–1142.

Van de Velde, W. (1990). Incremental induction of topologically minimal trees. In B. Porter and R. Mooney (Eds.), *Machine Learning, Proceedings of the International Conference*, Austin, TX, pp. 66–74. Morgan Kaufmann.

Vapnik, V. (1995). *The Nature of Statistical Learning Theory*. Springer.

Vitter, J. S. (1985). Random sampling with a reservoir. *ACM Transactions on Mathematical Software 11*(1), 37–57.

Vlachos, M., K. Wu, S. Chen, and P. S. Yu (2005). Fast burst correlation of financial data. In *Proceedings of the 9th European Conference on Principles and Practice of Knowledge Discovery in Databases*, Volume 3721 of *Lecture Notes in Computer Science*, Porto, Portugal, pp. 368–379. Springer.

Wagner, A. and B. Plattner (2005). Entropy based worm and anomaly detection in fast IP networks. In *WETICE '05: Proceedings of the IEEE International Workshops on Enabling Technologies: Infrastructure for Collaborative Enterprise*, Washington, DC, pp. 172–177. IEEE Computer Society.

Wald, A. (1947). *Sequential Analysis*. John Wiley and Sons, Inc.

Wang, H., W. Fan, P. S. Yu, and J. Han (2003). Mining concept-drifting data streams using ensemble classifiers. In *Proceedings of the ACM SIGKDD International Conference on Knowledge Discovery and Data Mining*, Washington, DC, pp. 226–235. ACM Press.

Wang, M. and X. S. Wang (2003). Efficient evaluation of composite correlations for streaming time series. In *Advances in Web-Age Information Management - WAIM 2003*, Chengdu, China, pp. 369–380. Springer.

Wang, W. and J. Yang (2005). *Mining Sequential Patterns from Large Data Sets*. Springer.

Wang, W., J. Yang, and R. R. Muntz (1997). STING: A statistical information grid approach to spatial data mining. In M. Jarke, M. J. Carey, K. R. Dittrich, F. H. Lochovsky, P. Loucopoulos, and M. A. Jeusfeld (Eds.), *Proceedings International Conference on Very Large Data Bases*, Athens, Greece, pp. 186–195. Morgan Kaufmann.

Widmer, G. and M. Kubat (1996). Learning in the presence of concept drift and hidden contexts. *Machine Learning 23*, 69–101.

Wolff, R., K. Bhaduri, and H. Kargupta (2006). Local l2-thresholding based data mining in peer-to-peer systems. In *Proceedings SIAM International Conference on Data Mining*, Maryland, pp. 430–441. SIAM Press.

Wolff, R., K. Bhaduri, and H. Kargupta (2009). A generic local algorithm for mining data streams in large distributed systems. *IEEE Transactions on Knowledge Data Engineering 21*(4), 465–478.

Wu, K., S. Chen, and P. S. Yu (2004). Interval query indexing for efficient stream processing. In *Proceedings of the ACM International Conference on Information and Knowledge Management*, Washington, DC, pp. 88–97. ACM Press.

Yang, Y. (2003). *Discretization for Naive-Bayes Learning.* Ph.D. thesis, School of Computer Science and Software Engineering of Monash University.

Yang, Y., J. Zhang, J. Carbonell, and C. Jin (2002). Topic-conditioned novelty detection. In *Proceedings of the 8th International Conference on Knowledge Discovery and Data Mining*, Edmonton, Canada, pp. 688–693. ACM Press.

Zaki, M. J. (2000, May/June). Scalable algorithms for association mining. *IEEE Transactions on Knowledge and Data Engineering 12*(3), 372–390.

Zeira, G., O. Maimon, M. Last, and L. Rokach (2004). Data mining in time series databases. In M. Last, A. Kandel, and H. Bunke (Eds.), *Data Mining in Time Series Databases*, Volume 57, Chapter Change Detection in Classification Models Induced from Time-Series Data, pp. 101–125. World Scientific.

Zhang, T., R. Ramakrishnan, and M. Livny (1996). BIRCH: An efficient data clustering method for very large databases. In *Proceedings of the 1996 ACM SIGMOD International Conference on Management of Data*, Montréal, Canada, pp. 103–114. ACM Press.

Zhu, Y. and D. Shasha (2002). Statstream: Statistical monitoring of thousands of data streams in real time. In *Proceedings of the International Conference on Very Large Data Bases*, Hong Kong, pp. 358–369. VLDB Endowment.

Index